RANDOM HOUSE

LARGE PRINT

AMERICAN CRISIS

AMERICAN CRISIS

—

ANDREW CUOMO

RANDOM HOUSE
LARGE PRINT

Copyright © 2020 by Andrew M. Cuomo

Published in the United States of America by
Random House Large Print in association with Crown,
an imprint of Random House, a division of
Penguin Random House LLC, New York.

Cover design: Christopher Brand

The Library of Congress has established a
Cataloging-in-Publication record for this title.

ISBN: 978-0-593-41026-4

www.penguinrandomhouse.com/large-print-format-books

FIRST LARGE PRINT EDITION

Printed in the United States of America

10 9 8 7 6 5 4 3 2 1

This Large Print edition published in accord
with the standards of the N.A.V.H.

Dedicated to the people of New York.

We're going to make it. We are tough. You have to be.
This place makes you tough, but it makes you tough in a
good way. I love New York because New York loves you.
New York loves all of you. Black and white and brown
and short and tall and gay and straight.
New York loves everyone.
It always has, it always will. At the end of the day,
my friends, even if it is a long day—
and this has been a very long day—love wins.

Always.

AMERICAN CRISIS

INTRODUCTION

I NORMALLY DON'T TURN OFF MY CELLPHONE when I sleep, because the work of being governor is literally twenty-four hours a day, and the phone pings all night long. If I'm really tired, I will turn it off, but that doesn't mean people can't get me; it's just harder. My office phone is always answered, at night by a New York State trooper. Callers must convince the trooper that their issue is really important. Some troopers are easier to convince than others. Some troopers decide that it's safer to put all callers through, but as I joke to my team, those troopers learn quickly that it is not in fact safer when they are then assigned to different duties.

When my cellphone rang late on March 1, I hadn't turned it off, but I didn't get to it in time. Moments later, the landline rang. It was Melissa DeRosa, secretary to the governor and my top aide. Brilliant, tough, indefatigable, and widely respected, she is the quarterback on my team and is responsible for managing all the pieces.

"Governor, I'm sorry to stalk you with the

multiple calls, but we just received a confirmation from Wadsworth." This was the New York State Department of Health's lab in Albany. "New York has its first case of coronavirus—a health-care worker who just returned to New York City from Iran. We believe the incident is isolated. I have Dr. Zucker on the other line. Can I conference him in?"

"Please put him through," I said.

As the state health commissioner, Dr. Howard Zucker, began to run through the patient's background, symptoms, and literal steps taken between landing at JFK airport and reaching her apartment in Manhattan, it seemed as though white noise washed over the line. I couldn't prove it, but I knew this wasn't New York's first coronavirus case. And I knew the country wasn't prepared.

The good news that night was that this was a fairly straightforward case, which would hopefully not cause great public alarm: The thirty-nine-year-old woman had traveled to Iran to provide health services and returned to New York feeling ill, but she knew to take precautions and did not come in contact with many people. She had been traveling with her male partner and had worn a mask. She took an Uber from the airport to her apartment and then called ahead to the hospital to make arrangements to be tested. In many ways it was the best-case scenario: an informed health-care worker who did the right thing.

However, even this single case in the state of New York presented complications and foreshadowed what was to come. What flight did she take? Could she have infected people on the plane? Who was responsible for contacting all the passengers on the flight? How about the Uber driver? Were the proper precautions taken at the hospital? These were the operational issues that we would need to figure out and standardize quickly, and they were mind-boggling when we considered the volume of cases we could anticipate given what we already knew about the virus.

A few weeks earlier, we had received the first taste of what was to come. On February 6, I was sitting at my desk in my New York City office at 633 Third Avenue in Manhattan working on a speech. My director of administration, Stephanie Benton, came in because I had an important call. Stephanie organizes the executive chamber operations and has been with me since I started as attorney general, fourteen years ago. She can juggle ten balls at a time and always does it with a smile. I am fully aware that my ability to function and get things done is dependent on Stephanie and the strong team around her.

On the phone line was Rick Cotton, the executive director of the Port Authority of New York and New Jersey, a powerful agency that operates bridges, tunnels, and airports, as well as the Port of New York. Rick called to tell me that federal

Department of Health and Human Services (HHS) officials had contacted him about passengers on a cruise ship nearby who they believed were positive for COVID-19. HHS wanted to dock the ship at a Port Authority facility and New York to take charge of the patients.

The novel coronavirus—formally the severe acute respiratory syndrome coronavirus 2 (SARS-CoV-2), which is the virus that causes the disease we've come to know as COVID-19—was at that time thought to be largely contained in China, with a few scattered cases in Washington and California. But this was the first case that would come knocking on New York's door.

When the call came in, the Ebola crisis from years earlier flashed in my mind—how we handled it, what went right, and what went wrong. In 2014, a health-care worker who had been helping out with an Ebola outbreak in Africa returned to New York after having contracted the disease. He rode the subway, ate in a restaurant, and visited a bowling alley before he knew he was sick. People got scared. Governor Chris Christie of New Jersey and I held a joint press conference, because we shared control of the Port Authority, to announce a policy to screen people at the airports and, if necessary, quarantine them. When another health-care worker arrived at Newark airport, also returning from Africa, airport officials ordered the woman held in quarantine in a tent at the airport, where she was given nothing more than granola bars and a cellphone, which she quickly used to call CNN. We hadn't forgotten the pitfalls of forced quarantine.

As would happen again and again over the course of this emergency, dozens of questions flooded my thoughts: What if the patients said they wanted to leave? What was the Department of Health's authority to hold patients? If patients agreed to come with us, where should we bring them? Do they need a hospital? Do the hospital and medical staff need to take special precautions? If we are quarantining them in a hotel, do we have the legal authority to force them to stay? Can they leave the hotel room at all? How do they get meals? Can housekeeping staff enter the room? What medical assistance do they need? How long will they be sick?

The questions were obvious, and the answers were few. HHS was alarmingly ignorant. In the end, the ship docked in Bayonne, New Jersey, and the four passengers who were transferred to a hospital for further evaluation tested negative, but the situation gave me the first true sense that we were on a journey to a place we had never been before. I sat back and wondered, how did the great United States of America get to this point?

When COVID first hit, it was inconceivable to me that the federal government would abandon its basic role of managing a federal emergency, but that is exactly what would happen as soon as they understood the depth of the problem, the

complexity of the solution, and the political pain
that needed to be endured in the coming weeks and
months. Before the extent of the crisis was revealed,
the federal government initially sought control.
The Centers for Disease Control (CDC) and the
Food and Drug Administration (FDA) were very
possessive of the initial testing strategy, deciding
who should be tested, when they would be tested,
when states would receive the results, and who was
being screened at airports and how. Making the
bureaucratic nightmare worse, every single test was
routed to a single lab in Atlanta—a lab that, by
the middle of February, had already been known
to return faulty results. It was clear that building
out testing operations would be key to controlling
the spread not just in New York but in the whole
country. You didn't have to have spent a lifetime in
government to know the system in place was set up
for failure.

Given the consistent irrationality of the Trump
administration, why would anyone think this
federal government would act responsibly or com-
petently? I had deep philosophical differences with
Trump before COVID began. I believed he was a
salesman who adopted hyper-conservative positions
to win as a Republican. I knew Trump from earlier
days in New York and was aware of his lifestyle. He
was anything but hyper-conservative. Trump had
no government experience when he took office,
and he was rarely involved in substantive policy

once he did. Most qualified professionals in the Trump administration came and left before their dinner got cold. Trump, from all evidence, believed the pandemic was just another public relations matter.

In February, before the first COVID case came to New York, I had already been tied up in my latest fight with the president, a very public, very ugly battle with the administration over the Trusted Traveler Program. Otherwise known as Global Entry, the program allowed high-volume travelers the convenience of skipping long lines at customs. As part of his election-year strategy focusing on deportation and immigration, Trump had his Department of Homeland Security (DHS) ban New York State residents from participating in the program. It was a blatant act of retaliation for a state law I had signed the previous year allow-ing undocumented immigrants to receive driver's licenses while shielding applicants' information from immigration enforcement agencies. While public health shouldn't be a political issue, with the Trump administration everything was political.

In retrospect, how ironic was it that the White House, which was initially so controlling, would soon run from the entire situation? In any event, I was already frustrated with their inability to make simple timely decisions about testing procedures and protocols. It was around this time that President Trump announced that Vice President Pence would head the White House Coronavirus Task Force. The Pence appointment was criticized not only because Trump made it but also because Vice President Pence, the former governor of Indiana, had been very slow to address or acknowledge the HIV crisis. Another criticism was that his appointment would politicize the task force when it would be better left to health professionals and substantive cabinet secretaries. On this I disagreed. I was a former cabinet secretary and have great respect for the position. They are weighty offices, no doubt. Confirmed by the U.S. Senate, they carry lifetime titles and are in the line of succession for the presidency. As Housing and Urban Development (HUD) secretary, I was thirteenth in the line of succession. If there were twelve simultaneous heart attacks, I would've been president of the United States. However, the COVID effort was going to be administration-wide and the vice president was in a much better position to command control over the entirety of the federal government. I publicly supported the president's appointment of Pence. I thought it was a positive sign that the president was putting his senior official in charge. I was wrong. I would be wrong many times throughout the crisis.

We were in a new moment in politics and government. There was no delay in communication. Everything was instantaneous. There were no letters or emissaries sent. I would do several media events per day. My words would immediately reach the White House, which would often immediately respond. Social media changed intergovernmental dialogue. I was direct to camera supporting Pence, and the White House would see it immediately. The White House was obviously appreciative of my position on Pence.

The last week of February, the vice president and I spoke, and we discussed the testing logjam. As a former governor, he understood the situation. He was also clearly navigating his federal authority for the first time. The vice president has no specific portfolio and no direct authority over an agency head. Of course, he has a great title, but stubborn agency heads could always pose a problem because they have ultimate constitutional legal authority. We needed Pence to intervene with the FDA to expedite the approval for New York to run our own COVID test. To my pleasant surprise he did, and the FDA approved New York's testing in its own laboratory.

As it turned out, that moment would change history. With the FDA approval, we could finally test for COVID in New York State, instead of shipping specimens to Atlanta one at a time. New York State had cut out the middleman, just in time for the call I was about to receive that Sunday night confirming what in my gut I already knew: Coronavirus had reached New York.

—

SO MUCH WAS UNKNOWN. In some ways I was not prepared for the moment, because no one could truly be prepared for the moment. In other ways, I have spent my whole life preparing for it.

I have a healthy cynicism about people in general and an unhealthy cynicism about politics and government in particular. But understanding people's experiences, motivations, and biases is always the starting point for me in judging what they have to say. So let me explain mine.

I'm sixty-two years old, and life has taken me up and down and all around. I grew up in New York City as an outer-borough, middle-class guy. I paid my way through school with every odd job imaginable: landscaper, night-shift security guard, mechanic, ice cream scooper, tow truck driver, and construction worker. I have been a campaign manager, started a nonprofit to help the homeless, served as an assistant DA, practiced law privately, worked in real estate finance, was a federal cabinet secretary, state attorney general, and now governor. I've loved and lost. I've lived through an embarrassing and very public divorce splashed across the front pages of the tabloids. I suffered the pain of feeling I failed my children. I was publicly humiliated by losing campaigns and was declared a political dead man. I suffered through my father's crushing political downfall and shared his grief and recriminations afterward.

I know my strengths and weaknesses. I want to get things done and be judged by results and by making a positive difference, and I can be obsessive in that pursuit. I have disdain for the shallowness and duplicity of political theater and no longer want to hold my tongue. I do not suffer fools gladly, gracefully, or patiently. I am an overprotective parent, and it frustrates and embarrasses my daughters. My natural instinct is to be aggressive, and it doesn't always serve me well. I am a controlling personality. At one time I opposed that characterization because it has a negative implication. But you show me a person who is not controlling, and I'll show you a person who is probably not highly successful.

I don't have what you call a balanced life either. I work all the time. Enjoyment for me is when I'm with my daughters or my family, and in the summer I spend time on the water with my brother and friends, but usually I just work. Being governor is a job that is never really done. If I'm not working, I always feel a tinge of guilt. The wheels in my mind never stop turning, so at night I think about the things I need to do the next day or go through the events of the day that just ended. I inherited this proclivity from my father, who was an even worse workaholic. When someone would suggest to my father that he take a vacation, he loved to say, "Why should I unwind? I will just have to wind myself up again." Then he would laugh. But living with a workaholic can be really boring.

I am a progressive Democrat, as that term used to be defined. I am frustrated by the incompetence of the government and distrustful of the motivations and ability of many politicians. I was raised at a kitchen table where my father talked about improving society in the teachings of Matthew 25 and **tikkun olam:** building community dedicated to doing justice and improving life for all. I deeply believe government is the best vehicle to advance that mission and that government service done well is an art form. But I also believe government service is a dying art, and too many seek office who do not possess the skills or knowledge necessary to actually make change or are motivated by personal rather than public advancement.

I spent eight years in Washington, and I have no desire to go back. There have been rumors during this crisis and before that I was interested in running for president. That is a natural suspicion: After all, Grover Cleveland and both presidents Roosevelt, FDR and Theodore, were governors of New York. My father, Mario Cuomo, talked about running for president, although he never did. But I have been definitive in my support of Joe Biden for president, and he is also a personal friend. But facts never get in the way of a good rumor.

I've worked with presidents, cabinet secretaries, governors, and world leaders, attended many meetings in the Oval Office, worked to pass many bills through Congress, was confirmed twice by the U.S.

Senate. I fought for and alongside underserved communities, reduced discrimination against the LGBTQ community, sued the KKK, increased federal aid to Indian reservations, rebuilt public housing across the country, designed a new model to help the homeless, served during national emergencies and disasters, as HUD secretary, worked in every state in the nation, and represented this nation in countries around the globe.

As governor for the past ten years, I've worked with Democrats and Republicans. I reformed the bureaucracy of government. I reduced taxes, passed nation-leading progressive legislation—from gun control to marriage equality, and from codifying a woman's right to choose to instituting the highest minimum wage at the time, free college tuition, and the nation's most aggressive environmental program. My administration has completed more major infrastructure projects than any other in modern history. I have an advantage in my position: I have nothing left to prove to anyone and find the plain truth liberating.

This is my second life. I lived and died a political death before my eventual rebirth. I ran for governor in 2002 and lost. Before that, my father had lost his reelection in 1994 after three terms as governor. My father and I spent many evenings sitting on the couch, watching a ball game, drinking a bottle of wine, and replaying the "game tapes" of our government careers, reviewing what we did right, what we did wrong. The advantage of retrospection is priceless, as well as painful. Over time, the petty day-to-day political pressures become irrelevant, and only the lasting contributions remain.

Our shared conclusion was that if we could somehow replay the game, we would play it much differently. My father and I agreed we would be bolder, take more risks, make more change, and make more progress by proving to the people that government can be effective and can actually make a positive difference. We lamented the time wasted catering to this official or that official. The lost opportunities of an overly cautious legislature. The frustration of a bureaucracy that didn't move fast enough to produce real results for people. If we could do it over again, we would get even more done, and those accomplishments would then build more support for government.

After all those nights on the couch, in 2006 I was reborn when I won the election for attorney general of New York. Dead politicians don't usually come back to life. I had a second chance, and I would do it right this time. As I called my father onto the stage that election night and held his hand high, I pledged that I would do it right for myself and for my father.

The political pundits get to write the eulogy once you are out of office, and my father's political eulogy was essentially that he gave great speeches but his government didn't produce major successes. In my father's case, the Albany reporter he respected the least wound up writing his actual eulogy for **The New York Times.** There is no justice. It was unfair as well as unkind. It was also untrue. But welcome to politics in New York. My father was interested in the articulation of government principles, but not to the exclusion of government implementation. I am committed to highlight both. I want a government that talks the talk and walks the walk. A government of principle that can also produce and improve people's day-to-day lives.

I intend to serve as governor of New York as long as the people will have me. My daughters are grown, their education is paid for, and I can pay for their three weddings. After I'm done as governor, I want to help my children in any way I can, and also buy a boat and go fishing. But for now, I have 19.5 million people counting on me. That is my priority. At the beginning of this crisis, I thought of FDR's words: "Courage is not the absence of fear, but rather the assessment that something else is more important than fear." There might be no good outcome, but I knew I could not live with myself if I stayed in the foxhole. The right thing to do in the coming battle was to step up and give it my all. There could be no ambivalence. Total commitment is always the first step.

Most Americans go to sleep at night thinking that the government is keeping this nation safe—that, God forbid, if a terrible disaster emerged, some authority with men and women in uniforms and equipment would show up to save the day. Sometimes that is not enough. I have been through hurricanes, floods, fires, and earthquakes. I know how fragile our social foundation really is. I have seen people panic and trample one another. I have seen civilization degrade when the instinct of self-survival takes over.

An airborne virus was one of the nightmare scenarios envisioned as a terrorist plot. It is easy to create chaos and overwhelm society with fear when people are afraid to breathe the air. There would be no good news with this virus and no good outcome. Schools and businesses would be closed. The economy would suffer. People would die. Nothing we could do would be enough. There was no possibility for victory, and even FDR and Churchill had at least the **possibility** of a successful outcome.

I knew this country was in trouble when COVID hit. It was divided and vulnerable, making it weak. A serious threat was inevitable, and when it came, we did not have the capacity to handle it. The only way to defeat the virus is for a united societal response where we all agree to protect one another. But the coronavirus is attacking us at an unprecedented time of partisanship and internal discord. Political, racial, economic, and geographic divisions are at all-time highs. The nation is more divided than at any time since the Civil War. The unity this nation has shown in the past when it was under attack, such as in World War II, is nowhere to be seen. When we are united, we are undefeatable. When we are divided, we are vulnerable.

Our ability to respond together as a society is dependent on the strength and the capacity of our government. Government is nothing more than the vehicle for collective action. Washington, Lincoln, FDR, JFK—these were great men made for the moment, or the moments made these men great. At this moment in time, this nation is led by neither a great government nor a great leader.

Still, there is reason for hope. In this crisis we see evidence that the virus can be defeated. New York State, a microcosm of the nation, has shown a path forward. We have seen government mobilize to handle the crisis. We have seen Americans come together in a sense of unity to do the impossible. We have seen how the virus is confronted and defeated. New York didn't do everything right, but there are lessons we can learn that will lead to victory.

MARCH 1 | 1 NEW CASE | 0 HOSPITALIZED | 0 DEATHS

———

"It was a matter of when, not if."

I T WASN'T LONG AFTER THAT EVENING CALL FROM Melissa that my office issued a statement reassuring New Yorkers that it was always a matter of when COVID would arrive in our state, not if, and now that it was here, we were managing the situation.

While New Yorkers are a diverse international community, they can still be a parochial bunch. There is an attitude that it's not real until it happens in New York, and until we had our first COVID case, our population was still fairly dismissive of the threat. Even with the announcement of the first case, New Yorkers had largely not yet reached a point of high anxiety. But I had.

We had no idea how bad the situation would become. For weeks, the federal authorities had told us to look to Asia and the West Coast of the United States, where the infections first surfaced, but what we would soon find out was that the coronavirus had come from the other direction and that travelers from Europe to and through New York had brought the invisible hitchhiker with them weeks if not months earlier, and it was already circulating among thousands who had not yet manifested the illness. In a retrospective interview given on June 26, Dr. Anthony Fauci, director of infectious diseases at the National Institutes of Health (NIH), acknowledged that the first wave of cases that hit New York was from Europe. "Everybody was looking at China and it came from Europe," Fauci said.

MARCH 2 | 0 NEW CASES | 0 HOSPITALIZED | 0 DEATHS

———

"It is deep breath time."

I FLEW DOWN TO NEW YORK CITY TO HOLD what would be the first daily press conference, or "briefings" as they would become known, about the arrival of the coronavirus. I had done them often as governor, usually at the state capitol in Albany, the main location for my operation. The capitol is a beautiful building first erected in the late nineteenth century and finished when Teddy Roosevelt was governor in 1899. At the time it was one of the most expensive public works projects in the nation. The press conferences are held in the official governor's office, called the Red Room, a magnificent space with wood paneling, red leather, and gold-embossed wall coverings, and they are always simulcast on the internet for anyone who cares to watch. However, before this year, not that many people were interested in the day-to-day operations of state government.

With me on the dais on March 2 were Dr. Zucker

and Mayor Bill de Blasio of New York City. While I was not the mayor's number one fan, a fact that was well known to the public, I made the trip to the city specifically to sit with him to show a unified front to New Yorkers. An informed, consistent message was important, so by doing this event with the mayor, I could make sure we were stating the same facts.

One of New York City's blessings is that it has some of the best medical institutions on the planet. Joining me were the top executives from Mount Sinai Health System, NewYork-Presbyterian Hospital, and NYU Langone Medical Center and the heads of the Greater New York Hospital Association and the Healthcare Association of New York State. I had met with them prior to the briefing because I wanted to make sure that we were coordinated in doing research and sharing the best information on a timely basis.

My plan for this briefing and all the ones to follow was simple: We would provide unbiased factual evidence explaining the virus and its progress. A single day's briefing means little, but constant reinforcement and updated factual data could present a story that the public could follow. Besides, matters of life and death tend to get people's attention. The main challenge for me was to communicate this data to the public in a way that would establish my credibility for providing timely information with transparency while also instilling confidence. My daughter Mariah said to me late the previous night, her voice clearly filled with anxiety, "Don't tell me to relax; tell me why I should be relaxed." She was right; it was an important distinction that I would remember going forward. I understood that people were anxious. The message I delivered was that this was "deep breath time." "Deep breath time" meant that I understood their emotions and I was not discounting them. But we could not act on emotion. We would act on facts.

This first briefing was the opening salvo in an ongoing discussion. In many ways I was reintroducing myself to the people of the state. Yes, they knew me, but today everything was different. We were going to a new and different place. Today, I was not just the governor; I was the governor in a historic crisis. If people didn't believe in government yesterday, they desperately wanted to believe in government today. Today, government mattered.

Initially, I had no expectation when we started that these briefings would be anything out of the ordinary. I was wrong. Within a matter of days, this mundane government procedure during pre-COVID times became something of a phenomenon, what became characterized as required viewing first for New Yorkers and then for the entire nation.

NEW YORK HAS A MUCH larger government than most states, with more depth and more resources.

Fortunately, when the virus arrived, we already had—in my opinion—the best team of professionals that has been assembled in modern political history. My team is a group of top-shelf individuals who could excel in any position in the corporate sector making millions; instead, they are public servants. And we knew one another like a basketball team that has played together for many years, how each person moved on the court and who should get the ball for the game-winning shot. My job as the leader of this team has always been to help them find the confidence to demand more from themselves and from the systems around them. Often, when people, especially bureaucrats, are faced with a problem, their first response is to list the reasons why something can't be done. My team does not accept no for an answer; they get to yes. So when COVID hit, I was confident that my people would face this challenge with everything they had and then some.

I was also confident in my relationship with the hospitals. I was confident in my relationship with the state legislature. I was confident in my relationship with local executives. Westchester County executive George Latimer, Nassau County executive Laura Curran, and Suffolk County executive Steve Bellone were in the hot seat handling their counties, but they are pros and we worked together well. Likewise, Buffalo mayor Byron Brown, Syracuse mayor Ben Walsh, and Rochester mayor Lovely

Warren were capable of handling the situation well. I was confident in myself to the extent that I had every experience one could have to be prepared. I was knowledgeable, even enough to know one could never be truly prepared. I was confident that we could do as good a job as could be done in the circumstances, but I was never comfortable with what the outcome might be.

The arrival of COVID also put New York State in direct engagement with the federal government in a new way. I had already been talking to them about COVID issues such as bringing testing capability to our state, but now the urgency went up tenfold, as did my relevance to the White House and their relevance to me.

Before this, I had probably been the most outspoken governor against Trump's policies. We fought on immigration policy, environmental policy, you name it. We had a number of nasty exchanges. I was enraged when he imposed the cap on state and local taxes (SALT) in his 2017 tax package. That policy increased the income tax on New Yorkers $14 billion. When we codified a woman's right to choose with the Reproductive Health Act in early 2019 in case Republicans did anything to overturn **Roe v. Wade** at the Supreme Court level, Trump attacked New York in his State of the Union address, ridiculously claiming that lawmakers in New York had "cheered" for a law that he said allowed "a baby to be ripped from the mother's womb moments from birth." He had also lobbed a series of tweets at me in early February, complaining, "Very hard to work with New York—So stupid. All they do is sue me all the time!" and "New York must stop all of its unnecessary lawsuits & harrassment, start cleaning itself up, and lowering taxes."

I found his constant pandering to the Far Right alternately disingenuous and repugnant, but today was a different day, and New York needed the federal government. As a former cabinet secretary, I knew what it could do, and I knew we needed its assistance. My personal feelings and politics were irrelevant. I would do my best to make the relationship work.

THE STATE'S WADSWORTH LABORATORY had the capacity to do about four hundred tests per day. Now that we had permission from the federal government to conduct tests ourselves, we announced the ambitious goal of increasing capacity to a thousand per day within a week and said that tests would be free to the public. Given the current state of testing in the United States, this number was ridiculed as pie in the sky by some folks, and several of my own team thought I was crazy for setting such a high goal. What we didn't know was that ultimately we would need to perform in excess of fifty thousand tests per day.

New Yorkers, some of whom can be a neurotic

group, were quick to analyze the potential exposure risk. For months, we'd thought the risk was from the West Coast, where it seemed the virus first took root in late January. The CDC was allowing tests only for people with symptoms who had recently traveled from Wuhan, China. Of the few people who were being tested, the nasal swab was performed in New York, then mailed to Atlanta. I knew we were in trouble when four of my family members called asking how they could be tested. Meanwhile, the World Health Organization (WHO) declared a global emergency on January 30, and San Diego and then San Francisco declared states of emergency in February. But the CDC had claimed there were no cases in New York. An FDA press release on February 4 said, "At this time, federal health officials continue to believe that the threat to the general American population from this virus is relatively low."

All through January and February, the Department of Health sent us updates of people under investigation, or PUIs, in New York. These were people who had traveled to Hubei Province in China or had had contact with a relative who had traveled and now had a temperature. All the tests went through the CDC in Atlanta. And every day, the New York State Department of Health would put out a press release saying, according to the CDC, there were no confirmed cases of COVID in New York. It gave people the sense that the situation was being well monitored, but it was completely false because there were so few tests and they were testing the wrong people! On top of that, they didn't know that the enemy had already been arriving from another part of the world, probably earlier than the first week in February.

Given the density and crowding of New York City, once the virus had officially arrived, the possibility of coming in contact with a COVID-positive person was very real. If a positive person took the subway, people immediately wanted to know what train, at what time, and what car. Maybe they had held the same pole in a bus or train as a COVID-positive person. Maybe they rode in the same cab. Maybe they were in the same Uber. The possibilities were endless, so we quickly instituted new cleaning protocols for public transportation, schools, and so on.

For months the federal government told us the COVID spread was from symptomatic individuals, that transmission was from sneezing, coughing, and touching contaminated surfaces. However, that was a half-truth. We would later learn that the virus also spreads from asymptomatic individuals.

Yet as early as January 27, a doctor named Camilla Rothe, exploring Germany's first coronavirus case, concluded that the patient was infected by a person from China. The doctor also found that the visitor from China exhibited no symptoms whatsoever. Thereafter there was a viral spread in French churches, Italian soccer stadiums, Austrian ski barns—all also apparently from asymptomatic or presymptomatic spreading. One of the first international outbreaks of the virus was on a cruise ship, the **Diamond Princess**. Interviews with the health professionals on the ship pointed to symptomless spread: Of the 454 people who tested positive, about 70 percent showed no symptoms whatsoever.

The health community debated the concept of asymptomatic spread for more than two months before they were willing to accept it. There were articles published in **The New England Journal of Medicine** as a caution to countries around the world. The World Health Organization noted in early February that patients might transmit the virus before showing symptoms, but also said patients with symptoms were the "main" cause of the spread of the epidemic. Chinese health authorities had also explicitly cautioned that patients were contagious before showing symptoms.

Why would federal health officials be hesitant to acknowledge symptomless spread? And why would the orientation not have been toward being overly cautious, assuming the worst, and acting accordingly? Because the ramifications were too colossal. If we assumed people must show symptoms if they were positive, it made the diagnosis and containment much easier. It also limited the population that required attention. If we assumed a person without any symptoms could be positive, massive amounts of testing would be required at extraordinary expense.

Too many federal officials were oblivious to the conversations about how the virus spreads. As is the case with the spread coming from Europe, if we had known that people without symptoms could spread the disease, we would've acted much differently and much sooner, and many lives would have been saved.

In the last week of January an adviser to the president, Peter Navarro, sent an internal memo that should have set off alarm bells. It said that the coronavirus was not contained to China and could possibly affect 200 million Americans. There are only 330 million Americans total. The memo went on to say the virus could result in one to two million lives lost—more casualties than have been sustained in any war the nation has ever been engaged in. Navarro is not a junior staffer. He is a senior political aide with direct access to the president. Who read the memo? What was done as a result of this memo? Absolutely nothing.

MARCH 3 | 1 NEW CASE | 1 HOSPITALIZED | 0 DEATHS

"Every day matters."

NEW YORK CITY IS UNIQUE, AND PEOPLE often assume that situations in New York City can't happen "somewhere else." When New York had its second positive case, this time in New Rochelle, in Westchester County just north of New York City, I knew that attitudes would change. Despite New Rochelle's proximity to New York City, it was really Anyplace, U.S.A. This area would quickly become the nation's first "hot spot," due in large part to the fact that patient zero, a lawyer named Lawrence Garbuz, was infected well before he knew it.

Patient zero attended a Bat Mitzvah ceremony and a funeral as a member of a congregation at a local temple, along with hundreds of other guests. In his other interactions over several days—working at his law office, taking public transportation, and visiting a doctor's office—he spread the virus to dozens of people. The New Rochelle man was the first known American "super-spreader," an infected person who happens to be in the company of a large number of people and can spread the virus in a short period of time.

If COVID could explode in New Rochelle, it could happen anywhere. I knew this would strike a troubling chord in people, and so I explained the situation carefully at my daily briefing. As I had the previous day, I presented the facts, including dates and medical information. I didn't hold back any information because I thought it was too difficult or frightening. It's not my place to filter or edit the truth. The people of New York are not children, and I am not their father. In fact, I don't even filter the truth for my kids. People will make the right judgment if they know the facts.

The facts from New Rochelle were startling. Patient zero was critically ill, and the virus was spreading like lightning. He could have been anyone's husband, brother, uncle, or friend. There was no malice or irresponsibility on his part. Not only was the situation in New Rochelle a wake-up call for people all over the state, it was the first time the state government needed to answer questions because the federal government was quickly doing an about-face on taking control.

A local doctor was among those infected soon after patient zero. We were telling anyone who tested positive that they couldn't go to work. Local health officials told him to shut down his office, but the doctor refused. He said closing would hurt his business. The state Department of Health also told him to shut down, and he said, "On what authority?"

That's when I heard about it. The last thing I wanted was a lawsuit, which would take weeks of hearings to get a resolution. We didn't have weeks. So I called him myself.

He wasn't impressed; in fact, he was really angry.

What mattered was persuading him to do the right thing, to protect other people, so I let him vent, and then I talked him through the reasoning. "We're all doing things we don't want to do," I said. "We have to do this." Finally, he agreed to close.

Next, we talked with local officials about shutting down the schools. The pushback was fierce. The Orthodox community didn't want to shut their schools, and they felt discriminated against. They were a sizable political constituency, and the local officials were intimidated. The head of the local public school board also called us, enraged. She said they shouldn't have to close, because the kids testing positive didn't go to the public schools. She emphasized how many of the kids in the public schools were food insecure and that school was a major source of meals. As a result, the state elected representatives were against shutting the schools, fearing it would be too disruptive.

What really stood out was that no one thought the outbreak itself was a big deal. So a few people got the bug, why shut everything down? It was the first manifestation of the disconnect people had about the threat. I realized we were going to have to make some incredibly tough decisions and work vigilantly to achieve public support for them.

We were already talking about creating a containment zone in New Rochelle, where we would close schools and religious gathering places and focus our testing on residents. Gareth Rhodes, a longtime trusted aide, and Melissa printed out a map and laid it on the conference room table. The three of us, along with the health commissioner, Howard Zucker, talked about how big to make it. There was no playbook, no guidelines coming from the federal government; it was up to us. We decided on a uniform mile from the center.

We got on the phone with Noam Bramson, the mayor of New Rochelle, and George Latimer, the Westchester County executive, explaining where the line was going to be drawn. Noam pointed out that the line went right through the middle of a golf course. "Do you know which side of the line the golf course clubhouse falls? Depending where the line is, a wedding this weekend may have to be canceled." All politics is local! We went back and forth negotiating but concluded we just had to make the zone indiscriminate and fair. We spent all day on the phone with businesses who called to say, "We're right on the line. What should we do? Should we stay open? Should we stay closed?" We said, look at the map and make a decision by your location.

At this point, it was only a few days since the first positive test, and no one had died. The president was saying this was a flu, that our concern was a Democratic hoax. There was a lot of skepticism from the public as well as officials. No one was ready to accept that they needed to change how they were living.

I knew we weren't going to get anywhere if we couldn't persuade people to accept the situation before we took action. So we scrambled to fly down and meet with the Westchester County local officials in person. The operational gymnastics of my travel and schedule were incredible. Every hour had to count. Jill DesRosiers is my unflappable chief of staff and has been with me for years. Annabel Walsh is my director of scheduling. She has the joy of talking to me twenty-four hours a day. I always try to get done more in a day than twenty-four hours permits. Annabel never fails to make sure it happens.

As we saw in Westchester that day, local parochial concerns would butt up against major, wide-ranging changes that had to occur in order to combat the virus. This pattern would play out over and over again in the coming weeks. Most local politicians seek to make people happy; that's the business model. If something doesn't make people happy, they don't want to do it. As we were instituting this lockdown on New Rochelle, one Democratic assemblywoman who represented Westchester came to my office demanding a meeting; then she simply sat in the second row at a press conference and scowled at me.

I would make my first major communications mistake when I used the words "containment zone." I also said I would call out the National Guard to help deliver food to students after we closed schools. The combination of the words "containment zone" and "National Guard" frightened people. To be clear, there was no actual "containment" of people; they could come and go as they pleased. The "containment" was of the virus. But the term was misunderstood, and I soon realized that a poorly worded phrase was very dangerous.

The quick escalation from mild concern to high anxiety surprised even me. People were panicking, asking, what if the shelves in the store were emptied and not refilled? What if the grocery store owner, truck driver, gas station attendant, cashier, stayed home because they were afraid of the virus? It is terrifying how quickly society can unravel. Communication was everything in this situation, and I couldn't make any more mistakes.

And in case you're wondering, the clubhouse was inside the line, and the wedding was canceled.

I AM A STUDENT of history, and it amazes me how the old adage "past is prologue" still holds true.

No matter how the facts change, the fundamental dynamic remains the same. I now live in the Executive Mansion in Albany. It is a great big old house that really should be a museum. Al Smith, TR, FDR, Grover Cleveland, and my father, Mario Cuomo, lived here. I think about them often— what they faced and what they accomplished.

There are two themes that differentiate periods of national accomplishment from periods of national crisis. First, the solidarity and unity of the American people. Second, governmental leadership and competence. Periods of great accomplishment occur when the country is unified behind a goal with inspired leadership and extraordinary government capacity. Problematic periods are a sign of a divided nation, social unrest, failed leadership, and an incompetent or corrupt government. Even with an external threat, the result is determined by the nation's internal forces.

COVID is in many ways a symptom and not the illness. The human body is attacked by literally dozens of viruses per week. A healthy body with a functioning immune system will fight off and manage the attacks. Science, in and of itself, has never killed a virus in the body, but science has worked with the human body to defend against attacks and managed to resolve them. A viral attack is most damaging when the body is weakened.

COVID attacked this country at a time of extreme weakness on every level. Since 2016, a political strategy of fearmongering and division has been furthered and normalized by President Trump. Behavior long festering underground has been validated and allowed to reach the surface.

In the years following Trump's election, racial and religious prejudices boiled over; the KKK removed their white hoods and took back to the streets. Unresolved tensions around policing and criminal justice were exacerbated. Inflammatory anti-immigrant policies have divided the nation. Anti-Semitism is increasing. Income inequality is at an all-time high. Discrimination in housing, education, and unemployment has deepened the divide. Hyper-partisanship and demagoguery are destroying democracy and have rendered government institutions paralyzed.

The degradation of our government is both an aggravating cause and a contributing effect of the country's division. Faith and trust in our government have continued to dissipate for decades. It is a self-fulfilling prophecy. People believe in government less, support government less, and thus government produces less.

I do not blame President Trump for creating this situation; that would give him too much credit. I do, however, believe the Trump presidency is the product of this downward trajectory. And, as a master marketer and salesman, he recognized, seized, and exploited it. A unified country that believed in itself and in the strength and capacity of government would never have elected Donald Trump. He is the symptom of an illness untreated.

Trump's slogan "Make America Great Again" was a dog whistle recalling a time of white dominance and small government. Trump sensed growing racial and economic divisions and discontent, and he capitalized on them. A unified country that believed in the strength and capacity of government would've repelled the Trump candidacy.

Trump senses the marketplace and rides the wave. He sees where the public is marching, runs to the front of the parade, and bangs the drum the loudest. We have reached a point where people don't even remember what government has accomplished. Generations have come and gone since government won wars, produced the GI Bill of Rights, passed Social Security and Medicare, built bridges and a national highway system, and enacted the Civil Rights Act.

If you don't believe government is capable of performing, you don't bother electing people who can make it perform. Trump never promised any positive performance. He never laid out an affirmative goal, mobilized public support, or developed the government that could achieve it. House Speaker Sam Rayburn used to say, "Any jackass can kick down a barn, but it takes a good carpenter to build one." He was right. Getting government to actually deliver a quality product on time is no small feat. Passing a new piece of legislation is not easy. Trying to move government quickly or precisely is like driving a tractor trailer on a race course. Its design is the obstacle. That does not mean it's impossible, but it is difficult.

I know the challenge well. I've spent much time in the bowels of the beast. As a young man frustrated with government's lack of performance, even when my father was governor, I set up a nonprofit to provide housing for the homeless and get them out of welfare hotels. I spent eight years at HUD, the most dysfunctional of all the federal agencies. I've spent ten years as governor. I know that government can make a difference. I also know all too well how hard it is, how much skill and effort it takes, and that government is only as strong and effective as the level of public support and unity it inspires.

IN MARCH THE STATE LEGISLATURE, which normally meets from January to June and recesses for the remainder of the year, was still in session. The key legislative action is normally the passage of the budget by April 1, but for years the state legislature never actually passed the budget "on time." It became a joke and a symbol of government dysfunction.

The truth is, the budget is hard to pass because it allocates every dollar of the state's $175 billion. The two houses of the legislature have their own priorities, and each region of the state has competing priorities. Upstate New York and downstate New York are very different places. In years past, it was such a difficult equation to solve that the governor and the legislative leaders gave up. It was not unlike the federal government, which doesn't even try to pass a budget anymore and just rolls forward with what they call continuing resolutions, which are slight modifications to the existing budget.

IN THE PRECEDING THIRTY YEARS, governors had passed an on-time budget only seven times. Batting .233 is barely acceptable in baseball but certainly not in government. When I took office, I took it as a personal mission to get it done, to demonstrate government credibility. We did that. I've passed an on-time budget every year of my administration, the first time one administration has done this in more than fifty years. Having said that, I acknowledge that getting a significant piece of legislation passed is still no small feat. Now, with the first "hot-spot cluster" in the country, we needed to pass a plan for how the state would handle the COVID crisis.

The governor's legal power to handle a "disaster" was actually very limited and amounted to basically expedited procurement. It's a law that was constructed in a different time for different situations. I told the legislature that this situation would dwarf anything we had seen in New York, including the devastation wrought by Superstorm Sandy in 2012 and the two terrorist attacks on the World Trade Center in 1993 and 2001. I told them that without the legal responsibility to handle the situation, I would not represent to the people of the state that I was in charge. If 213 members of the legislature wanted to manage the COVID situation, God bless them. I wouldn't take on the responsibility without the authority. I wasn't bluffing. Any other arrangement would be chaos.

I knew confidence in government in the middle of an emergency was a tall order. What we were attempting to do was virtually impossible. I would not ask the people of the state to trust me if I didn't know I could deliver. Allowing different local governments to put different policies in place, often inconsistent with surrounding policies, is asking for chaos. To handle the emergency unfolding in front of us, I needed the authority to make decisions for the welfare of the entire state.

Many politicians think they want control, but they don't really want the responsibility that comes with it. They do, however, want control of the microphone. I have seen too many situations where a politician will adopt a different policy from a neighboring jurisdiction just to be different. No one gets a headline by saying, "We're doing the same thing as everyone else." I have made this mistake myself before. But the virus does not respect city or county boundaries or even state boundaries. We were watching the situation unfold in California with caution as different cities and counties took different actions, with some declaring emergencies and restrictions and others not, while a confused public tried to understand which path was correct.

The legislative proposal we put forth accomplished two goals: fund coronavirus as a statewide emergency and give the governor power to set statewide policy. It was obvious to me that this was the only way to proceed. But it would not be easy with the legislature, where politics often drive lawmakers to "bring home the bacon" for their local district, be that government funds, patronage, or political power. And as I said, one part of New York State is very different from another.

As an elected official, I'm less worried about political consequences and more worried about the governmental consequences. At times, my father and I had both made the mistake of focusing on the immediate politics of a situation, and I would not make it again. I am focused on the real-life effects that will be judged by the history books or judged by me when I'm sitting in my rocking chair explaining my actions to my grandchildren. I was not playing politics with COVID. All that mattered was that people would die or lives would be saved.

The Speaker of the assembly, Carl Heastie, and the senate majority leader, Andrea Stewart-Cousins, are good politicians, and they are also responsible government leaders. They knew what needed to be done and how we needed to do it. I told them that I would not be taking significant actions without consulting them; our relationship had proven productive for the state in the past and would again.

The day after our first COVID case, the legislature passed the law giving the governor emergency powers to handle the crisis. If the legislature had not passed the law, I would not have had the power to do what I would soon do. There would be no executive order closing businesses or schools, no order requiring masks or social distancing. The legislature still retained their authority, and they could override any executive order with a simple majority vote. The law was smart, and it has proven successful. It might not have been politically smart for me, because it made me personally responsible for all the difficult decisions ahead.

MARCH 6 | 22 NEW CASES | 5 HOSPITALIZED | 0 DEATHS

———

"I'm urging reality. I'm urging a
factual response as opposed to an
emotional response."

AFTER THE FOURTH OR FIFTH DAY OF
briefings, I knew that I would be doing
them every day for the foreseeable future. I stuck
to the format, because I thought consistency of
presentation was effective and offered its own kind
of comfort to viewers; they knew what to expect.
That's why we tried to do our briefings at the same
time every day, unlike the chaotic and rambling
briefings the White House staged at varying times.
Our briefings were at 11:30 A.M., and generally I
could be back in the office at about 1:30 P.M. Then
the operational focus began.

On Friday, March 6, while New York still had
very limited testing capacity, we could test beyond
the restrictive criteria that the CDC had put out.
I announced in my press conference who would
be eligible, including New Yorkers with symptoms

who had traveled from hot-spot parts of the globe and contacts of known positive cases. Later that day, almost as if in response, President Trump, while touring the CDC headquarters in Atlanta, said that "anyone who wants to get a test can get a test." Of course, this was not true and sowed further chaos and confusion, and our social media team had to work overtime to clarify who was actually able to get a test in New York State.

By this point, we had put together the New York State Interagency Task Force to focus on testing priorities, quarantine, and containment tracking, including our health commissioner, Dr. Zucker, and three of my all-stars: Linda Lacewell, superintendent of the Department of Financial Services; Gareth Rhodes, deputy superintendent and special counsel of the Department of Financial Services; and Simonida Subotic, deputy secretary for economic development. Simonida went to Wadsworth to oversee their work to increase capacity. Linda focused on the daily reporting and monitoring hot spots. Gareth focused on building lab capacity.

THERE WAS NO BLUEPRINT for this undertaking. No governor had faced this challenge. But in some ways it was basic. For me, it was about developing a relationship, and a relationship is based on trust and trust comes from the truth. If they did not trust my credibility, they would not trust me, the information

I gave them, or my proposals. The same way I cannot deliver a speech that I have not written because the words must be mine, I would not be effective in communicating the facts of COVID if I didn't understand them, and I didn't know if I could learn them quickly enough. We consulted with experts from many different organizations, hoping to find consensus to guide us. These included researchers from the WHO, for the international perspective; the public health school at Drexel University in Philadelphia; the SUNY Albany research center that works with the Department of Health; the renowned modelers from Imperial College in England; and global experts including Dr. Michael Osterholm, an epidemiologist and director of the Center for Infectious Disease Research and Policy at the University of Minnesota. It was a great network of people who were all doing this for free.

Unfortunately, every expert had a different position on the "facts." My goals were to speak to all of them and to ask the questions savvy New Yorkers would ask. To research the actions of other countries to determine what worked and what didn't work. To research past pandemics to see what we could learn.

I then presented what I'd learned to the people in a totally transparent manner because I knew long before this crisis happened that trust has to be earned, competence must be proven, credibility must be established. The briefings needed to do that.

The founding fathers were right: Government can be an instrument for social progress. If that foundation is successfully created, there is no limit to what society can achieve. However, the founding fathers assumed public trust and government competence. Today we live in a hyper-partisan divided world with so much of our "news" and information coming from biased sources. We get conservative facts from Republican news channels, or we get liberal facts from Democratic news channels. That news is funneled through social media echo chambers by algorithms that target and cater to specific people inclined to believe it. And then we wonder why the public is fragmented and disillusioned. No one knows what and whom to trust. I would have to convince people that I was delivering an unbiased truth with facts. The people needed to trust me on this before I could ask them to act.

As the days passed, it was clear that this wasn't just about my ability to garner the attention of people so I could present this troubling and complex information. We would also need support for drastic remedies while not causing panic. We were already talking about precautionary quarantine, mandatory quarantine, and mandatory isolation. It was all frightening. It was a fine line to walk, and my message would not be going out in a vacuum. The president, vice president, and their federal mouthpieces were all communicating. Other governors, mayors, and public health officials were communicating. Cable news was providing around-the-clock coverage featuring every talking head in the country. Different states and cities were taking different actions. People were confused by the divergence of opinions, which only vindicated their cynicism about government.

Most of all, I was concerned about public panic. I had seen it before when I was at HUD. I'll never forget the images I witnessed during one hurricane warning in the Southeast, people blowing through red lights at intersections with a policeman banging on the hood of a car to avoid being run over while trying to direct traffic. Panic is the real enemy, even more than the initial disaster. Once people are panicked, there is chaos. A natural disaster can be managed; a panicked population cannot.

Counties around the Bay Area were among the first in the country to take decisive action, and it sent ripples of fear across the nation. The mayor of San Francisco announced a "shelter in place" policy on March 16. Shelter in place was originally used in the 1950s in anticipation of a nuclear attack. In San Francisco, it was first used as a cautionary alert in anticipation of a possible earthquake. The policy literally means to seek out shelter in an interior windowless room in your home and remain there until the "all clear" sign is given. It was a startling and frightening concept, especially for those of us old enough to remember the nuclear attack drills in elementary school when we were sent to the basement of the school to hunker down. This wasn't what Mayor London Breed intended; she meant simply that people should stay home. But the headline traveled across the country. I could see fear in the people around me, their eyes widening with anxiety. Communication is an art form, especially when emotion is running high; I'd already got in trouble when I used the term "containment zone" in New Rochelle. When we issued our own order in New York on March 20, I would speak about "staying home" and "pausing," which I considered more comforting terms.

This was a highly emotional time. We were navigating the unknown. People would be afraid and isolated. I wanted to say to people, you are not alone, I am here with you. I will be here with you every day. I will do my best to inform myself, and I will tell you everything that I know without any political filter. We will make decisions together, and even if we disagree, you will know why we are doing what we are doing, and you will know that what we are doing I believe is in our best interest. I wanted people to understand that even in this time of slanted "news" on both sides of the political spectrum, unvarnished truth still existed, and they could find it with me. There was no example that I could follow. FDR's fireside chats were the only parallel I could find.

A lot happened before the 11:30 briefings every morning.

The numbers came in around 3:00 A.M. Melissa

would get on the phone with Gareth and Dr. Jim Malatras between 4:00 A.M. and 5:00 A.M. to talk about them and what needed to be included in that day's presentation.

Gareth is thirty-two years old and started working for me when he was twenty-two years old. During those ten years, he left to attend Harvard Law School and ran for Congress. Bright, hardworking, and effective, he is a superb manager who makes the bureaucracy produce. It is an art form. You can be both charming and purposeful.

Jim has been with me even longer and is one of the best policy minds not just in New York State but far beyond. When I was attorney general, Jim helped write the law that helped local governments consolidate, and went on to serve as director of state operations. Jim is a workaholic with an exceptional sense of humor. He has a PhD in political science—so while he is technically a doctor, he is not what I consider in a public health crisis to be a "real doctor," a fact that I pointed out in my briefings, much to the chagrin of PhDs nationwide.

Melissa would text me the numbers so that I could look at them as soon as I woke up at 5:00. When I got to the office between 6:00 A.M. and 7:00 A.M., there was a stack of paper—testing numbers, hospitalizations, hot spots. I would pepper the team with questions and then write the whole presentation by hand myself. It was important to me that everything I conveyed at the briefings was logically organized and in my own words. And I'd draw the visuals for each of the twenty or thirty slides for that day. One day I wanted to visualize the threat facing New York's hospital system, so I sketched a tidal wave representing COVID cases cresting upward, and in the sea below, a hospital. I can't claim to have much talent as an artist, but I knew the information I wanted conveyed. I would note where the clicks went to advance the text or slides in the PowerPoint; I held the clicker during the briefing, so those were important. Noah Rayman, Will Burns, and Jack Davies—three of the smartest, hardest-working, and most reliable aides anyone could ask for—would scramble to bring the entire thing to life, complete with graphics, charts, and art, to convey the day's message.

As time went on, the team wanted to use more modern visuals on the PowerPoint, with different colors and fonts. They thought ours looked straight out of the 1960s. But I didn't want to make it look slick. I wasn't trying to sell anything.

After the presentation of the day's facts and numbers and statistics, I would offer my personal take on how we were doing, under a banner on the PowerPoint slide that said "Personal Opinion." When I was afraid and I was frustrated, I said that. I did not know what tomorrow would bring. When I was sad, especially when the fatalities began, I communicated honestly and extemporaneously exactly what I was feeling. All we can do is our best, and all I could do was my best. I vowed I would work as hard as I could, be open and honest and present every day.

We also had to coordinate the voices within this state. New York has the same political divide seen in the rest of the country. We are a majority Democratic state, but we are about 40 percent Republican. There is New York City, but there are also rural counties that have more cows than people. All politicians want to dictate policy for their jurisdictions, but it was vital that government speak and act with one voice. Different or competing plans would only further confuse an already frightened public and further erode confidence. While we have our political differences, in New York we lived through the experience of 9/11 together, and most understand that at a time of emergency, building unity and commonality are the primary responsibilities of a true leader. Fortunately, in the face of this unique challenge, 90 percent of the politicians in New York were collegial and helpful and eager to cooperate. In truth, I suspect they were happy to let us lead in those days when all the news was bad. We would have to deal with harsh conservative elected officials in upstate New York who followed the Trump doctrine of denial. Downstate, we would have to deal with Mayor de Blasio, who was quick to make public pronouncements despite his having no authority under the law to do so. And I was sure that sooner or later we would run afoul of President Trump. He used the partisan divide to insulate himself and demonize any contrary voices. He would surely accuse me of playing politics as soon as what I was saying was not convenient for him.

I am not a typical politician. If I were, I would have run for president. Period. I had to make sure that it was clear that I had no agenda besides helping New Yorkers. This was not about me, it was about them. And there was no politics at play. I am a Democrat and a proud Democrat. I am the son of Mario Cuomo and a proud son. But I am first and foremost governor of all New Yorkers.

A rumor would emerge in mid-March after the briefings had become popular nationally that I might be interested in being vice president on a Biden ticket. Although I specifically denied it several times, the rumor was difficult to kill. I could anticipate President Trump's tweet: "Andrew is just running for vice president." Nothing was more important to me than my ability to do my job in this moment. Therefore, in Shermanesque, absolutely clear, and specific language, I would repeatedly state that I had no political aspirations beyond being governor of New York. I would not run nor accept the nomination for vice president. Never satisfied, the New York press asked the next question: "Did I want to go to Washington in a Biden administration?" My answer was again definitive: I wanted no position in the Biden administration; I was governor of New York. I would not let politics get in the way. If they wanted to attack my analysis or plan, they would have to do it on the merits.

"I have officially declared a state
of emergency."

O NLY SIX DAYS AFTER OUR FIRST REPORTED
case in the state, we got word of two confirmed cases in Saratoga County, thirty miles north
of Albany and at the foothills of the Adirondack
Mountains. One of the patients was a pharmacist
who had been working out of different pharmacies,
so he was in contact with hundreds of people in the
area. That changed the tenor of fear upstate.

Meanwhile, the virus was spreading in Westchester, following the trail of patient zero.

The following day, a Sunday, we got in the helicopter and visited the main lab at Northwell in
Nassau County, one of the largest hospital systems
in the state. We were federally authorized to conduct
tests only at the state lab at Wadsworth, but not at
Northwell and other labs, although I already knew
we needed to utilize them. The early kits provided by
the CDC produced false positives, and even when

the kinks were corrected, the CDC didn't have the capacity for the number of tests we needed. The WHO had been offering test kits to "underresourced countries" but deemed wealthy countries like the United States capable of developing their own.

We still needed FDA approval before we could run the test that Wadsworth had developed at other labs in New York State. Dr. Dwayne Breining, executive director of Northwell Labs, showed me the instruments that, once the FDA approved, would be used to run the Wadsworth test, doing a few hundred a day and requiring a lot of labor and time. Next he showed me a machine called the Hologic Panther, which was a fully automated high-throughput machine and capable of running thousands of tests per day—but would need separate FDA approval! Seeing this machine, I knew we hadn't been thinking big enough. We didn't just need the FDA to approve our private labs to run the Wadsworth test; we also needed them to approve fully automatic testing on machines like the Panther, and fast.

Back in Albany, I inquired about what might be done to get fully automated machines like the Hologic machine I had seen at Northwell up and running. I was told that Roche, a Swiss company with a U.S. headquarters and manufacturing facility in Indiana, was in line for FDA approval of its fully automatic testing system in the coming days. This would be a major breakthrough that would allow one machine to do thousands of tests a day. I spoke with Matt Sause, CEO of Roche North America, on the phone along with Joe Lhota and Bob Grossman of NYU and Steve Corwin of NewYork-Presbyterian.

"Matt, how many Roche instruments can you get to New York and how fast?"

He agreed to have several delivered within the next week along with the chemical reagent allocations that would be a critical piece of ramping up early testing.

When visiting Northwell, I had made the case for the FDA to approve the lab to run the Wadsworth test, as well as approve several other of the state's most sophisticated labs. Hours after the event ended at Northwell, the FDA approved Northwell's lab to use the Wadsworth test. In thanking the FDA for their approval of Northwell, I noted that it was a good first step, but they needed to go further and expedite approval of the fully automated machines like the ones made by Roche and Hologic that would exponentially increase our testing capacity.

———

"New York Empire State. Progressive capital of
the nation. You are a problem solver."

I WAS JUGGLING THE BRIEFINGS IN THE
morning and then the operations in the afternoon. For me the two functions demanded two
very different aspects of my personality. The briefings required me to be calming and confident and
emotionally connected. The operations meetings
needed me to be persistent, detail oriented, and
aggressive. Switching gears quickly that way was
not easy.

In a situation where everything is out of control, we seek to control anything we can. I needed
something that I could actually control and get
done myself, and quickly. One of the significant
issues was that stores were running out of hand
sanitizer. The fear of the virus was everywhere by
this point, and the immediate response was to stock
up on disinfectants, cleaning products, and hand
sanitizer. The government had suggested using it as

a precaution in addition to regular and thorough handwashing, and now you could not find a bottle on store shelves. On the internet a bottle that sold for $3 before the pandemic could now be priced as high as $50. The media was reporting on the scarcity, which only further increased the growing anxiety. Hand sanitizer is important, but washing your hands is just about as effective. If you want to be hypercautious, you can wash your hands with some alcohol.

I wanted to show people—and myself—that I could actually solve a problem, even if the problem was just the availability of hand sanitizer. I also needed a break from what I was dealing with. The first order of business was to find out what exactly hand sanitizer was. I figured it couldn't be that hard. It turned out hand sanitizer is more complicated than you think. I called several manufacturers (yes, me), and it turns out there is a variety. There are different scents and differing lotion capacities. A good hand sanitizer not only cleans your hands but also leaves them feeling soft and smooth. My hands have never been soft and smooth. I was interested only in the virus-killing capacity of hand sanitizer.

Someone suggested I contact our prison industry division, which employs prisoners to make various products, and it turned out that the prison industries program already made hand sanitizer. Who knew? Prison industries made a number of products including industrial cleaners, furniture, and clothing. And yes, they made hand sanitizer. Problem solved. Now we just had to focus on bottling and distribution.

Not so fast. It turned out the hand sanitizer made by prison industries was 50 percent alcohol based. The CDC had said that for hand sanitizer to be effective against COVID, it had to be at least 70 percent alcohol based. I called the CDC to figure out where they got the information leading to the 70 percent figure, but after being transferred to eleven different people, I gave up. I concluded that we would make hand sanitizer with a 75 percent alcohol base to be safe.

The prison industries made products for large-scale commercial use. Therefore, they used large drums to contain their products. We had to retool the industry. We needed small bottles and new equipment to fill the bottles. We needed additional holding tanks and large quantities of alcohol and lotions. It also appeared that alcohol was in short supply—of course, because all the manufacturers were increasing hand sanitizer production in an effort to meet soaring demand. After calling a dozen suppliers, I secured a significant amount. I spent hours getting the entire operation in gear, but it was actually a worthwhile distraction, though I could not have done it without Kelly Cummings, my director of state operations. As crazy as this hand sanitizer project was, Kelly never flinched and made it all happen.

Our hand sanitizer was called New York State Clean. It came in several sizes, including an easy-to-use gallon jug. Over time, we produced millions of bottles. You couldn't walk around New York without seeing a New York State Clean hand sanitizer bottle. We flooded subways, buses, and more with free hand sanitizer.

But make no mistake, our hand sanitizer has no floral scent. It smells like embalming fluid and has a slight burn to it. After application one is tempted to make sure the skin is still intact. But it surpassed CDC guidelines and resolved the anxiety people had about running short of hand sanitizer.

Of course, in New York you get criticized for everything. There were complaints that it was an exploitation of the prison population to have inmates making hand sanitizer. I agree inmates are paid too little for the work they perform, and I have supported a higher minimum wage for inmates. But the fact that the prisoners were already making hand sanitizer and had been for years fell on deaf ears. The fact that the prison industry program was voluntary also fell on deaf ears. But as I have learned, an executive must make a decision that is right even if not everyone agrees. It is a difficult balance to do the right thing rather than the popular thing when your position is dependent on support of the people. The only path and rationale that I have found is to always assume that you are serving your last term and that what matters most is your legacy of success and integrity. There are no great political leaders who have followed the course of political expediency. There may be long-serving politicians who followed the path of political expediency, but none whom I would call great.

TRICKY CURVEBALLS COULD BE thrown at us at any moment, making an impossible situation even more difficult: For instance, Rick Cotton, the executive director of the Port Authority, tested positive for COVID. Rick, like me, is not a young man, and I had asked him to keep an eye on the airports when the crisis first started unfolding. Rick's agency, the Port Authority, has administrative responsibility for the airport facilities themselves, even though the federal Department of Homeland Security and Customs and Border Protection had screening jurisdiction. I felt personally responsible for Rick getting infected because he was there night and day at the airports under my instruction. He was at home and doing fine, but it was still scary, although a photograph of him in his silk bathrobe snapped by a photographer lurking nearby when he opened his door to accept a delivery ended up gracing the pages of the **New York Post** and lightened the moment. True to form, even with COVID, Rick looked good. Nonetheless, I was asking people to literally risk their lives.

As we could see the oncoming wave of infections

slowly building, I boiled down my role to two parts. I had to communicate with the people of the state the scope of the problem and the plan forward. And I had to marshal a government that could actually execute the plan. The last time government needed to rise to a challenge of this magnitude was when the federal government had to retool the economy to produce tanks, missiles, bombs, and guns and draft an army for World War II. Government doesn't do big, bold things anymore. It doesn't even try. The lack of national unity and the lack of a competent government go hand in hand. One precedes the other.

This was beyond the scope of a state government and would have been highly challenging even for a competent federal government. The systems and functions necessary to fight a virus don't exist. There is no adequate operational public health system in this country. Large-scale testing for a disease and contact tracing exist only in textbooks. No government in this country is capable of building new hospital structures on an emergency basis. We don't have the manufacturing companies to make new medical supplies. Government is not equipped to develop and build large systems quickly. But, I told myself, we are where we are. The moment is here, and we will fight the battle with what we have.

I assumed and hoped the federal government would do its job. I at least assumed the federal government would try to help. I prepared a small note card on one of the first days that I carried with me at all times. It reminded me of the four priorities I must focus on: First, communicate with the public and develop a relationship of trust so they accept and follow the plan. Second, focus on government operations necessary to execute the plan. Third, get as much help from the federal government as possible. Fourth, keep my head focused and in the game, and stay positive. It all sounded so easy at the time.

———

"When you politically interfere with science,
that's when you tend to make a mistake."

I CALLED INTO MY CONFERENCE ROOM THE leadership of the Wadsworth Center, Dr. Michael Ryan, Dr. Jill Taylor, other health department officials, and members of my executive team including Melissa, Gareth, and Simonida. I began the conversation with my usual salutation: "Pardon my ignorance, but I don't know what I'm talking about and I have to be educated. So excuse me if I ask simple or stupid questions." First question, "What is large-scale testing?" The blank faces let me know that we were in trouble.

Wadsworth had done groundbreaking work over the years. However, the lab does not do high volume or mass testing, and that was exactly what we needed.

"This doesn't work," I told the team assembled around the big table that was in my father's conference room as well. When I became governor, I asked the Office of General Services if they had any idea where my father's conference table was. They found it in a warehouse in Schenectady.

The conference room is filled with other things that are meaningful to me. There is a humidor gifted to me by President Clinton and a piece of original terra-cotta from the New York State Capitol roof signed by a workman in 1867. On the wall hangs an original sepia-tone poster from FDR's reelection campaign in 1930 that reads, "Re-elect Governor Franklin D. Roosevelt for Progressive Government." I also have the official Senate roll call from my confirmation as HUD secretary in 1997 and the flag that flew over the Capitol in Washington that same day, a gift from the late, great senator Ted Kennedy.

Sitting at my father's table, surrounded by these mementos, I was reminded of my father telling me that in the midst of the daily tumult, as difficult as things seemed in the moment, tomorrow will come. It also reminded me that it's not about the destination; it's about the journey. There will always be more to do. There will always be more to accomplish. There will always be more wrongs to right. But we do the best we can every day, and we are committed to the battle.

"A week ago, I said we'd be doing a thousand tests a day. How do we bring this to scale? Forget a thousand a day; we need to be doing ten thousand or more a day."

Several people in the room looked at me as if I were asking for a cure for cancer by 10:00 that night. My role in meetings like this is to be the aggressive CEO. I have a policy I've named "constructive impatience," which promotes an aggressive posture in problem identification and resolution. Unlike at the morning briefings when I was trying to be calm and assuring, in these meetings I was more activist and probing; in other words I could be a pain in the heinie. That's why I called these meetings "peeling the onion." They are to strip away issues to get to the essence of the matter, and someone usually cries in the end.

In large institutions and organizations, people often create a culture that is nonconfrontational and adopt a behavior of avoidance. That can be the enemy of problem solving when time is of the essence. The Department of Health's senior team were all experienced long-term civil servants. They knew the state health regulations backward and forward. They had worked in the bureaucracy for years and were well versed in the culture. The Department of Health developed and promulgated regulations, but they were not known for rapid deployment or rigorous timelines. That mentality was incongruous with the skill set necessary to address COVID.

The FDA had approved Northwell to test after my Sunday visit and this afternoon had authorized just a handful of other labs—NewYork-Presbyterian, Memorial Sloan Kettering, University of Rochester Medical Center, Roswell Park, and SUNY Upstate Medical University—to test. But this was still not getting us to where we needed to be.

"How many labs do we have in New York State?" I asked. Again, blank stares. No one was sure. "About two hundred," Dr. Ryan said. "How many of those labs can test for COVID?" Silence. Then Dr. Ryan spoke up with a suggestion. "Of the two hundred labs, there are about twenty-eight that are the ones we know and trust completely."

I asked Melissa to put together a team to immediately go make phone calls to each lab. I have total confidence in Melissa, and it is a great luxury for me. I asked Dr. Zucker to call the FDA that night to ask for the ability for Wadsworth—not the FDA—to approve each of these labs to test, removing an unnecessary roadblock.

At the end of the meeting I said, "Well, one thing is clear: It's up to us."

MARCH 11 | 44 NEW CASES | 32 HOSPITALIZED | 0 DEATHS

———

"New York State is going to take matters into its own hands."

WE ANNOUNCED THAT THE PUBLIC COLLEGES would be closing for distance learning for the remainder of the semester. We'd already recalled students in study abroad programs; now teachers and administrators were nervous that students at upstate schools might be visiting family downstate for spring break, or hitting the beaches in Florida and Laguna Beach, and then unwittingly bring the virus back to campus. At first, we talked about moving up spring break, but we realized that we'd need to shut campuses down for two or four weeks at minimum, and there wasn't much school year left anyway, so we said, "Forget it, let's just close."

Closing state colleges was my signal to private colleges that they should consider the same. Many people thought I was overreacting, but I would rather err on the side of caution. I would prefer to be blamed for unnecessary inconvenience than have to give condolences to the grieving parents of a dead student.

SOME ON THE RIGHT were blaming China for allowing the virus to spread. Trump wasn't helping by constantly referring to it as "the China virus." On March 10, an Asian woman in Manhattan was attacked with a punch in the face for not wearing a mask. Masks weren't yet required for everyone, so this was clearly someone targeted for her ethnicity. It was another caution to me about the delicacy of society's emotional response and how quickly fear turns into anger. The communication strategy was everything.

MARCH 12 | 56 NEW CASES | 47 HOSPITALIZED | 0 DEATHS

"Reduce the spread of the disease to make sure
that you can treat the number of people who
get infected."

EVERYTHING WAS RAMPING UP AT LIGHT
speed: the public anxiety, the avalanche of press
inquiries, the challenge of coordinating hundreds
of local governments and school districts. Each
hour brought dozens of new issues to light, none of
which were readily answered.

The increase in the number of cases in less than
two weeks since the first case was alarming. We were
watching the health system in Italy melt down and
starting to talk to hospitals about developing surge
capacity, increasing ventilator supply, setting up
temporary hospitals, and possibly canceling elective
surgeries, which would free up a lot of beds. We
were also very aware of the deaths in the nursing
home in Washington State; early in the outbreak—
before a single person had died of COVID in
New York—we required our nursing home staff to

wear masks, be monitored for symptoms, cohort residents with COVID separate and apart from noninfected residents, and allow no visitors except in possible exigent circumstances.

We announced that gatherings with more than five hundred attendees must be canceled or postponed. As part of that, we shut down Broadway theaters. Initially, the theaters wanted to operate at half capacity, but they soon capitulated to our full closure, in part because that way they'd be entitled to insurance money, which would save them from bankruptcy.

When we announced that the St. Patrick's Day Parade would be postponed, a reporter from the **New York Post** complained, "There are a lot of people who love the parade." She was right: New York loves parades. Almost every group has its own parade. We have the Celebrate Israel Parade, the Greek Parade, the Columbus Day Parade, the West Indian Day Parade, the National Puerto Rican Day Parade, the African American Day Parade, the Pride March. The parades are a symbol of our diversity and a sign of respect for every member of our New York family. The St. Patrick's Day Parade is one of the oldest and largest parades. Not only is it a tribute to the Irish community, but it is also a favorite of the Catholic Church. I am Catholic but have had my issues with the hierarchy of the Catholic Church. I support a woman's right to choose and marriage equality. The Catholic

Church is vehemently opposed to both. New York was the first big state to pass marriage equality legislation that allowed same-sex couples to marry, and the Church never forgave me. It didn't really matter that the Supreme Court of the United States went on to find prohibition against same-sex marriage to be unconstitutional; the Church still didn't let me forget. I remember attending a service with my daughters at a church in Mount Kisco the Sunday after passing that law. The priest gave a homily about how reprehensible marriage equality was. We got up and left in the middle of the service. This was after we'd had to leave our previous church because the congregation gave the priest a hard time for letting me attend services there because I was divorced. I also had refused to get an annulment that would have made my children illegitimate. I had also advocated for and signed the Child Victims Act into law, allowing people who were sexually assaulted by a member of the clergy to sue for damages. This law had significant financial ramifications for the Catholic Church.

My father also supported a woman's right to choose, and at the time the Catholic Church threatened my father with excommunication. My father was raised on the old Baltimore Catechism; by those rules, if you were excommunicated, you could not get into heaven. Purgatory was the best you could hope for. But then the Church eliminated purgatory as a concept, and now you had a real conundrum. It hurt my father deeply, and he gave a famous speech at the University of Notre Dame explaining how he reconciled his Catholic faith with his public duty as governor. But these were old and deep wounds.

The tension with the Church was personally painful to me as well. As a former altar boy raised in Catholic schools, I will say that their displeasure still resonates to this day. Postponing the St. Patrick's Day Parade was going to make a bad situation worse, I feared.

In retrospect, shutting down the parade was an obvious move to make, but at the time, when all of this was still new and unfolding, the critics were loud and had a lot of support. St. Patrick's Day is a high holy day in New York. However, the history and facts were undeniable. In the 1918 flu pandemic, Philadelphia allowed a parade in support of Liberty Bonds for World War I, which increased the spread of the virus exponentially. Even during these early days of the coronavirus, we had seen that allowing large celebrations to go on in other states resulted in long-term damage and even death. New Orleans had allowed Mardi Gras celebrations to go forward in late February, an "epidemiologist's nightmare," as The New York Times put it.

At this point the federal government hadn't even put forth national guidelines to establish which activities were safe and which should be prohibited, leaving decisions to state and local governments.

This has its downsides. Local politicians are focused on their smaller, regional constituencies, which means making decisions that offend the local community is not easy. National guidance can be helpful. Also, when I get to the pearly gates, I don't believe postponing the St. Patrick's Day Parade will be at the top of the list of reasons why I am denied admission. At the end of the day, the hard decision was the right decision, and the history books will make the ultimate determination.

The St. Patrick's Day Parade highlighted an ongoing major tension in taking action. I wanted to be aggressive in combating the virus, but we could not get ahead of the degree of public acceptance and compliance. If the public refused to follow an executive order, it would all be over. They would then disregard all the difficult executive orders, and we would be powerless to enforce compliance. I needed to bring the public along with me. If we canceled the St. Patrick's Day Parade but people showed up anyway, it would signal a major problem. Fortunately, the officials involved in the parade were all too willing to support my decision as long as I went first and took the heat.

MARCH 13 | 102 NEW CASES | 50 HOSPITALIZED | 0 DEATHS

———

"At times of crisis you tend to see what people are really made of."

W E DID THE MORNING BRIEFING FROM NEW Rochelle, which now had the highest cluster of cases in the country. We had already closed the schools there and banned large gatherings, and the National Guard had come in to help clean and distribute meals to people in quarantine.

I felt it was important to let people know that basic security was in place and life's essentials would be intact. I ordered a ninety-day moratorium on any eviction for nonpayment of rent due to lack of income from being laid off or furloughed from work. People would have a place to live. I also ordered that no public utilities could be turned off. People would have electricity and phone service. We announced the state would establish emergency food banks so no one would go hungry. We also announced that unemployment benefits would be immediately available so that people would have money in their pockets.

Later in the day, I spoke to both the vice president and the president about our ongoing testing needs, and they finally approved New York's request made earlier in the week to be able to approve any lab in the state to do COVID testing—a real breakthrough that practically took the FDA out of the lab-approval equation for New York. This enabled us to start activating our network of 250 local labs across the entire state, a game changer particularly months later, when long lag times from the major national labs slowed down the reporting of test results. This Friday we had hit our goal of a thousand tests a day, and with the ability to activate our local labs ourselves, we set a new testing goal for the next week: six thousand a day. We would beat this goal, hitting ten thousand tests a day by March 20, and would be doing twenty thousand tests a day by the beginning of April. But critical days had been lost as we sought federal approval.

On Friday, March 13, Roche's fully automated test was approved by the FDA. As other governors and elected officials scrambled to get in line to buy a Roche machine, New York was already on our way, installing the new machines we had secured earlier from Roche that days later would be doing thousands of tests per day. Bizarrely, at the White House press conference when President Trump announced that the FDA had approved Roche's fully automated system, he noted the approval would allow "1.4 million tests on board next week and 5 million within a month. I doubt we'll need anywhere near that." The comment underscored the skepticism from the very top about the seriousness of the virus and was a reiteration of Trump's stated belief that this would just "go away." Laboratory capacity was only one element. We needed testing sites for people to get swabbed in every corner of the state, more testing equipment, and a steady supply of collection kits and testing reagents, and we would also have to enlist and coordinate all the local departments of health in every county of the state. It was going to be a nightmare, period.

That day, the federal government also declared COVID a national emergency, after outbreaks of cases in more than twenty states, and two days after the World Health Organization affirmed we were in the midst of a pandemic.

SOMETIMES, THE DAY'S EVENTS required a second briefing. I wanted to publicly thank the president for allowing us to increase our testing capacity because I knew he needed to hear my gratitude if we were going to continue to work together. I was also beginning to suspect that there were thousands of cases of COVID we didn't know about because our testing was so limited. It was then that I shared my personal testing saga.

My three daughters are Cara, Mariah, and Michaela. Cara and Mariah are twins, twenty-five years old, and Michaela is twenty-two. Cara and Mariah graduated from college two years ago and were living in Manhattan and starting their professional careers pre-COVID. Michaela was to be graduating from Brown this year. I am blessed to say that I have a beautiful relationship with all three. It is true what they say. The years from about fifteen to about twenty-one can have their challenges, but sanity eventually returns: for both parents and children.

Cara called me and said one of her mother's friends tested positive for COVID. And the wheels began to turn. Michaela was still at school in Rhode Island but came back and forth to see me in Albany. Cara and Mariah went back and forth and saw me often as well. The detective work of contact tracing fell to me. First, we needed to get my ex-wife, Kerry, Cara's mother, tested, because she had definitely been in contact with a positive person and that was the protocol. In the meantime, those people in contact with Kerry needed to be quarantined.

After several conversations involving exquisite cross-examination, I learned that Cara had also been in contact with Kerry's friend. Cara didn't tell me that in the first conversation, because it was a fleeting contact that she didn't consider significant. But when you don't know exactly how the virus transmits, there is no way of telling what an "incidental" contact is.

Cara had to be quarantined for two weeks alone in her Manhattan apartment. She was not happy about this and considered it the "heavy hand of big government," which is even more complicated when the heavy hand belongs to your father. This experience showed me how difficult and disruptive quarantine would be for an individual. Two weeks alone in an apartment is a big deal. We were two weeks from our first case. No quarantine of any scale had been put in place in more than a hundred years. Let's just say it took numerous conversations to convince Cara that she needed to comply, and I could just imagine how hard this was going to be when we were trying to get thousands of people to quarantine when I did not have the advantage of the parental pulpit, however minimal that may be.

I called Michaela, who was at Brown, and she said she had just been with her mother the day before. While Cara was adamant that she was fine and this was all unnecessary, Michaela went the other way. COVID, in many ways, is a Rorschach test: Different personalities respond differently. It turned out that after Michaela had been with her mother, she had five other friends over to her apartment for the evening. She was worried that maybe her mother infected her and that Michaela had infected her five friends. I tried to calm Michaela and tell her that her mother was being tested and we would know in two days and then we would decide what to do.

Michaela did not want to wait two days, so she contacted all five friends immediately and told them to assume that they had the COVID virus. The five friends then got on the telephone and communicated with all the people they had been in contact with. They were college students and attending class, so I'm sure those calls involved dozens of people. Michaela was distraught and said she would stay in home quarantine and wait for the results of her mother's test.

I then called Mariah. Her reaction was to be upset that she had been subjected to the situation through no fault of her own. She was surprised by the randomness of the circumstances and was not happy. Mariah wanted to get tested immediately and have definitive answers. The fear of the unknown and the loss of control this virus spreads truly wreak havoc.

The person I was most concerned about was Cara because she had direct contact with a positive person. Given the incubation period, the fourteen-day quarantine was the smartest path. I would talk to Cara a couple of times a day. She watched my briefings because she had little else to do and was literally a captive audience. COVID now had her full attention. It felt so unnatural for me to have a daughter in distress and not be able to do anything to help her—to not even be with her, not be able to see her and hug her, and to know that she was alone.

Meanwhile, my mother, Matilda, is eighty-nine years young and in a vulnerable population for the coronavirus. I hadn't been able to see her since this started. Although I'm careful, my job puts me in contact with many people, and I would never want to infect her.

She had been living on her own since my father passed, with home health aides coming to help out, but that became a risk in itself, because the aides could bring the infection in. So starting in early March, she alternated going back and forth staying with my sisters, Maria, Madeline, and Margaret, a doctor.

Every day I called her, and every day she asked, "When is this going to end?" It's not that she didn't like staying with my sisters; she just wanted to be in her own home. She wanted her independence. Like so many people at the beginning of this crisis, she had a hard time comprehending how serious the threat was.

My sisters would tell her, "Andrew says you can't go home yet, it's too dangerous." I understood why they would blame me: I wasn't in the room!

My mother would say, "I'll be careful. I don't have to be here. I want to go home."

I would insist, but I had to strike a delicate balance. In her book a son doesn't have the right to tell his mother what to do. Nor is she that impressed with the concept of a "governor" as having any special authority over her, be it a husband or a son. My mother can still be very tough. I learned New York tough from her and my dad.

I knew many people were having similar conversations with their own parents, and I communicated that in my briefings. It was another way we were all in this fight together.

This is the cruel torture of COVID. Patients alone in hospitals, seniors alone in nursing homes, disabled people alone in group homes. Yes, it was for the best, but it is a terrible human toll. Can you imagine being in a hospital emergency room not knowing whether you will live or die, no family around you, and the nurses and doctors you see are wearing so much protective equipment that you can't even make out their faces? Terrifying, but that's what so many people experienced and continue to live through.

Because I grew up the oldest male in an Italian house with my three sisters, my instinct is to protect. My father was not around much; he worked all the time. And I mean all the time—seven days a week from when I was a child. He left in the morning before we woke up for school and came home after we were asleep. Sunday evenings he was supposed to be home by seven to have dinner. Even that deadline was often missed. Because of that, I was always rigorous about making time for my kids. When they were with me, I would be home by 5:00 P.M. I'd often drive back and forth from Albany to Westchester in a single day to see them.

My mother and my sisters relied on me. With my three daughters now, my natural orientation has never changed. I have to be careful how I express things because my daughters are always setting traps for me to fall into so they can accuse me of "paternalism," which is totally impolitic now. In my family, the line between parental responsibility and female empowerment must constantly be navigated.

While Cara is twenty-five years old, a Harvard graduate who has traveled the world and is smarter than I am, she is still my daughter. Cara is independent and resourceful. She is a strong, principled personality and has a great, dry sense of humor. I would say that she got it from me, but that would offend her. She also has an infectious laugh. There was no logical reason why she was not totally capable of handling this situation, or any situation, herself. Cara, more than the other two, bristles at my overprotective tendencies. I did the same with my father. But emotions are not logical. I felt powerless to help her, and it hurt me. At my briefings, I talked about how this saddened me and frightened me at the same time.

It appeared at the time that young people were relatively unaffected. But I knew too well that we didn't really have all the facts and the conventional wisdom was false comfort because it was constantly evolving. This was an emotional experience that we were all going to go through. There is comfort in knowing you are not alone in your emotions. You can validate emotions without validating the fear. Easier said than done, but that's where I needed to bring myself to be able to help other people get through this.

Luckily, the situation with Cara turned out fine. After several days of anxiety and fifty-seven telephone conversations, everyone was negative. Michaela had to call back her five friends, who then had to call back the dozens of people they contacted. The experience graphically illustrated for me how difficult this was going to be: the personal anxiety, the explosive expansion, the rush on testing, contact tracing, the anxiety of the unknown, the parental panic. For me, the lasting feeling was fear.

———

"Nobody believes there are only five hundred
cases of coronavirus in New York today. We
believe there are thousands of people who have
coronavirus, maybe tens of thousands."

EXACTLY TWO WEEKS AFTER OUR FIRST case, we reported our first death from COVID-19—an eighty-two-year-old woman in Brooklyn with emphysema. The situation felt urgent in a whole new way, especially because it came right on the heels of the scare with my family. This was also the same day we closed the state capitol, because members of the assembly tested positive, and that sent shock waves through the whole government.

People around me were getting tested, and we were socially distanced from one another during meetings and in the Red Room. We changed the staffing around the governor's suite. But the fear was everywhere. When someone handed me a document, I wondered, can I get COVID from paper?

—

MY FATHER ONCE SAID to me that it's hard to find a person who can come up with new good ideas, and it's also hard to find a person who can implement good ideas. But it's impossible to find a person who can do both. After all those sad conversations on the couch with him recounting our failures, I knew the right formula, impossible or not. It was doing both: doing the briefings in the morning and management efficiency in the afternoon.

Every day was developing the same rhythm, alternating between two main functions: communications and operations. Communications was preparing for the briefing, doing the presentation, answering the press questions. I had a great team, but not being able to gather all of the relevant people in a room and hold a proper face-to-face meeting was a real obstacle.

The operational issues were also hampered by the fact that the line where state responsibility ended and federal responsibility began was very unclear. And the federal government was not saying. Later, I realized they just didn't know.

We were attempting to outline the entire system that would need to be in place to deal with the virus itself. Of course, there were secondary consequences driven by the economic fallout and social issues, but the first priority was to handle the pandemic.

The medical response would start with intake facilities, testing facilities, quarantine facilities, hospital capacity, hospital equipment, and medical staff. Every element of the system posed a problem. Either the scale was nowhere near adequate, or it didn't exist at all.

There were so many questions: How large would the universe of infected people be? How many people could be infected, and how many people would we need to treat? The challenge was driven by quantity, and we needed a number.

Several firms were doing projection models of the rate of infection. Models provided specific ranges and dates for the spread, the rate of transmission, the number of hospital beds needed, and the number of deaths anticipated. There were so many projections that we had hired the consulting firm McKinsey to review all the models and give us a workable range.

Modeling the spread of the virus is a little less precise than modeling weather patterns; at least forecasters can point out the number of variables. In the coronavirus projections, the variable was human behavior. There is more data available on wind patterns than on possible human responses.

The U.S. models had the advantage of being able to study the spread in the countries that went before us, like China, South Korea, Italy, and others in Europe, to get a sense of what was going to happen in the United States, and New York in particular. All the models were extrapolating out from the current viral transmission rate, and the main variable was how successful the closedown and social distancing policies would be. No one really knew, including me.

Every society is different, and our success was wholly dependent on what people themselves, rather than governments, chose to do. If people took the threat seriously, it would be one situation. If people were dismissive, there would be an entirely different outcome. In many ways the operational needs would be linked to my success in communication, because the more people were persuaded to follow our policy prescriptions, the lower the infection rate and the smaller the scale of our operations.

The White House Coronavirus Task Force had made a truly startling projection at the beginning of March, when the CDC suggested a minimum of 2.4 million Americans would be hospitalized and a maximum of 21 million. The tenfold range did not build confidence in the model, but even the minimum projection suggested catastrophe. Two million Americans hospitalized is staggering when you consider there were only 925,000 staffed hospital beds in the nation, and most of those beds were already used on a daily basis.

Again, in retrospect it is easy to see how dysfunctional the federal situation was. Their own projections of potential hospitalizations would have panicked any rational federal official. The president was in denial about his own experts' projections. On March 6, he said, "It'll go away," and later, after Dr. Fauci testified to Congress that the country was "failing" when it came to testing, Trump said of the virus, "We stopped it."

We needed to know the realistic range for New York so I could understand what we were really dealing with. The best estimates suggested that the state would need 110,000 to 140,000 total hospital beds in a day at the apex. I was shocked, because in total New York State has only 53,000 hospital beds and 3,000 ICU beds. The nightmare scenario was overwhelming the hospital system, and that's what we were watching on the nightly news in Italy, where people were dying in the street unable to access medical care, morgues were overwhelmed, and coffins were stacked in churches awaiting lonely burials after funerals were declared illegal. I knew that once the hospital systems became overwhelmed, lives that could have been saved would be lost. Compounding this was the concern that if the hospital system was overwhelmed, people suffering normal health emergencies, such as heart attacks and strokes, could not be treated.

There was no way that we could dramatically increase the number of hospital beds, although we were trying. I posed another option to the experts: What if we were more effective in changing human behavior? Could we reduce the number of those being hospitalized? But the experts did not believe it was possible to change social behavior quickly enough to make a real difference in the numbers. The news was so bad that it was almost inconceivable. I was stunned.

I called the president and explained the scenario. He was pleasant enough, but he just didn't want to hear it.

The truth is, I didn't want to hear it either, but I did. I met with my team every afternoon as soon as the briefings were over, and we went over dozens of what-if scenarios. It was clear we had to try to reduce the transmission rate, and at the same time we had to figure out a way to build hospitals in three weeks.

I was beginning to understand that this conversation with the people of my state was different from any conversation had in generations. This was not about normal government issues of budgets, taxes, roads, and bridges. This was about life and death. This was as real as it gets. No one knew the future, and no one knew how many would die.

I had an interesting conversation with a woman who had been watching the briefings. She said she was taken with the fact that I was "unflappable." "Unflappable" is a word that can mean totally different things to different people, so I asked what she meant. She said that I didn't seem "scared" about COVID.

"I don't mean to disappoint you," I said, "but you couldn't be more wrong."

She was surprised.

"I am more frightened about COVID than almost anything in my life," I said. I once had a serious health scare with Mariah when she was severely burned as a toddler, but second to that I have never been more frightened.

I had already been thinking about what dimension of the COVID crisis frightened me most. I think it was the "fear of the unknown known," as the expression goes. There were existing facts about this virus that we just didn't know yet, but I was sure that we would know in the future. Then, with the advantage of hindsight, we will say we should have made different decisions, such as asking people to wear masks sooner. A factor driving the fear for me was that the "facts" were already changing. The worst was the reversal on the belief that asymptomatic people couldn't spread the virus. We would have operated much differently if we had known that earlier. What else will we find out six months down the road?

The former defense secretary Robert McNamara talked about the "fog of war" in explaining his actions during Vietnam. What would the "fog of COVID" turn out to be? Will the antibodies have a secondary effect on people who were infected? Was there a drug that could have helped? Will the virus mutate and come back like the 1918 flu pandemic? Will a second wave be even worse?

I had this conversation with my daughters one

evening while sitting around the dinner table. They asked me how I seemed so calm at the briefings when they knew how anxious I was. I said to them, you can feel fear, but acting on fear is different. Even being governed by the fear is different. I think it is disingenuous when people say they weren't afraid in a situation that would normally trigger fear. Fear is a normal and healthy response to the appropriate stimulus. If you don't feel fear, you don't appreciate the consequences of the circumstance. I told them to confront the worst-case scenario and make peace with it. Resolve the anxiety. I understood the projection models. I knew how bad it could be. The questions are what do you do with the fear and would you succumb to it. I also told my daughters that there are little things you can do to help with the fear when you are speaking in public. Control your breathing by taking long deep breaths. Fill your stomach when you inhale. Don't drink coffee. I would not allow the fear to control me. The fear kept my adrenaline high and that was a positive. But I would not let the fear be a negative, and I would not spread it. Fear is a virus also.

I think people are often stronger and more capable than they realize. Insecurity causes them to underestimate themselves and is self-limiting. It also prevents them from pushing hard enough to reach their full potential. Many people are more powerful than they are in their day-to-day lives. If you never push yourself to your limit, you don't have to acknowledge your limit—that's the good news. The bad news is that you don't realize your full potential. For most people, this is a choice we make subconsciously.

Sometimes life brings you to a point where you either give up or push harder and dig deeper to find an unrecognized strength in your character. My divorce, political loss, and public humiliation did that to me. It was terrible, and it all happened at once. My life was upended: no home, no job, no prospects, my reputation trashed, my family embarrassed. It felt at the time as if things couldn't be any worse. It wasn't just my perception; objectively, it was a very bad time for me. I knew I had a choice: I could either give up, or I could look inside and work through how to change.

When I was starting to get stronger, after my darkest days, my father said to me, "What you went through was really brutal, and I told your mother I wouldn't blame him"—me—"if he spent the rest of his life on a barstool." He didn't mean it literally, but was just communicating that he felt my pain and respected my resilience. He was not the most emotionally fluent man, but I heard him and I appreciated his sentiment.

The adage "That which doesn't kill you makes you stronger" is true, and many people are stronger than they know. They just need the reason to reach their true limits. I also believe we are better, kinder, and more loving than we realize. Showing love makes us vulnerable, and we don't want to be vulnerable. We are also socialized to think showing love is showing weakness—especially men. I have gotten past that. I am an emotional person and I show it very openly in my personal life.

After what I went through, I became much more emotionally expressive. I wanted to fully communicate how I felt and understand the feelings of others. I try to ask questions to understand what makes other people tick. But in politics, I have remained what I would call emotionally reserved. Politics can be nasty. Opponents seize on any weakness. The press is always looking for any controversial statement or action to exploit. They said Vice President Al Gore had no sense of humor. They were wrong. I know him and he is as smart as people think he is and as honorable, but he is also witty and funny. He is a respectable pool player, too, and I have lost money to him. So why doesn't he show that side of himself in public? Because it is perilous. Emotion in politics is a risky proposition. It can always be misconstrued, and there are many forces looking to do just that.

This crisis, and the briefings, communicated my genuine self publicly. The trauma we were dealing with was emotional. It was driven by fear, anxiety, loneliness, and doubt. Quarantine specifics and testing protocols were not the only major issues to be processed. People were on emotional overload. How do you help others deal with the sense of fear and vulnerability? Show your own vulnerability first. Discuss your emotions and fears. And that's what I did in the briefings. It was authentic and real. I felt the same emotions so many people were feeling, and I would acknowledge them and show them. It was risky to do this, but I didn't really have a choice. First, I am emotional, and the situation did not allow me control or reservation. Also, I needed to connect with people where they were. I had to go to them—they would not come to me. If I was going to succeed, I would have to try. If it didn't work or backfired, I would fail. But if I didn't try, I would fail anyway. It was an easy choice.

That's where I was. If I expressed vulnerability and emotion and got criticized or mocked, I could handle it. I had been mocked before and survived. My kids would still love me. But if I didn't connect emotionally with the people, they would never have the trust and confidence in me to follow my proposals. To believe in me, they had to know me as a person and not as a government official. In the briefings I spoke the way I would speak to a close friend or to my daughters. I said the same words that I said to my mother and brother. Everything I communicated was true, unrehearsed, unscripted, and spontaneous. If people rejected me, so be it. That's the only way I could do it. I gave my heart in the briefings and people gave me theirs. The letters, emails, smiles, and thumbs-up on the streets were them showing their love because I showed my love.

And there is nothing better. I learned that even in the public arena vulnerability is always worth the risk, because without it there's nothing. I learned that in the right circumstances people can reach a higher level of trust and goodness. Sometimes it just takes the other person to go first. So I'll go.

GOOD QUARTERBACKS IN FOOTBALL can throw the ball brilliantly but can also take off and run the ball. I had always striven to be a "complete" government official. I worked to connect with people, motivate people, and drive a dialogue. But I also wanted to be a great executive with a government of extraordinary performance.

It quickly became clear that the claim that we had fifty-three thousand hospital beds in the state was misleading. The "state" had only a couple of thousand beds in public hospitals. The vast majority of beds in the state are owned and controlled by private hospitals, and each one is its own corporation with a board of directors or trustees, its own clientele. They had never been "controlled" by the state. The state government is their regulator, meaning the Department of Health promulgates regulations about safe operating conditions and also regulates certain financial aspects, but they are private entities in competition with one another.

There was the additional complication that most of our cases were in downstate New York, and many of the hospital beds were in the suburbs and upstate. Planning for an available capacity of fifty-three thousand hospital beds assumed you would be controlling all the beds statewide and that a patient from any area of the state could be placed in an available bed anywhere in the state. That is not how the system worked. Patients picked their hospital. There had rarely been a situation where an individual showed up at one hospital and was sent to a hospital in another region of the state. But we had no choice. I couldn't just sit there and pray, nor could I continue to ask the federal government for help that I couldn't count on coming.

I began calling the leaders of the major hospitals. Some of them had been with me during the first virus briefing on March 2. I have known many of the hospital administrators for years; once again, personal relationships are always most important. I explained the situation and the options. I wanted them to understand how dire the potential consequences were. For them to accept state control of the private health-care system would be a major hurdle. When they heard the numbers from the projection models, they understood why we needed to take such dramatic action. They didn't like it at all, but they couldn't deny the reality. We were all watching the collapse in Italy and the crushing impact on its health-care professionals. They did not want to be part of an international story of the failure of one of the greatest hospital systems in the world. Their bread and butter was people coming from all over the planet for treatment in their facilities. There were also significant financial concerns. I told them that we would need to agree to work together and get through the crisis and then they needed to trust me that we would work out the finances.

The individual phone calls to the biggest players laid the groundwork for their buy-in so that when we brought in the leaders of other hospitals around the state on group conference calls, every hospital knew its competitors and colleagues were in the same situation.

My first specific request bordered on the insane: Every hospital had to increase its capacity by 50 percent and stop elective surgeries to free up existing bed capacity. The 50 percent increase in capacity would take the entire system from about fifty-three thousand beds to seventy-five thousand beds. Even seventy-five thousand beds was only about 60 percent of the projected need.

The challenge to the individual hospitals was overwhelming. A hospital with two hundred beds would need to create an additional one hundred beds. Hospitals are normally highly regulated with specific requirements as to room size, staffing ratios, and so on. Now we were telling them to double the number of beds in some rooms, convert cafeterias to congregate areas, and find space wherever they could. For them it was an earthshaking proposition.

The second component, ending elective surgery,

would begin to reduce the current hospital population to make room for the COVID patients who were just days or weeks away. Elective surgery is also the primary source of income for hospitals. I explained that our plan assumed we had fifty-three thousand beds, all empty, so we had no alternative but to start creating capacity.

While many of the people I talked to said such an increase was impossible, I told them that impossible wasn't an option. After much discussion, we had consensus support. It was a relief to see that even large institutions, when they understood the consequences, were willing to accept major change. This was critical because if they had sued to stop me, they probably would have been successful, at least in the short run, and that's all we had—the short run.

———

"The curve is not a curve, the curve is a wave,
and the wave could break on the
hospital system."

THERE ARE SEVERAL MAJOR FACTORS TO consider when you close schools. You stop providing food for many students who rely on school lunches. The teachers in the school have concerns for their own health separate and apart from the students'. The teachers' union is very strong and influential with state and local politicians. At first, the unions were allied with local school districts and the state education department in saying, "You are out of your mind; you cannot close the schools." Children staying at home for long periods of time raises socialization and mental health issues. School districts are proudly locally run, and when the state or federal government makes a decision concerning schools, they often organize the parents in opposition.

As usual, some people wanted schools open and

some wanted schools closed tomorrow. It wasn't that easy. My grandfather had a great expression: "When you don't know what you're talking about, it always seems simple." Here's a question that illustrates how complicated the decision is: If the governor concludes that in the middle of a pandemic safety dictates he must close the schools, who does the most pivotal conversation include?

A. The local politician
B. The local teachers' union head
C. The local PTA
D. The local health commissioner
E. The local school board
F. The local hospital staff

The answer is F.

The most essential conversation around closing schools in the midst of a pandemic is, will the hospital staff show up for work if their children are at home? All other issues involve levels of political opposition, but the availability of hospital staff means life or death. In the situation we were facing, one needed to conclude that the politics and press coverage were irrelevant, as any disruption would cause opposition. To me there were only two relevant factors. Was it the right decision for the safety of the children and the school staff? And, if schools were closed and students were at home, would the nurses, doctors, and hospital staff need to stay home and take care of their children and therefore disrupt the operations of the hospitals and health-care facilities?

The majority of health-care workers are in working families without significant resources. Many earn near-minimum-wage salaries. Nurses are often mothers who are also working to manage households. If the health-care staff needed to stay home to care for their children and families, it would be a major problem. By definition, the intensity of the health issues driving the closing of the schools would be creating unprecedented demand on the local health-care system.

The same situation was presented for many of the essential workers. Police, firefighters, truck drivers, blue-collar workers operating vital systems—how did they take care of their children who would now be home?

That was the riddle that we had to solve. Where could we find large-scale childcare facilities to provide for the children of essential workers so we were sure they would show up for work? If we were going to close the schools immediately, we would need to set up large-scale childcare operations for the children of these essential workers. To do that, some schools would need to serve as safe childcare centers, and some teachers would have to staff them. In some cases, we would bring childcare workers to hospitals, so workers didn't have to go out of their way to drop their children off. We would need to open them on a regional basis and make sure the essential workers in that region understood their availability and were comfortable with the arrangement before we could actually close the schools. This all had to happen very quickly.

The teachers' and health-care unions have great reach and credibility with their members. If I could fashion a solution with them, they could quickly communicate to the membership and serve as credible validators of the system's safety. Many of the other essential workers also were members of powerful unions. As always, relationships matter. There would be no contracts or documentation, this would all have to be done on a handshake. We would need to understand that the situation would change going forward, that issues would pop up that we did not anticipate, and that we must deal with one another in good faith.

Sometimes, but not often, there is an advantage to being old. I had worked with the leadership of the major unions for many years. We knew one another well and trusted one another on a personal level. And this would have to be personal. Normally, a small change in work rules would be negotiated for weeks. In this case we would be setting up an entirely new system overnight. The relevant teachers' unions are run by Randi Weingarten, Andy Pallotta, and Michael Mulgrew. The main health-care union is 1199 and is run by George Gresham. I had worked with all of them on many issues. Recently, we had all gone to Puerto Rico to volunteer to help the island deal with Hurricane Maria.

I had a series of frantic phone calls over two days, most ending with the same phrase: "Don't worry, we will figure it out." As a result, New York State had a new system of childcare facilities managed by teachers and day-care providers that could provide for the children of classified "essential workers." In a normal situation, what we did could take literally years to complete; we did it in three days.

People can rise to the occasion. If they understand the issue and the consequences, they can step up. We tend to assume people will be self-interested, exploitive, selfish, and difficult. Maybe it doesn't have to be that way. If one person lets their guard down first, it makes it easier for others to respond in kind. Maybe we can establish a precedent in which each of us operates from a place of decency and mutuality.

Two weeks after I started doing my daily briefings, with three COVID deaths, on March 15, we announced the closing of schools in New York City and Westchester, Nassau, and Suffolk counties. The following day, we announced the closing of schools in the entire state. Even though the action was highly disruptive, people accepted it because they had been following the information I'd been sharing every morning. Many of the districts' officials did not want to close, and they did not appreciate my newfound control over them. But the people of the state understood the necessity and supported my decision. I also ordered nonessential New York State workers to work from home. As with the closing of colleges, government action would set a precedent for policies that I hoped private companies would follow.

Never in modern history has government ordered businesses, schools, and private institutions to close. State government has never issued stay-at-home orders, not even during the 1918 flu pandemic, when schools and theaters were allowed to stay open. With each state determining its own path, the inevitable incongruous decisions would lead only to confusion and decreased support from the people. If the federal government established a national standard, it could ease the burden on state leadership and increase popular support. The federal mandate could have easily set an infection rate, hospitalization rate, or death rate by percentage of population that would've triggered a state to shut down. The federal government has the expertise in global health pandemics. State and local health departments do not.

WE CONTINUED TO WATCH what was going on in California and Seattle, and what we saw was disturbing. Even more disturbing was watching China and Europe. Italy was in the worst situation, with an overwhelmed hospital system that prompted officials to lock down much of the northern part of the country, including Milan and Venice. Even China—where government control is total—was having trouble executing coherent procedures to safeguard the population. Imagine how hard it would be in our situation where you must actively persuade people to follow the policy rather than simply dictate it. I had been speaking to every expert I could get on the phone. Would we have to do something like Italy and China were doing? The answer was yes, but the drastic measures that they said may be required seemed almost impossible. How do you "close down" society? What does that even mean?

It turns out that when people say close down, they don't really mean close down. They mean closing down "unnecessary" economic and social activities. "Unnecessary" is defined as any functions not required for basic social stability. Again, there was no existing blueprint, but when we started discussing the list of "basic" activities, the list actually got quite long. Society still had to be stable and functioning. Public transportation would need to continue. Grocery stores and pharmacies would need to remain open. Doctors' offices and the health-care system would be essential. Delivery services, utility services, emergency home repair services, stores that sell home goods, police, firefighters, some government workers but not all. It was a substantial list.

Discussing the ramifications of the closures, I became deeply troubled. Talk about a tale of two cities: This would be a tale of two economies and two types of workers. The phrase for the employees of the basic services is "essential workers." An essential worker may sound like a nice title, but it is really anything but glamorous. The essential workers are the structural framework for the service economy. They are the backbone of New York. They are the blue-collar working folks we too often take for granted. In New York City, they are not the fancy Manhattan residents or the Wall Street bankers. They are Queens, Brooklyn, the Bronx, and Staten Island residents, outer-borough Latino, Asian, Black. They are the hardworking, struggling families. Why is it that the poorest among us are always asked to pay the highest price? These are the people our society always seems to forget. They are working, so they are not on public assistance or Medicaid. But they are barely making it. The last national "disaster" was the 2007 housing collapse and mortgage fraud scandal, when these people lost the equity in their homes while the federal government bailed out the big banks with their tax dollars. I am from Queens. I grew up feeling that I was from a different class from the Manhattan elite. As attorney general, I had brought actions against companies like AIG and Bank of America, which took the federal bailout funds and paid million-dollar bonuses to the same executives who created the scandal in the first place. No one bailed out the working families in the outer boroughs who saw their home values depleted.

My father's voice rang in my ears. The system was rigged. One set of rules for the rich and powerful and another set of rules for everyone else. Whatever the situation, it seems working families get the short end of the stick. The powerful institutions work together to protect themselves and their friends, and the government is their unwitting or, even worse, conscious ally.

But in many ways this situation would be more devastating than the Great Recession of 2008. This was not just about unfair economic gain or loss. We would be asking one group of workers to put their lives at risk so that another group, the "nonessential workers," would be able to stay safe at home. It is a gross injustice and manifestation of the inequality in society. I couldn't get past the feeling that this was just unfair.

How could I even explain this when the time came, and it seemed certain that it would soon. I would need to tell the people of the state that the situation was incredibly dangerous and would require drastic action that was without precedent. We would need to close down business and social activity because it was unsafe. However, essential workers still needed to go to work because we needed them to do their jobs. They would have to deal with the risk that they might get sick and bring the virus home to their families. There was no alternative. If the essential workers didn't show up, there would be anarchy. Imagine a situation with no police, no food, no public transportation. What if I asked the essential workers to continue working and they determined it was too dangerous? The ethical, moral, and practical issues continued to multiply. I struggled with these questions night after night when I reviewed the decisions I'd made that day and considered the decisions that awaited me the next. I talked to any number of people, and everyone had a different opinion. In bed when the phone was finally silent, I would rerun the whole day one more time in my mind like a video replay. It came down to judgment calls about life and death, and every one of those calls could be second-guessed. The only certainty was that I had to make decisions now and move.

MARCH 16 | 294 NEW CASES | 158 HOSPITALIZED | 6 DEATHS

———

"When we say these facilities close down at 8:00 P.M. tonight, they will then remain closed until further notice."

W E REACHED OUT TO THE GOVERNORS OF the surrounding states, most notably Phil Murphy of New Jersey and Ned Lamont of Connecticut, who joined me at the day's briefing. Melissa spoke to their respective chiefs of staff numerous times a day, and I spoke with both men directly. It was helpful to have leaders from the neighboring states to bounce things off, because they were facing the same challenges we were. It also gave me comfort to talk to people in a similar position. We could commiserate. Many people in New Jersey and Connecticut commuted to New York for work, and their infection rates were spiking in tandem with ours. If the federal government wouldn't come up with a national policy, then we would come up with our own regional policy. This would do two things. First, it would give people a sense of comfort that they were not alone because their neighbors were taking the same actions. Second, it would avoid people traveling from one state to another state to "shop" for activities, goods, or services they might need. Together, we took the most dramatic action to date, instituting uniform closures to take effect that night: The restaurants, bars, movie theaters, gyms, and casinos in all three states were closing at the same time, and all gatherings would be capped at fifty people.

I do a lot of work with Governor Murphy and Governor Lamont, and they are both good men. Last year I invited Lamont to go salmon fishing with me on Lake Ontario. In addition to the opportunity to spend some time together away from meetings, the trip was meant to highlight the great fishing in upstate New York. We chartered a boat, and we planned a brief chat with the press when we got back to the dock.

It was getting close to the time that we were supposed to return, but we had a major problem: We hadn't caught any fish. And there was no way I was going back to face the press on the dock without fish. I told the captain showing up empty-handed would be bad news for the state of New York, and he knew that it would not be great for his business either. I was ready to jump overboard and dive down to see what I could find. Luckily, we landed a fish before I had to do that. But one fish isn't really enough for two fishermen. We needed another one.

The press was already waiting on the dock, but I was committed to that second fish.

Miraculously, as we were pulling in to harbor, we saw the pole bend and the line take off; we caught our second fish. The poor charter boat captain was so relieved I thought he was going to cry.

WHILE WE WERE MAKING this progress at the state level, we were still operating in the absence of federal leadership and coordination, and that day Trump went as far as to tweet, "Just had a very good tele-conference with Nation's Governors. Went very well. Cuomo of New York has to 'do more.' " I tweeted right back, "I have to do more? No—YOU have to do something! You're supposed to be the President."

The president had finally instituted a partial European travel ban on March 12. But it was too little, too late. The virus had been silently circulating in the New York region for weeks, if not months. If the federal authorities had realized this basic reality—that the virus would have traveled from China over the course of weeks—we could have screened or stopped European travel much earlier and saved thousands of lives.

The ban was fatally flawed—announced by the president only two days before it was to go into effect. This late notice drove thousands of Europeans and Americans in Europe, many already sick with the virus, to rush to the airports to find seats before they would be locked out, causing crowding in airports in both Europe and New York. Customs and Border Protection checks at New York airports also shuffled thousands of travelers into tight waiting areas, further spreading the virus.

To be clear, New York's problem was caused by federal negligence. New York was ambushed by COVID. I believe that this was on par with the greatest failure to detect an enemy attack since Pearl Harbor. The Japanese fleet sailed for twelve days and got to within two hundred miles of Pearl Harbor without being discovered. The U.S. Pacific Fleet was all gathered in a dense configuration totally unaware. COVID attacked from Europe, landing at the crowded JFK and Newark airports, infecting the dense Northeast. The historical echoes continue. The morning of Pearl Harbor the Americans had detected and captured a Japanese submarine just off the coast. Despite the submarine capture, the U.S. commander, Husband Kimmel, did not react quickly to the imminent threat. Likewise, the federal government knew in December 2019 that COVID was in China but did not react and did not realize that the virus had traveled to Europe and then took flight for America. By the time the European travel ban was put in place, the virus had been coming to New York for more than a month. After Pearl Harbor, FDR marshaled and mobilized Americans for the war effort; we would now need

New Yorkers to mobilize to take on this challenge. The failure to detect the enemy in Pearl Harbor cost 2,400 lives. The failure to detect COVID in the northeast United States would cost ten times as many lives.

THEY SAY PRESIDENT TRUMP is a voracious consumer of television news. From my interactions with him, they are right. He knew what I had said on television news shows better than I did; that became the medium for engagement. The only thing he responded to was public pressure, so that's what I would use. I'd been pushing for federal assistance, including for two items on the top of my agenda: increasing testing capacity and the creation of additional hospital beds. We were also asking for ventilators. A substantial percentage of COVID patients required ventilators, and just providing a bed and staff would be useless without them. But there was another immediate challenge to address: the shortage of personal protective equipment (PPE) such as masks, gowns, and face shields. The increasing volume of patients at hospitals and the new testing facilities were consuming large quantities of PPE. We were facing both a national and a global shortage. I had personally contacted a number of suppliers across the country, and they all had the same story: They were merely distributors of the product; American companies were not major manufacturers of PPE. The main manufacturing was all done in China, and China was worried about China.

I talked to the White House about possible assistance from the national stockpile or assistance in organizing the supply chain. I asked the president to invoke the Defense Production Act, which would allow the government to mandate that private manufacturers produce the reagents needed for tests as well as masks, gowns, and other PPE. Trump thought it was too heavy-handed to force the private sector to do something, that it would look like "big government," which was anathema to conservatives. He insisted that this was not their responsibility, and he considered my request an intrusion.

The White House was still making every effort to further distance itself from any operational responsibility. President Trump's abdication exacerbated states' capacity to address the crisis, and this was a battle states could not win on our own. This left me no other option but to go public. Traditional discussion and negotiation never worked with Trump; nothing mattered to him other than the conversation in the media.

I've worked with government on every level for many years. Dealing with the Trump administration was a new experience. For all the interchange, there were very few policy or program discussions. In fact, the most relevant and effective conversations were those conducted in the press. For them, every issue was just another public relations issue.

So as the old saying goes, "When in Rome." My briefings were garnering tremendous attention. They were broadcast live on national networks for up to two hours per day. We had tens of millions of viewers. I would then do one-on-one interviews with up to ten shows per day. This would get not only the president's attention but also that of the people around him.

I was getting much more press attention in recent weeks—obviously because New York was a hot spot, but also because of the practical realities of COVID. Because the news shows were doing everything remotely, there was no need to travel to the studios, which was a major intrusion in the day. This meant that from my own office I could just do a digital connection with network after network. During COVID, we could book the interviews in an hour. And COVID was such an all-consuming topic that news stations were open for comment virtually twenty-four hours per day. So if the best way to communicate with the federal government was through the media, I would do just that.

Donald Trump did not have the only microphone. I had one too. And I had something else: credibility.

I had started by publishing an op-ed in **The New York Times** on March 15 that was a direct appeal to President Trump asking for a modicum of federal assistance. I argued for a national strategy, the deployment of the Army Corps of Engineers, assistance in increasing the nation's testing capacity, and the institution of federal standards for cities and states to shut down. "The scarcity [of hospital beds in America] portends a greater failing and a worse situation than what we are seeing in Italy, where lives are being lost because the country doesn't have the health care capacity," I wrote. "States cannot build more hospitals, acquire ventilators or modify facilities quickly enough. At this point, our best hope is to utilize the Army Corps of Engineers to leverage its expertise, equipment and people power to retrofit and equip existing facilities—like military bases or college dormitories—to serve as temporary medical centers. Then we can designate existing hospital beds for the acutely ill. We believe the use of active duty Army Corps personnel would not violate federal law because this is a national disaster. Doing so still won't provide enough intensive care beds, but it is our best hope." The article was widely covered, but the White House did not respond. They were clearly trying to let it pass. I had to make sure it didn't.

I did a round of media appearances and then decided to do an appearance on my brother Christopher's show on CNN. I knew this would attract attention in and of itself: both positive and negative. Trump allies would criticize us, saying that it wasn't in keeping with objective journalistic ethics. I have no problem with that criticism because neither Chris nor I ever pretended that this was an objective interview. The conversation was between two brothers—what viewer would be confused?

I also found it laughable that Fox broadcasters would feign objectivity when the entire network was essentially an apparatus for the Trump campaign. The on-air dynamic between Chris and me was provocative. If other reporters were as direct and obnoxious in their questioning as Chris was, it would be unacceptable. But Chris didn't have to be especially respectful, which generated a much more honest, candid, and hard-hitting discussion. Likewise, I could have a more forthright tone and be less politically sensitive. It was probably the most straightforward and informative discussion I had in the hundreds of media appearances that I did on COVID.

The show really did help get good information to people, but it also did something else. It made people smile, and a smile can be the best therapy. Chris is very funny. He's the baby of the family and naturally irreverent. He could get away with it because by the time he was born, my father was much more tolerant than he had been with me. My father allowed himself to enjoy Chris and even encouraged his humor. My brother has never been in public service nor had to deal with the scrutiny of having every word and every action examined by a hostile press corps. I am funny. Many people don't know that I'm funny. But I am. Actually, I am very funny. But you're not supposed to be too funny as a governor.

When Chris and I are together, usually, it's during those few times in my life when I'm not in public and there is no one there to judge. We're normally on a boat fishing or at a bar having a drink. Although we were on national TV, our natural rhythm came to the forefront. He teased me, as is his way, and I reacted, as is my way. Because it was his show, the odds were in his favor, and I was in a no-win position. He is my little brother: When he attacks me, it's cute; when I attack him back, it's not cute. But it worked and provided respite for people overwhelmed with heavy news.

The president, however, hates CNN and Chris in particular. I don't think the president hates me as much as he hates Chris, but it depends on the day. Chris has done some tough pieces on the president, but nothing that wasn't fair. That doesn't matter; with the president, everything is personal. There are no principled disagreements, only personal disagreements. The president, when he is upset, likes to refer to Christopher as "Fredo," a character in the **Godfather** movies. Let's just say Fredo was not the favored son in the movies. But more, in my opinion, it raises the negative Italian stereotype of the Mafia.

Fredo is a Mafia reference that strikes many deep chords for me. First, that I should cause the

Fredo reference to be repeated bothers me because I am inadvertently causing my brother pain. If the president wants to hit me, then hit me, but don't hit my brother to cause me pain. In actuality, it is a very effective device because his attacks on my brother caused me more pain than any direct attack on me would cause. To the extent that Trump is aware of this, it is really nasty. As usual, his attacks would then be repeated by the **New York Post.** I doubt that President Trump and Rupert Murdoch are empathetic enough to appreciate how effective these attacks actually were.

The Mafia stigma is one of the most painful and vicious of anti–Italian American stereotypes. I fought it all my life as my father had done before me. I speak about it often to the Italian American community. The **Godfather** movies and **The Sopranos** all reinforce the stereotype of the Italian as the criminal and the thug. Some people repeat the stereotype out of ignorance. The **Times Union** in Albany published an insensitive column about Fredo, for which they were unapologetic even after Italian American organizations publicly complained. Some people just don't appreciate how offensive stereotypes can be. As a New Yorker, I learned at a very young age that different religions and ethnic groups have their own experiences that must be respected. People who did not grow up in a diverse community don't have the same level of sensitivity. Also, people who never felt the sting don't appreciate the pain. I thought the Mafia stereotype might have died with my father. But the Fredo incident and its coverage said that it is alive and well.

I will fight it with all my might every time it raises its ugly head, just as I fight negative stereotypes and discrimination against any American. Any politician will tell you it's not smart to fight with people who "buy ink by the barrel." I know it's not smart, but I also know it's right. In my place in life, "right" is more important than "smart." Maybe if I do my job right, the negative Italian stereotype will die with me, and my children won't have to fight the battle or feel the pain.

BUT PUTTING THE FREDO references aside, it was the plain facts that I laid out on Chris's show on CNN that evening that were damaging to Trump. No other country's federal government walked away from the national crisis as ours had. Every other country has been led by its national government. Only the United States would come to adopt this fragmented, every-state-for-itself approach.

I hit Trump and the federal government with both barrels. At least the federal government could help us with resources. Even if you say the states are responsible for the front-line attack, couldn't the federal government at least help with supplies? Trump not only watched the news shows but also closely followed their ratings. The show I did with Chris that night got very high ratings. It succeeded in getting Trump's attention.

———

"What are we doing? Everything we can."

MINUTES BEFORE MY DAILY BRIEFING, I received a phone call from President Trump. He was not happy.

The president had obviously seen the interview I did with Chris.

I tried to slow him down. "Mr. President, you're a New Yorker. I'm a New Yorker. I told you what I needed, I asked you to mobilize the Army Corps of Engineers, I asked you **before** I wrote it in the **Times**, I talked to you **before** I went on CNN. This is about the people of New York, this is about saving lives, and I can't do it alone! I need the resources of the federal government—you have the army, you have the Army Corps of Engineers, you have FEMA, you have the Department of Homeland Security—use them!"

The president was angry.

Rather than continue to fight with him, I appealed to him as a president and also appealed to his politics. "Mr. President, I will work with you," I said. "I'm not running against you; I'm not running for anything. All I care about is getting the people of New York through this crisis."

I meant every word. I said, "I'm going to do my briefing in a few minutes. Let someone watch and tell you what I said. I will go first in the spirit of good faith."

When I hung up the phone, Melissa was standing in my office looking upset. "I don't understand why you're trying to work with him," she said. "It's like Lucy with the football. It's impossible; **he's** impossible. We should just go out there and say exactly what this is: The president of the United States won't help."

I understood her frustration, but this was about getting help for our state and saving lives.

I called for the team to enter the Red Room for the briefing—one I knew the president would be watching. A couple of minutes into my remarks I looked directly into the camera, and I did exactly what I said I would do, intended to reach an audience of one:

What does government do in this moment? It steps up, it performs, it does what it's supposed to do. It does it better than it's ever done it before. What does government not do? It does not engage in politics or partisanship. Even if you are in the midst of an election season. Even if you are at a moment in time and history where you have hyper-partisanship, which we now have. The president of the United States, Donald Trump, it is essential that the federal government works with the state and that this state works with the federal government.

We cannot do this on our own. I built airports; I built bridges. We have made this government do things that it's never done before. This government has done somersaults; it's performed better than ever before. I am telling you, this government cannot meet this crisis without the resources and capacity of the federal government. I spoke to the president this morning again. He is ready, willing, and able to help. I've been speaking with members of his staff late last night, early this morning. We need their help, especially on the hospital capacity issue.

We need FEMA. FEMA has tremendous resources. When I was at HUD, I worked with FEMA; I know what they can do. I know what the Army Corps of Engineers can do. They have a capacity that we simply do not have. I said to the president, who is a New Yorker, who I've known for many, many years. I put my hand out in partnership. I want to work together 100 percent. I need your help. I want your help, and New Yorkers will do everything they can to be good partners with the federal government. I think the president was 100 percent sincere in saying that he wanted to work together. In partnership, in the spirit of cooperation, I can tell you the actions he has taken evidence that. His team has been on it.

Shortly after the briefing, the president called again. He said the Army Corps of Engineers would be contacting me immediately to set up a meeting and that the USNS **Comfort** would be on its way, too.

So far, so good. But tomorrow would be another day.

MARCH 18 | 1,009 NEW CASES |
496 HOSPITALIZED | 4 DEATHS

——

"We are responding to science and data.
There's no politics here."

SECRETARY OF DEFENSE MARK ESPER WENT ON
Fox News and confirmed what he and I had
just discussed over the phone. "I had a call with
Governor Cuomo, and we had a very good conversation," Esper said. "What he sees is a deficit in
hospital beds in New York State as he looks ahead
to what may be coming. I gave him my full commitment that we would get the Corps of Engineers
up there to assess the problem and see how we can
help out."

On Wednesday, March 18, I met with the leader-
ship of the Army Corps of Engineers, including
Major General Jeff Milhorn, Lieutenant General
Todd Semonite, Colonel Thomas D. Asbery, and
Anthony Travia, in my conference room in Albany.
We discussed various ideas, including converting
dormitory buildings, hotels, and vacant state build-
ings into field hospitals. My guiding principle was

the urgency and scope of what needed to be done. While hospitals were expanding their own capacity by 50 percent, bringing us to nearly seventy-five thousand hospital beds, and elective surgeries were being postponed to free up space, we were still tens of thousands of beds short of what we might need.

Following the meeting, I assigned the commissioner of the Division of Homeland Security and Emergency Services, Major General Patrick Murphy, a seasoned pro, and Gareth Rhodes to work with the Army Corps of Engineers to make sure they had all they needed to get the job done. A "site inspection team" including members of the Army Corps, led by Colonel Tom Asbery, the head of the Army Corps's New York office, and state officials from the Department of Health, Dormitory Authority, Office of General Services, and New York Power Authority, was dispatched on Thursday to more than twenty sites around the downstate area to evaluate properties, including the dormitory complexes at SUNY Stony Brook, CUNY Hunter, CUNY City College, and the Fashion Institute of Technology, for their fitness as field hospitals. Thursday night and into the early hours of Friday morning, the team prepared copious reports on the benefits and drawbacks of each facility.

And despite growing public awareness of the severity of the situation, we were still fielding complaints from people who were upset that their favorite restaurants and bars and gyms were closed. I made it clear that people shouldn't be upset with their local officials. They should be upset with me; I made these decisions in the best interests of the entire state.

MARCH 19 | 1,769 NEW CASES | 617 HOSPITALIZED | 22 DEATHS

—

"It is a war in many ways and government has to mobilize as if it is a war."

PROVIDING ESSENTIAL SECURITY FOR FAMILIES continued to be a major concern. We needed to assure them that their basic way of life would be maintained until we got through this. I had previously ordered a ninety-day moratorium on rent eviction, and now I signed an executive order giving all homeowners a ninety-day grace period from any mortgage payments. If a homeowner was suffering a financial hardship from COVID, the bank must allow a ninety-day forbearance. The banks would eventually get their money, but no family would be unnecessarily displaced.

You hear about the isolation of leadership. Now I understood it. In the heat of battle, one must make decisions seeing the full field and the entire context. Many observers and pundits bring only a particular perspective and therefore find it easy to criticize, but I tried to hold every scenario and every concern in my head at every moment. We needed to slow the virus spread. There was no way our hospital system could manage the volume every model had projected. The nightmare of people dying in hospital corridors we were seeing in Italy loomed. We would have to move heaven and earth to create more hospital beds faster than any state in the nation, but it still would not be enough. Therefore, we needed to reduce the viral spread more than any of the experts thought was possible.

The "closedown" strategies, theoretically, could do just that: reduce activity and reduce the spread. But it wasn't that simple. Pundits will say in hindsight that we should have closed earlier. But they are missing an important point. Government can announce drastic and dramatic policies to close down and reduce activity. The intelligent question was, would people follow them? It is naïve to think that government could order the most dramatic behavior change in modern history and assume all people would salute and follow the order. This is not China. This government has no ability to enforce closedown rules on 19.5 million people. State government has only about six thousand troopers, and local governments' ability or desire to use their police to enforce unpopular directives is uneven at best. As we would learn, government couldn't even keep young people from gathering at bars! Compliance would be essentially voluntary. Mask wearing, social distancing, and stay-at-home orders would have to be socially accepted. The public would need to agree that the policies were necessary, which means they had to be educated to that realization.

Further compounding the challenge was that we had to inform them of the drastic consequences without panicking them. The calibration needed to be exquisitely balanced. Panic and chaos would be harder to manage than COVID. The information had to be communicated in a measured way, but quickly. Also, "government" writ large was offering mixed messages. The federal government was saying that COVID was not a major threat, so why would the public accept drastic action? One message from me and a different message from Trump could create a political divide. I had to first earn the trust of the public and gain unprecedented credibility to overcome the intense politics and mixed messages of the time. I studied other governments' actions. California had fifty days to socialize the notion of a shutdown to the public after its first case. That was a long time. I didn't have that luxury. I would need to move faster.

Communicating facts and authenticity, and taking daily incremental closedown actions correlated to the new information on the increasing threat: every day more cases announced, every day ratcheting a closedown. I closed down 50 percent of nonessential workers, then 75 percent. On March 20, only nineteen days from our first case, we announced a 100 percent closedown. People virtually unanimously supported it, and compliance was nearly universal. It was truly incredible.

In retrospect, I wonder if I could have accomplished achieving credibility with the public and getting them to understand the need to close down even faster than nineteen days. The truth is, I will never know. The stakes couldn't have been higher. The risk was that if I announced closedown orders before the public was ready to support them and they rejected them, all would be lost—we would be worse off. Once the public lost trust in me or disregarded my proposals, the entire effort would be derailed. I believe I moved as quickly as I believed and felt I could, given the balance I needed to maintain, but it is impossible to know.

The risk of losing the public cannot be underestimated. In the end, we did what many thought was impossible, faster than any government had done it at the time, and faster and more effectively than any of the experts thought we could. Amen.

———

"When we look back at this situation ten years
from now, I want to be able to say to the people
of New York, I did everything we could do."

COVID LITERALLY AND FIGURATIVELY CHANGED
the entire atmosphere of social interaction.
You couldn't shake hands and were afraid to
touch another human being. Our team couldn't sit
in meetings together or share a meal. We conducted
meeting after meeting on Zoom, but it's not the
same as a human interchange. People had to think
before they touched the doorknob. No one knew
when and where the enemy would strike again.
While we were being careful in my operation, my
first priority was to get the job done, and I couldn't
do that in a hermetically sealed bubble. Nor did
I want to. It was important for me to try to project a sense of normalcy, even though that was far
from what we were experiencing. My staff and the
press who covered us were already nervous after

two members of the New York State Assembly had tested positive the weekend before.

That Friday at 5:15 A.M., my phone rang. It was Melissa.

"We have a situation, but I want to start off by saying that I'm calm and everyone is calm, and it's all going to be fine," she said, the tone of her voice suggesting that the person she was trying to reassure was herself.

"It's Caitlin," she said. Caitlin Girouard, our press secretary, was primarily based out of New York City but had spent the last several days in Albany as part of the all-hands-on-deck effort.

"Caitlin? What's wrong with Caitlin?" I asked.

"Well, really it's the whole press office, but primarily it's Caitlin," Melissa continued. I could hear the panic in her voice. "She wasn't feeling well yesterday afternoon, so Peter [Peter Ajemian, our loyal and reliable deputy communications director] sent her home. I thought he was being dramatic, but agreed it was better to be safe than sorry."

I cut her off. "And what information do we have now that we didn't have yesterday afternoon?"

"Last night, she had a fever. So Dr. Zucker thought it was best that she take a coronavirus test; the test came back positive around 11:00 last night, but to be absolutely sure Dr. Zucker had them do a second test."

"Okay, and?"

"And it was negative. So there we are. And yes, we are having her tested a third time to find out exactly what is going on. We don't know at this moment definitively if she is sick or not. That being said, for the last several days she has been sitting in the press office, which, as you know, could generously be described as a sardine can, with nine other staffers," she continued at a frenetic pace.

"The belief is that if she got sick, it happened over the weekend when she was in New York City. I've carefully retraced your movements and my movements for the past four days, and the reality is that neither of us has been near her, but I've spoken with Dr. Zucker, and he thinks, again, out of an abundance of caution—just out of an abundance of caution—we have to quarantine every single person in the press office and a handful of the advance staff who she came into contact with. So there it is—you know everything I know."

"Okay, deep breath. I'll be in the office in fifteen minutes."

By the time I arrived in the office a few minutes later, it was clear the staff had been up all night. Linda Lacewell, one of my longest-serving aides based in New York City who had recently been parked on the second floor of the capitol to help manage the crisis, had already put a wave of new protocols into motion. Linda is a former federal prosecutor who worked with me in the attorney general's office. As a lawyer, she has a rare combination of talents: facility with the law and with managing people. After the attorney general's office, she had left to take a great gig in her home state of California. A few months after her departure I called her up and said, "You have to come back, I really need you." She came. If you understood the bond that we develop working together the way we do, you wouldn't be surprised. I work with a group of people who would do anything for one another, and they do.

LINDA HAD CREATED A list of staff people deemed "essential," who were permitted to work from inside the capitol, and another much more modest list of staff labeled "essential essential," who were allowed to enter the contained suite of offices connecting my office, Melissa's office, the conference room, and the Red Room. A crew of maintenance staff would arrive by 7:00 A.M. to clean surfaces.

That morning represented a critical juncture in other ways as well. It was about communicating to 19.5 million people that the virus had reached a point of spread that required dramatic action; I was asking New Yorkers to stay home. And I was, by extension, telling millions of them that they were about to lose their jobs. Today wasn't about me or my staff's behind-the-scenes drama. Today was about delivering truly tough news to New Yorkers and hoping they would follow it. We would see if the public really trusted me and were ready to sacrifice.

The sudden increase in cases was jarring, and the progression of the incremental actions had reached a climax. It was time to announce New York State on PAUSE (the acronym stood for Policies Assure Uniform Safety for Everyone), which banned all nonessential gatherings, established social distancing requirements, and closed 100 percent of nonessential businesses. We had already started the process gradually, so people could get used to the idea.

Closing down society is easier said than done, and many politicians didn't appreciate the complexity of the issue. First, you can't close down until you have all the precautions in place and have thought through all the ramifications. Closing down is not a press release; it's the most complex government policy we have ever instituted. Necessary functions must continue or you risk anarchy. Contact must be made with all the main system operators so they know what is coming and are prepared for it. If a closedown order is going to impact the workforce or management of an essential system, you'd better know in advance.

Second, the public must comply, and that means they have to be socialized prior to the announcement through a gradual process that communicates the increasingly dire nature of the situation. Communicating the seriousness haphazardly causes panic, but communicating it incompletely causes people to refuse to follow the order. Again, New York's closedown accomplished these prerequisites within only nineteen days. And it had never been done before.

After we made the announcement on Friday the twentieth, we had two days to decide what exactly was "essential" versus "nonessential" before the order went into effect on Sunday. In government, we use these terms during events like snowstorms, when travel is perilous. You don't want people on the roads, but the government needs to operate, so who are the most essential people to allow the government to do its work? Everyone else stays home.

But now we were dealing with the entire private sector. I sat at my conference room table with Melissa as well as Robert Mujica, the state budget director, and other members of my team to go through a list of industries, one sector at a time, deciding which businesses were so "essential" they could not be closed. As budget director, Robert does all finances for the state. He is a sphinx. The man's face never moves. He is inscrutable and unrelenting, and as tough a negotiator as I have ever encountered. Robert is not a pol, he's a pro, and he manages the state finances almost single-handedly.

The decisions weren't always obvious.

I was inclined to close as near to everything as possible, because every person who had to go to work was putting their life at risk and I wasn't going to ask that of one more worker than I absolutely had to. On the flip side, we were also deciding who was about to lose their jobs. There are, for example, more than 100,000 employees of gyms in New York State. Gyms were about as high risk as they come and would likely be closed for a long time.

Food, health care, pharmacies, and supply chain industries were essential; that was easy. But when Robert argued that dry cleaners were essential, I thought he was crazy. There's nothing essential about dry cleaning. "You're just saying that because you don't want to do your own laundry," I teased him. But the truth is, as he explained it, police and other uniformed personnel need dry cleaners for their uniforms, so they stay open. Verizon stores were essential because people need to be able to repair or replace broken cellphones. I objected to liquor stores staying open, but I was overruled, the argument being we had to be consistent about food and beverage businesses; if you could sell beer at a convenience store, then liquor stores should be allowed to stay open. That was also why we changed the law to allow restaurants offering takeout to offer alcoholic beverages, which had the added advantage of making people a little happier being stuck at home.

As dramatic as New York PAUSE was, the facts had led to the inescapable conclusion. I did not have to convince the people of the state. I believed they would have taken the same action if it were put to a vote. There were still voices in opposition, primarily those on the Far Right. Trump was fanning the flames against government and business closures. But the overwhelming majority of New Yorkers— Democrats and Republicans—knew where we were and what we must do. Closing down the state through the New York PAUSE order was accomplishing the first essential task: communicating the extent of the problem, the urgency, and solidifying New Yorkers' support for my plan to accomplish mission impossible.

Aside from asking everyone who could stay home to do exactly that, I implemented Matilda's Law, named after my mother and directed at seniors like her and everyone else in a vulnerable population, which limited home visitation to immediate family members or close friends in order to protect them. In a way, this law felt like a culmination of the daily conversations I had with my mother explaining how we were trying to keep her safe.

During the briefing that day, the main message I wanted to convey was the need for everyone to be safe, and that the only way to do that was together. The human toll all of this was taking was never far from my thoughts. "People are in a small apartment," I said at the briefing, my voice breaking with the emotion of it. "They're in a house, they're worried, they're anxious. Just be mindful of that. Those three-word sentences can make all the difference. I miss you, I love you, I'm thinking of you, I wish I was there with you, I'm sorry you're going through this, I'm sorry we're going through this. That's going to be a situation that's going to develop because we're all in quarantine now." It was a very emotional moment for me, and it was later reported that I shed a tear. I do know that I welled up with emotion that day.

I also needed to strike the right balance between disclosing to the public the potential of someone in our office having coronavirus while still protecting that person's privacy and not overhyping what could just as easily come back with a negative result.

At the end of the briefing, as I began to get up from my chair, I dropped the news that a member of our press office was exhibiting signs of coronavirus, adding that we would be quarantining employees of the entire office.

Looking back, I'm not sure it was the most artful way to disclose that information, particularly to a group of reporters who had spent the last twenty days huddled in the Red Room with my press staff, but as we had been learning, sometimes there didn't seem to be a "right way" to do anything.

It felt as if the ground were shifting beneath us. The final test on Caitlin came back that she was COVID positive. The virus could infect anyone, and its reach did not discriminate. And regardless of perceived power or access, with too few tests and even less information, our entire press office would be quarantined for the next fourteen days.

The burden I asked people to shoulder—quarantining as a precaution after coming into contact with a positive case—was now one my entire press team would experience every day for the next two weeks. By talking about this publicly, I wanted to show New Yorkers that I was in that journey with them, experiencing it, feeling it, suffering it, just as they were. They say relationships take work. My relationship with the people of the state was vital, and I was willing to put in the work.

MARCH 21 | 3,254 NEW CASES |

1,406 HOSPITALIZED | 12 DEATHS

—

"I don't believe this is going to be a matter of
weeks. How long and how well it takes to get
through this is up to us."

THERE WERE NO DAYS OF THE WEEK—ONE
day just blending into the next. One crisis
blending into the next. But these days were also so
extraordinary on so many levels. They really pushed
people to the brink and gave them a glimpse of their
souls. It's relatively easy for people to be nice and
functional when things are going well. But when
the pressure is on, you really get to see what people
are made of. It's like a piece of marble that has a
fine crack in it. It's almost invisible and blends into
the pattern. But when that marble is under pressure, that crack can explode.

I was operating on multiple tracks. One, communicating with the public to keep them informed
and calm. Two, revamping the government to
functionally perform the incredible tasks of building hospitals, creating testing capacity, and finding

medical staff, ventilators, and PPE. Three, dealing with the federal government—not an easy task. And four, personally confronting the stress, pain, and death all around me.

FOR THE FIRST TIME in a long time, all three of my daughters were in Albany with me. Michaela would finish her classes online and, like so many other seniors, miss out on graduation festivities. My daughters are young, tech savvy, and cool and often tease me about being out of date. They would tell me, Dad, this tweet could be better, or give me advice about how to communicate with people their age. They would say, "This picture would be a great 'latergram.'" I still do not know what that means. So I asked Mimi Reisner, my social media and messaging guru, to make them part of the social media effort, helping to communicate the information and connect with people who don't normally engage with government. Having them around grounded me and gave me comfort, reminding me what's important in life and how meaningless so many things become when faced with grave danger. At dinner each night, I'd ask them what they did that day, but what I meant was, what did they think of the day's briefing?

As anyone watching the briefings knew, Mariah wouldn't come to Albany without him: the Boyfriend. I begrudgingly agreed that the Boyfriend could come. The Executive Mansion has twelve bedrooms, and he got the one on the top floor with the twin bed everyone says is haunted. I assure you, that was a coincidence. The Boyfriend, who shall remain nameless unless and until the relationship proceeds to an impending formal status, is a genuinely nice and talented fellow. He is a gentleman, which I cannot say for all boyfriends. Luckily, my daughters have an overprotective dad. They don't always believe that it is lucky for them. But sometimes dads just know best.

Cara worked on finding PPE to purchase for the state, calling all over the world. Michaela worked on organizing mental health providers and setting up a hotline that provided mental health counseling and support services. Mariah worked on social media and video advertising to encourage wearing masks and social distancing.

In the normal course of life, my girls would never have spent weeks with their old man in Albany. After this crisis I am sure they never will again. They are birds who have flown from the nest with much to do. I see myself in them all the time. It seems life repeats itself.

What I wouldn't give to be able to sit at home with my old man for just one more day. To have him back, hear his voice, touch his face, and hold his hand. We lost him six years ago. He was ill and debilitated, and his quality of life had degenerated. In many ways he just didn't want to go on. I told him how important it was for him to stay alive and how much we all needed him, and he scoffed at my argument. So I resorted to making it personal. I told him I was several weeks away from Inauguration Day for my second term and I needed him to help me work on the speech. But he was too smart for me, and he rejected that, saying that he would be there for his son, to hear my inauguration speech. I looked at him and I said, do you promise? He looked at me and he said he promised. My father never broke a promise to me, nor I to him. January 1 was the day of my inauguration. I gave the speech, and he heard it over the telephone. One hour after the speech he passed away. True to his promise, always.

Since he died, when I have a special or difficult day, I wear my father's shoes: literally! It sounds ridiculous I know. My father wasn't a material person and we didn't have many objects to remember him by after his death, but he loved shoes and I wear the same size as he did. My mother gave me my pick. My father's love of his shoes stemmed from his growing up during the Great Depression era, when shoes were precious, so he bought quality shoes and took excellent care of them. I once heard my father talking to Harry Belafonte about how they shined their shoes, and the method was so intricate that it sounded absurd. My father shined his own shoes on a weekly basis. As a kid, I would help him. He would explain the process to me:

saddle soap first, then mink oil, then regular polish, and then neutral polish; brushed and buffed and only cedar shoe trees, of course. Plastic shoe forms were for amateurs. My daughters were particularly fascinated with the "filling your father's shoes" psychological angle, but I wanted them to know how important he was to me and how much comfort I still take in feeling that he is with me. I only hope that my daughters can get that sense of comfort from me when I'm gone. It's said that "the spirit" lives. I believe it does. I am not sure my father would support everything I do in his shoes, but he would appreciate what they mean to me, and he would love that I still shine them the same way he taught me. Brushed and buffed and cedar shoe trees, of course.

———

"We will overcome this and America will be
greater for it, and my hope is that New York
is going to lead the way forward—
and together, we will."

NOTHING WAS EASY, AND THERE WASN'T A
moment to breathe. Even if we had some
good news to share in the briefing in the morning—
where I had found some sliver of light in the grim
statistics to share—as soon as I got back to the
operational table, the ugly reality of our situation
would slap me in the face once again. To avoid
the tidal wave crashing on our hospital system in
a few weeks, we had to get the viral transmission
rate down, but none of the experts thought we'd
be able to get it to a manageable level. We had to
double—if not triple—testing capacity to have any
shot at controlling the virus and quickly create tens
of thousands of new hospital beds. All of which
would be a feat to rival Jesus's loaves and fishes.

And then there was the issue of ventilators. I had

never heard so much about ventilators and never wish to again. They are complicated pieces of technology and cost about $15,000 each, pre-COVID. Every hospital had some, but no hospital had many. In the normal course of business, they are not used that often. In total, statewide we normally have approximately four thousand ventilators, and by this point in the crisis, due to our purchasing efforts, we had between five thousand and six thousand.

It didn't take long for me to figure out that this was not just a New York problem. Every state in the country needed ventilators, but New York needed them the most urgently. The American companies that made ventilators were overwhelmed and could not increase supply quickly enough to come close to meeting the demand.

The main manufacturer of ventilators is China, but obviously China also had a tremendous need for ventilators. Besides that, every country and every state was trying to buy ventilators from China. The cost for a ventilator ran as high as $50,000. Competing states were bidding against one another to acquire the scarce resources. I had conversations with other governors about the situation, which we all agreed was ridiculous, but we had no choice.

Experts estimated that we would need at least an additional thirty thousand for the ICU beds. The federal government theoretically had an emergency stockpile of medical supplies including ventilators, and so the states, especially those with the worst caseloads, deluged the federal government with requests for ventilators. But, as we soon figured out, the federal stockpile had only about ten thousand ventilators—for the entire nation.

On this point, President Trump got very defensive once again. He took the request for ventilators as a personal attack. In this hyper-partisan environment, the blame game was in full swing. In reality no one was to blame for not having an ample supply of ventilators. No one could have predicted this virus and its particular effect on the respiratory system that would require the specific type of equipment.

Trump mocked my request for thirty thousand ventilators during a phone interview with Sean Hannity. Never mind that we were both using the same projection models and therefore had the same numbers. I could sense the president's position was hardening. He saw this as a no-win situation and more and more took to denying the problem. COVID was "just like the flu." COVID would "magically disappear." The "warm weather will kill the virus." The president responded as if these requests for ventilators, hospital beds, and testing were all political attacks.

When the NBC White House correspondent Peter Alexander asked him what he would say to Americans who were scared, he shot back, "I say that you're a terrible reporter . . . I think that's a very nasty question."

For me the situation was simple. Either we could provide hospital beds with ventilators, or more people would die. Either we could persuade people to stay home and reduce the viral transmission rate, or more people would die.

I called everyone I knew with contacts in China to help us buy more ventilators. At the same time, I asked engineers and medical technology experts to figure out other options. Northwell Health designed a conversion of BiPAP machines, which are normally attached to a mask that goes over the face to provide oxygen, so that they could be used as ventilators. This would increase our capacity by about six thousand.

One design firm created modifications so that one ventilator could serve two patients. An emergency physician in Detroit named Dr. Charlene Babcock had posted a video on YouTube that showed how to split ventilators so that they could serve four patients instead of just one, so my team tracked her down at the hospital where she worked, and I called her. We were getting messages from people saying, "I've got a guy who has a guy who has ventilators." We chased down every lead and dealt with anyone who would talk to us, including the Chinese and Qatari governments.

In the worst-case scenario we would have to use manually operated rubber bags. This is what you would see in the old movies: patients in beds with plastic covering over their noses and mouths attached to rubber bags being squeezed by people sitting next to the beds to assist inhalation and exhalation. We purchased six thousand of the bags, and we explored training members of the National Guard to manually operate them, which is harder to do than you might think. We tested it and it was too difficult for one person to squeeze for more than an hour, so next we talked to people about making machines that could squeeze them automatically. I tried to squeeze the bag for a period of time and thought, this is never going to work. We were desperate. I was desperate. Here we were in the greatest country in the world talking about squeezing rubber bags to keep people alive.

Another complication was that hospitals across the state would need to share excess ventilators on an as-needed basis. Most of the hospitals in the state agreed. One hospital system in western New York refused, saying they might need them. It was an unkind gesture and threatened the spirit of cooperation. Some upstate politicians were also quick to seize the moment as an opportunity to divide New Yorker's upstate from downstate. Several upstate politicians started a campaign saying, "Upstate lives matter." It was totally contrary to the sense of sharing and community we'd been trying to build from the beginning; it was straight out of the Trump playbook.

But the positive reactions in people overwhelmed the negative. When the news of the perceived "selfishness" was publicized, I received a call from a nursing home in the upstate town of Niskayuna outside Albany offering thirty-five ventilators to help. How great! A nursing home, one of the most vulnerable places, made a gesture to say, "I hear your negativity, and I respond with love." I returned the ventilators myself to the nursing home on Easter to say thank you, and the staff and patients all came to the windows. The episode was a little litmus test of what would win, the devil or the angel. You have the devil on your shoulder, you have an angel on the other shoulder, and the devil is generally easier to motivate. I had been trying to talk to the angels, and the angels were winning; then some politicians saw an opportunity to get the devil all fired up. The devil lost at the end of the day.

MORE THAN EVER, I was getting the growing sense of being on our own in New York. Trump never pretended to be a leader who could bring the country together in a moment of national crisis. In fact, I believe he relished his role as "divider in chief." It fit his personality. He was angry and resentful, and he communicated it. Nor did Trump ever suggest he believed in government capacity or that he himself could provide government stewardship. In many ways his response to COVID was predictable. At the same time, we still needed federal help whether he liked it or not.

With Trump, it's always about his ego. When one accepts that is when one knows how to deal with him. While he has no patience for the operations of government, he does like the bright lights and big stage and enjoys the optics of associating himself with the military.

I had met with the Army Corps of Engineers in Albany on the eighteenth, and we sketched out a simple plan. The state would identify sites and coordinate with existing health-care facilities to provide staff, and the Army Corps of Engineers would manage construction of temporary field hospitals. We took an aerial tour identifying large sites near existing hospitals. We identified four locations where the Army Corps of Engineers could construct thousands of temporary beds: SUNY Stony Brook in Suffolk County, SUNY Old Westbury in Nassau County, and the Westchester County Center—a regional balance that together with the Jacob K. Javits Convention Center in Manhattan would cover the entire downstate area, with each facility being able to treat at least a thousand patients. In the end, the military also agreed to provide a thousand medical personnel to help staff the Javits Center, which would be the largest facility.

NEXT I SPOKE TO the Federal Emergency Management Agency (FEMA) administrator, Peter Gaynor. I had worked with FEMA extensively when I was in the federal government in the 1990s. When FEMA is well operated, it is a beautiful thing, but when FEMA fails, it is a catastrophe. They show up either immediately before or immediately after a disaster. They have to be prepared for the unexpected, and they have to be able to deal with whatever peculiar circumstances develop.

In many ways FEMA is the antidote to a dangerously slow federal bureaucracy. They can mobilize quickly, command other agencies, be the central point of contact for local governments, and expedite procurement mechanisms. FEMA and the Army Corps of Engineers are the one-two punch for the federal government in an emergency.

The COVID crisis exposed the good, the bad, and the ugly in so many ways. Pressure tends to do that. And when the pressure was on during COVID, FEMA crumbled. The ventilator issue was a pure procurement and supply chain issue. It was a unique and unexpected challenge, but in an emergency you must expect the unexpected. FEMA was dreadful. Not only that, but on PPE procurement, personnel deployment, and ground transportation FEMA was incompetent.

As for the White House, the most productive person I could find there was Jared Kushner. He had a difficult time with the press. As the president's son-in-law, he was a natural target; the arrangement was peculiar and open to criticism of nepotism. In his position, he inherited all of the president's enemies, and the media had reported that he was resented by many of the president's staff.

Jared was from the private sector, so his natural orientation was the "end justifies the means." He was focused on production, and by definition he would run afoul of the bureaucracy. When I went to work for my father as special assistant during his first year as governor, I faced many of the same dynamics. Jared needed to get things done in the federal bureaucracy, but he didn't know how. He knew if they failed to produce, it would be blamed on the president. On the other hand, if he bumped heads with the bureaucracy to accelerate production, the bureaucracy would bite back. It was a no-win situation for him and he knew it, but he pushed anyway.

I saw him as the key to New York getting anything from the federal government, because we weren't getting anything from FEMA or HHS, the agencies that should have been helping. What's right is right. He was attentive and he delivered. Jared was the person who eventually produced the PPE, ventilators, and military personnel for New Yorkers, and I am grateful on their behalf.

MARCH 25 | 5,145 NEW CASES | 4,079 HOSPITALIZED | 75 DEATHS

——

"It is that closeness, that concept of family, of community. That's what makes New York 'New York.' And that's what makes us vulnerable here."

T HE PRESIDENT SEEMED TO BE EVEN MORE firmly planted in denial. His problem was obvious: The number of cases kept rising, as well as the number of deaths. I believe he didn't know what to do, but he really didn't want to do anything anyway.

His credibility was also falling at a faster and faster rate. On March 24, the president had proclaimed that he wanted to have the country opened up and the economy "raring to go by Easter," which was less than three weeks away. He also said, "We are beginning to see the light at the end of the tunnel." I was still amazed at his disconnection. How could he say these things, and how could his staff let him say them? I was watching the numbers and knew the facts better than anyone and was stunned by his statements. I asked myself, "Does he know something that I don't know? Does he have inside scientific knowledge? Or can he really be that dangerous?" As time went on it became clear that indeed he did not know anything that I didn't know.

It had been more than three weeks since our first case, and all the news was increasingly disturbing. There is only so much bad news you can take without a semblance of hope. For me the courage and generosity of people brought the light. Their positive energy sustained me. At one of the daily briefings, I had asked retired health-care workers in New York State to volunteer to assist, and I said that we would reinstate their licenses as nurses and doctors if they came back to help. I also asked health-care workers across the country who were not busy to come and help in New York. At the time, I had no realistic expectation that a significant number of people would be volunteering from across the country to come to New York in the midst of this crisis. But I was just plain wrong. Amazingly, within just weeks, nearly one hundred thousand people signed up to help. How incredible! One hundred thousand health-care professionals willing to step into dangerous, overcrowded, ill-equipped emergency rooms driven only by love.

I was so touched and humbled I spoke about it in the briefing. Their actions put my contribution into perspective. I was in a comfortable office with all the equipment I needed. I didn't have to look in the eyes of a dying patient. These people, including more than thirty thousand from other states, had no obligation to show up, but they did. Imagine the size of the heart and the capacity for generosity it takes for a person from another state to willingly step into the fire of the COVID crisis in the global hot spot. It was truly humbling.

I should have learned to never underestimate the courage and love of Americans. After 9/11, people also came from across the country to help New Yorkers. They just got in the car and came to help in any way they could. And within the state, when downstate coastal areas were hit by Superstorm Sandy, people drove from upstate just to be there to help, console, and support. These are powerful reminders of the essential goodness that is in most people. Why can't we appeal to the good in people more often? Why does government so often bring out the bad?

I had begun speaking to governors all across the country, regardless of political party, because many of us were facing the same challenges and were trying to work together. Of course, our closest relationship was with New Jersey and Connecticut, but we talked to everyone. Oregon sent us ventilators. Governor Mike DeWine from Ohio told us they had a company making washing machines that were proven to disinfect masks.

All states had a PPE shortage, testing shortages, equipment shortages, and we were all trying to find someone we knew in China. Many states do not have the government capacity of New York State, and even we were struggling. It was clear that a number of states would have serious issues. It was infuriatingly obvious that making fifty states compete against one another for scarce resources was a cruel form of the Hunger Games. Why would one nation deliberately cause its member states to compete with one another for the equipment necessary to save lives? Why force us to compete when our instinct is to cooperate with one another? We knew what was ahead, and it was clear there was a better way to address it.

The scientists were all predicting the same basic national phenomenon. The virus would move across the country much like a storm hitting certain areas hardest at certain times. The virus would peak in a rolling wave. The most problematic time was at the high point of the infection rate. A state government could manage a low infection rate, but when its hospital system was overwhelmed, it could no longer manage. That was the point when procuring equipment, ventilators, staff, and hospital beds was beyond the capacity of any state government.

That day I recommended that the federal government organize the states to participate in a "Rolling National Deployment Plan." It would have been so easy and would have made a tremendous difference. The experts had predicted that there would be a period of time between peaks in different states. In other words, New York would peak and a few weeks later Illinois and a few weeks later Oregon and so forth and so on. Because we were at our peak, I was asking other states to send us equipment and help. I told them that we would reciprocate and send staff and equipment when they hit their peak. If the federal government were to institutionalize this approach, it would allow one state to receive assistance from the other states when it was in dire need and likewise contribute assistance when its peak passed. It was the extension of the policy we were implementing within our state at the time. The statewide system moved the resources across the state as the need presented. A competent federal government should do the same for the nation, and I knew that the states would have been receptive and cooperative. Of course the idea went nowhere. Prophetically, months later, when our peak had passed and our infection rate was very low, we did just that. We were available to help other cities and states who were just hitting their peak, and we did.

Imagine how much better America's situation would have been if the federal government had just organized states to do mutual aid. How many lives could we have saved?

ON MY VISITS TO MANHATTAN, the empty streets were striking. I had never seen anything like that before. I didn't want people to give up on New

York City. They needed hope for the future. We announced a working group that would start preparing for New York's reopening, identifying ways to immediately jump-start the economy. We could institutionalize lessons learned through the crisis and build back better. Every storm has a silver lining, and when you must rebuild, it would be foolish to just replace. We should take the opportunity to enhance and progress. If your home is destroyed, you don't replace the kitchen with the same kitchen; you replace it with a better kitchen. We closed the economy; when we reopen the economy, it will be better than before. I had worked on rebuilding after many disasters in the federal government, and the message "Build Back Better" brought the impacted community hope. It was also totally true.

The president was becoming increasingly aggressive in his push to reopen the economy, and he was casting cautious governors as the problem. Once again Trump was blind to the actual consequences of his pronouncement about reopening by Easter. If governors followed Trump's advice, they would be walking into a trap. Accelerated reopenings would not in fact help the economy but rather hurt it by increasing the viral transmission spike. Other countries that had been reopening had been seeing dramatic spikes in their infection rate that resulted in hot spots popping up. Reopening wasn't that simple.

I was just as eager to reopen as Trump was, but

the real question was not whether we reopen or not; the smart question was how. We announced a committee that would begin working on it full-time. My two former top aides, Steven Cohen and Bill Mulrow, both of whom served as secretary to the governor, would take charge. I'd worked with them for years and they were great. While I was focused on the immediate COVID issues, they would liaise with the business community to discuss the aftermath, whenever that would be!

It was truly a family affair. My brothers-in-law also pitched in on the effort: Brian O'Donoghue worked with Bill and Steve day and night to assist in the NY Forward initiative while Kenneth Cole worked with his designer contacts to track down PPE while launching the "How Are You, Really?" campaign to destigmatize mental health challenges. Howard Maier had a great background in advertising and would tell me how my communication efforts were being received. My cousin Matthew Cuomo, a highly talented attorney, moved into the mansion for the month of March to help stand up hospitals.

At this moment, the number of cases was still going up, so we were very much focused on reducing the spread and protecting vulnerable people. But we would run two operations in parallel. One would be dealing with the crisis of today—testing, hospital capacity, PPE, and ventilators—while one would be preparing for the reopening tomorrow.

"This is a moment that is going to

change this nation."

THE JAVITS CENTER HAD BEEN TRANSFORMED into a field hospital in just a week, and it gave me hope that we would be saving lives. Normally home to everything from the New York Boat Show to Comic Con to the New York International Auto Show, the center was now a twenty-five-hundred-bed hospital with medical staff coming from the military, the National Guard, and Northwell Health. We were still weeks away from the predicted apex of the curve. Estimates said it could take several weeks to reach the maximum hospital need, but we had to be ready.

Hopefully, we still had a chance to reduce the viral transmission rate so that we would not hit the maximum hospital need. However, we had to be ready for the worst-case scenario, which was that we would overwhelm the hospitals and need the emergency beds. Javits would be one of those emergency facilities that I hoped to God we would never need.

At Javits, we wanted to avoid the "hurricane shelter" imagery that was ingrained in so many of our minds when we saw the images of the Superdome in New Orleans after Hurricane Katrina: rows and rows of cots as a shelter of last resort with conditions deteriorating by the day. It was critical that the Javits Center and other facilities be as close to real hospitals as we could get them, both to deliver the quality of care expected in a state with a globally renowned health-care system and to alleviate the trepidation and fear patients or their families would naturally feel when being told they were being transferred to a "field hospital." Conveniently, the Javits had hundreds of exhibit-booth room dividers that could be repurposed to build individual rooms with curtains for doors. My daughter Michaela worked with Gareth to prepare individual rooms to be welcoming to patients—including a welcome gift of a jar of honey from the bees on the roof of the Javits. But make no mistake, there was no denying or masking what Javits would actually be. It was the place of last resort. It was a place that you didn't want to need.

Walking around Javits, I could see on the faces of National Guard members that they were scared. They were mostly young, in their twenties, white, Black, brown, from all over the state. Some of them had worked on previous disasters with me and approached me, saying, "I was with you in Buffalo." "I was with you on Long Island." They had just gotten an extensive briefing about what to do and not do, what not to touch, what to wash. I'm sure their families had said to them, "Do you really have to do this?" I knew how they felt. Between the empty city outside, the thousands of green uniforms and Humvees and military jeeps, and the vision of row upon row of hospital beds, it felt like the end of the world. I wanted them to know I knew they were scared, and it was okay, and how proud I was of them for showing up anyway.

As I was doing the briefing from Javits that day, what people couldn't see on the television was that sitting in front of me were hundreds of National Guard and army personnel. In my remarks, I was speaking directly to them. I knew everyone was anxious and they were looking for guidance and comfort. I wanted to energize them and thank them for their courage. I said,

Ten years from now you'll be talking about today to your children or your grandchildren and you will shed a tear because you will remember the lives lost. You'll remember the faces and you'll remember the names, and you'll remember how hard we worked and that we still lost loved ones, and you should because it will be sad. But you will also be proud.

I had an issue close to home as well. A couple of the state troopers on my security detail tested positive. My state police security detail is critical. When I was at HUD, we had tremendous logistical support from the U.S. Marshals and military. Now that I'm governor, the state police provide all logistical support. While security is the priority for the state police, my priority is my ability to travel and actually get to places. I know I present them challenges. On a sunny day, life is easy, but if there is an emergency, I want to be on site. In emergencies, I want the first responders to know that I respect them and understand their sacrifice. Snowstorms, hurricanes, prison breaks—whatever the situation, I need to be able to get there. New York State is large, and in the midst of an emergency that's often easier said than done. Sometimes it is a scene from **Planes, Trains and Automobiles**. The state police have been extraordinary. The superintendent is Keith Corlett, who worked his way through the ranks. The deputy superintendent is Kevin Bruen, who is experienced in all aspects of criminal justice. And the head of the detail, Major Vincent Straface, served on other governors' details and has been with me from the beginning of my first term. He knows that as soon as a situation develops, we will need to be on site ASAP. Their support has allowed an additional dimension to my role as governor. I would never be comfortable as an "armchair general." I won't ask anyone to put themselves in a situation in which I'm unwilling to put myself.

The challenge presented by troopers testing positive for COVID was obviously a new one. Being in a car, a closed environment, is a huge risk for contracting COVID.

ONCE AGAIN, I WAS on notice to see if I was infected. The constancy of people around me getting infected created its own anxiety and was a reminder of how real this threat was. It seemed every few days someone close to me, or someone I was just with, tested positive. I was always wondering if I had gotten infected. Between the lack of sleep and the anxiety, I often thought I was coming down with it. It was another mind game for me to resolve. Ironically, I never did get COVID—so far! After we discovered the risk of being in a car with other people, we decided I would drive myself. There was actually a silver lining for me. I like the ability to drive and move around alone. I am very aware of the "bubble" that executives can become trapped in. I've seen presidents, mayors, and governors become isolated to the point where they are talking only to a small cadre of sycophants. I enjoy walking the dog, going into a store and meeting people casually, and having candid conversations. It keeps me grounded and in tune with what people feel. I learn what they actually think about what I am doing and what they are concerned about. It also reminds me that being governor is a temporary state. Always remembering my experience and my father's experience after losing office, I am acutely aware of the difficult return to reality upon leaving office, so I don't want to leave reality in the first place!

MARCH 28 | 7,681 NEW CASES | 7,328 HOSPITALIZED | 209 DEATHS

———

"You go to war with what you have,

not with what you need."

T HE FIRST SLIDE OF THE POWERPOINT said, "Today is Saturday," and everyone at the briefing laughed. After a month in the land of COVID, with everyone confined largely to home for weeks, no one knew what day it was anymore. There was no workweek as we knew it. There was no weekend. Every day was the same, like the movie **Groundhog Day.** You stayed home with your family, maybe you had some Zoom meetings if you were able to work remotely, maybe you had a Zoom cocktail hour with friends, maybe you helped your kids with their distance learning. But the usual cues for the days of the week were largely gone. Rush hour? Gone. "Today is Saturday" went viral, and we would do that every Saturday thereafter. How do we know if it's Saturday? Because Governor Cuomo says it's Saturday.

———

A NEW CHAPTER OPENED in the COVID story when Congress was preparing to pass the CARES Act.

Even at this time of crisis, the process was mired in politics. The Republican Senate didn't want to give federal funds to Democratic states for the simple reason that it wasn't in their political interest. Even in the middle of a historic world pandemic, Republican senators could not see beyond their own self-interest.

Trump personifies this divide, and his affirmative hostility to New York has long been a fundamental problem for me. Everything Trump did to New York was a negative. His tax reform plan of 2017 included ending the deductibility of state and local taxes, which hurt New York more than any other state. It also hurt other Democratic states, including California, Massachusetts, Michigan, Illinois, New Jersey, and Connecticut. It was the height of Republican hypocrisy. It turns out that the party that is against redistribution of income is only against redistribution if they don't benefit. SALT took tax dollars from Democratic states and gave them to Republican states. It was redistribution on steroids, and it was vicious to New York.

Senator Daniel Patrick Moynihan was obsessed with the fact that New York State contributes more in tax dollars than any state in the United

States. And he was right. We contribute more to the federal government than we get back, and our differential is the highest in the nation. New York subsidizes Kentucky, Florida, Alabama, Tennessee, and most of the Republican states. The Republican senators Mitch McConnell from Kentucky and Rick Scott from Florida are the greatest hypocrites, because their states get much more in federal funds than they contribute. This is nothing new and has been a long-term issue. However, the SALT provision and tax reform increased this disparity by forcing New York to contribute an additional $14 billion to the federal trough. I have been working to get the SALT provision repealed since it was passed three years ago. To further compound the injustice, after the COVID pandemic, Congress's first piece of legislation bailed out all the classic Republican donors—wealthy businessmen.

Even at this critical moment, their bailout legislation did not assist state and local governments, which fund essential services like police and firefighters—the very essential workers we were now relying on. Why? Because the states that had the highest number of COVID cases were Democratic states. McConnell was quoted saying he didn't want to "bail out blue states." Bail out blue states? It is the blue states that have supported his state for decades. In addition, all economists say that you cannot maximize an economic recovery without state and local governments functioning.

I have been in many negotiating sessions on many levels with many private sector and political leaders. In certain ways, the easiest personalities to negotiate with are the most extreme. Effective negotiating requires one to understand the situation from the other person's point of view. The old expression "check your ego at the door" is profound. If you can check your own and only seek to understand what drives the other person, you can succeed in the encounter. With Trump I had no ego. His attacks don't bother me, and his praise doesn't flatter me. The only question was how I could get him to help New York.

In most dealings between adversaries in government, there is a line that you don't cross. But with the Trump administration, there is no line. If something is in their political interest, they are capable of doing anything with no ethical or moral boundaries. I had seen it firsthand.

We had been in a court battle with Trump's Department of Homeland Security over the Trusted Traveler Program (a.k.a. Global Entry). I have dealt with DHS extensively over the years, and I knew its leaders were blatant political operatives. Since New York had implemented a policy of giving driver's licenses to undocumented people earlier in the year, DHS had barred New York residents from gaining global entry, unless we would give up our database, which was in effect a list of all undocumented people in the state with home addresses and pictures. We refused. The Trusted Traveler Program had absolutely nothing to do with access to driver's licenses for undocumented people, and DHS admitted it. I was amazed that Chad Wolf, the acting secretary of the Department of Homeland Security, and his deputy would stoop to such a low level. It was clearly unethical and possibly illegal conduct on their part. I'm not sure if they are ignorant or arrogant or both.

The Trump administration had previously instituted policies that have been much more damaging to New York than the Trusted Traveler Program, including SALT. They refused to fund Amtrak's train tunnels cross the Hudson, which were vital not just to New York but to the entire northeast corridor from D.C. to Boston, and withheld the funding to extend New York City's Second Avenue subway line. They gratuitously denied approval of an air train to LaGuardia Airport and a congestion pricing plan for the Metropolitan Transportation Authority (MTA). The suspension of the Trusted Traveler Program was relatively small compared with those issues, but again for me their actions were reprehensible and represented a pattern of unethical and possibly illegal conduct.

BACK IN FEBRUARY, I'd called the president and attempted to explain the Trusted Traveler situation to him, but it was complicated, so I asked for a meeting. That trip down to Washington, D.C., was memorable.

My special counsel, Beth Garvey, and I took off from Albany in the state plane. We had left promptly and had scheduled additional time so we wouldn't be late. On the way there the pilots told me there was a strong headwind and we were likely going to be late. At this point in my life, there is almost nothing that anyone could say to me that would surprise me.

The state plane is a flying jalopy, acquired as part of a purchase of federal surplus property. It is a forty-year-old twin-engine prop plane that seats about five people. You get in it and feel as if you are sitting in a tube of toothpaste. I have history with this plane: It was the backup to the governor's plane when my father came into office in 1983. His regular plane was a G1—a Grumman 1, the approximate size of the current G4s or G5s. It sat about sixteen people and was quite comfortable. In my father's last election, his opponent made a campaign issue out of the use of the state plane and then sold it upon taking office. But the new governor still had to travel and couldn't buy a new plane, so the state then purchased several helicopters to replace the G1. The helicopters were fine to operate between New York City and Albany, but are not really functional, as they can't make it to the western part of the state and can't fly in any bad weather. So any airplane travel had to be done in the original backup to the G1, the plane I was in today.

In 1982, I was working for my father as a special assistant to the governor, and I had recruited my friend at the time Tim Russert to join as press secretary. Tim and I had taken this plane to Buffalo, Tim's hometown, to do an official event. After the event, which was after five o'clock in the evening, Tim wanted to show me some of Buffalo's special places. A couple of those special places were dining establishments that also served beverages. Afterward we got back on the plane to fly to Albany, and the pilot said that there were some storm clouds en route but that he thought everything would be okay. Some storm clouds turned out to be near-hurricane-force winds. The plane bounced like a basketball going down the court. At one point, Tim and I were launched from our seats and hit the ceiling with full-body force. In fairness, the pilot did say to keep our seatbelts buckled, but we missed that point.

The bouncing airplane and the beverages from Tim's select Buffalo spots, combined with several dozen buffalo wings between us, were a toxic brew. By the time we got back to Albany, we were both a shade of green. I remember Tim getting off the plane swearing that he would "never get on that piece of s— again." That same plane is what I fly in today. I'm sure Tim is looking down and enjoying a hearty laugh.

The plane should be retired. It has had to make

a number of emergency landings, and every legislative leader who has been on it has commented that it needs to be replaced. However, given the political pressures, I don't want to be in a situation where I'm justifying to the public why we spent millions of dollars on an airplane. It just sounds offensive.

With the headwinds, the plane was traveling at half speed. I felt I could have driven my car faster.

It felt as if the flight took a week. Plus, I hate being late because it's disrespectful. We landed with minutes to spare, and after a maniacal car ride we made it to the White House on time.

Joining us at the White House meeting with President Trump about the Trusted Traveler Program were the acting Department of Homeland Security secretary, his deputy, the chief of staff, the counsel to the president, and some other people I didn't recognize. I explained how the Trusted Traveler Program was totally disconnected from the issue of turning over the undocumented driver list. The president listened and understood. The Homeland Security secretary was incapable of explaining any plausible rationale to connect the two issues. The president said at one point that he understood that DHS wanted leverage over me and was using the Trusted Traveler Program to do just that.

For the president, making a deal and using leverage are his basic modes of operation. He had ostensibly written a book, **The Art of the Deal**, that celebrated the practice. But in government, you are supposed to make decisions based on an issue's individual merits.

If I wanted the Trusted Traveler Program, I would have to give them the undocumented driver list. This was not leverage; it was extortion. The fact that I had the conversation in the Oval Office in front of top staff and lawyers and for no one to be appalled by it was breathtaking to me.

In my mind, this was the fallout of Trump being let off the hook by the Republican Senate in the impeachment trial. His administration thought they could now act with impunity. And it was all I needed to know about the people I was dealing with. There was no way that I would give them the undocumented driver list; it would be a feeding frenzy for ICE. And this would not be the last they heard of the matter. This was reprehensible, unethical behavior at best, and I would not let them get away with it.

Months later, on the afternoon of July 23, my phone rang. It was Alexander Cochran, my Washington representative, who had worked with me since HUD, who together with Sarah Paden, a top talent who is as sharp as a tack, manages federal affairs for New York State. "You're never going to believe this," Alexander said. "The Department of Homeland Security just issued a statement saying they are allowing New York back into the Trusted Traveler Program."

We had been fighting with the Department of

Homeland Security over the program for months, and then that day, out of nowhere, they issued a statement making the incredible claim that they'd just learned that New York was not the only state that shielded undocumented driver records from the federal government, and therefore the punitive action against us couldn't be justified? The statement was absurd. This was a major issue in the country. Everyone knew how many states had those laws. We had discussed it many times—even on television.

I was happy that the program was reinstated, but the entire thing didn't feel right. Something was up. Then, that night, a **New York Times** story broke: The U.S. attorney's office filed a motion late in the day to officially drop the case. They admitted in the filings that DHS officials not only made numerous false statements to justify the department's banning of New Yorkers from the Trusted Traveler Program but did so knowingly. The office went even further, apologizing to the state of New York for having had to unlawfully undergo the ordeal.

DHS lied and they got caught.

The next morning, I held a press conference and laid out my case against DHS. It was extortion and abuse of power by the federal agency. I called for a congressional investigation and said that New York State would pursue civil damages from the Department of Homeland Security. What they did to New York in this instance was emblematic of the rampant abuses the citizens of this country have endured. It had to be stopped.

Congressmember Bennie Thompson, head of the DHS oversight committee and a real professional, sent a letter saying that he would do an investigation. It will be revealing. I had had a meeting in the Oval Office on the matter. They all knew what DHS was doing. DHS acting secretary Chad Wolf and his deputy, Ken Cuccinelli, were only the hatchet men. They were handed the ax. I hope justice will finally be done.

I could tell the DHS scandal made them nervous. First, having a U.S. attorney's office refuse to represent the federal government because a federal agency was lying is very serious. I had never seen it before. Second, the prospect of a congressional investigation with subpoena power is also worrisome. One subpoena to Chad Wolf and Ken Cuccinelli and I am sure they would list a number of people who knew about the issue and who were part of the fraud and abuse. Shortly after my press conference on the DHS, I received a call from people in the White House who said they were willing to reopen discussion on the Second Avenue subway project. The Second Avenue subway project is the extension of the subway from 96th Street to 125th Street. It has always been a joint federal and state project. In the normal course of business, it would have been funded by the federal government years ago. But with this administration, where everything is political and personal, they have refused to fund it because New York is a Democratic state. I had been pushing them literally for years to fund the project, as well as others. They never say no, but then it never happens either. I keep expecting a different outcome. In any event, I believe their purported reopening of the Second Avenue subway discussion was intended to slow me down from pursuing the DHS scandal. That's not going to happen.

IN LATE MARCH, the number of cases in New York was spiking but remained low in the rest of the country. Governor Ron DeSantis of Florida complained that New Yorkers were bringing the virus to Florida. Florida is a key electoral state for President Trump, and Governor DeSantis was very much a Trump supporter. In fact, to secure a political advantage, President Trump had just changed his residency from New York to Florida. After DeSantis's statements, the president's aides started to talk about limiting New Yorkers' ability to travel. At first, we didn't take them seriously, but with a Trump White House you have to be constantly on guard because they were capable of anything. There was also a White House–driven theme emerging that COVID was a Democratic state problem, not a Republican state problem. Governor DeSantis's remark was another manifestation of this theme, and it was conceivable that targeting New York would be advancing this political narrative.

I have found that when two discrete situations coalesce, it can present a third, different, and worse problem. This was about to occur on March 27, when Governor Gina Raimondo of Rhode Island, a Democrat, said that she was wary of New York's high infection rate. That weekend, there were reports of Rhode Island police and National Guard troops pulling over cars with New York license plates. I feared that if a Democratic governor of a nearby state established a blockade against New Yorkers, Trump would seize upon the opportunity to expand on the blockade. This was all the stuff of nightmares.

When they were young, Michaela and Cara watched the movie **I Am Legend,** which caused Michaela to have nightmares for weeks. I remember having to explain to her how it was just a movie and it could never happen in real life. Now the movie was coming back to me. In it Will Smith is a doctor who is working on a cure for cancer when a virus is released that turns people into zombies. When the federal government realizes the virus is in Manhattan, they blow up the bridges and crossings leading to the island to isolate the virus—leaving the population trapped.

Now I could see Trump blockading New York State. If the Rhode Island governor could station police at the border, why couldn't Trump station Customs and Border Protection officers at the New York borders? Department of Homeland Security would jump at the chance to be able to stop every vehicle entering or leaving the state. They could check citizenship and have a field day for deportation. Trump could use it to highlight his claim that COVID was a function of Democratic states and big Democratic cities, and he could say he was protecting the good Republican states from being infected. He would be a hero in Florida.

I was surprised that Rhode Island would take such a measure without at least talking to me. I called Governor Raimondo and expressed my displeasure and concern with her actions. A quarantine was one thing. Other states have done it. A blockade is something else. I made the point that many people from Rhode Island traveled into New York for business and pleasure. We would later impose a quarantine on Rhode Island, but if we were to set up blockades, it would be detrimental to both states.

Within minutes our worst fears came true. The news reported that while boarding Air Force One, President Trump said he was considering a blockade for all of New York—referencing his conversation with Governor DeSantis. It was a dramatic, obscene threat; there haven't been blockades in this country since the Civil War. And the psychological damage and resulting stigma that such a move would cause New York would be devastating.

I had spoken to President Trump earlier in the day about additional aid for the state, in the form of temporary hospital beds. He never mentioned anything about a blockade. But that meant little.

The truth is, it would have wreaked havoc in the financial markets as well. Wall Street is the financial center of the world. To blockade New York is to effectively close Wall Street and the markets. I knew that was the only thing that would stop Trump. Any political benefit he would get in Florida would be overwhelmed by the political cost he would pay for causing the markets to plummet. But he had to hear the message.

I called Rich Azzopardi, my communications guru, and told him to set up whatever television interviews he could get as soon as possible. About fifteen minutes later I was live on CNN being interviewed by Ana Cabrera. She asked me first about Rhode Island, and I said, "I think what they did was wrong. I think it was reactionary. I think it was illegal but we will work it out amicably, I'm sure . . . If they don't roll back that policy, I'm going to sue Rhode Island because it is clearly unconstitutional." Ana then asked me about "Trump's newly floated New York lockdown," and I said if it happened, the stock market would "drop like a stone . . . It would be chaos and mayhem and that would drop this economy in a way, I think, that it wouldn't recover for months if not years."

The sensationalism of Trump's proposal was not lost on the press, and my remarks generated a firestorm. About thirty minutes after my CNN appearance, Melissa walked into my office and told me that she had heard from Rhode Island that they would reverse the executive order. That night the president reversed course on the idea of a New York blockade via tweet.

———

"Everyone is afraid."

T HERE WAS A FRESH RUMOR ABOUT A NEW possible COVID drug nearly every week. And there were constant conversations about the race to a vaccine. People were so desperate to find a cure they seized on any ray of hope. The president encouraged drug companies to work diligently, but he didn't really have to. The billions of dollars that a company that develops the cure to COVID-19 will make are likely incentive enough.

The Trump administration was suggesting that we would have a vaccine by the end of the year. This would be perfect timing for the Trump administration, because it would offer optimism through Election Day. Yet they had scarce facts. Even if development of a vaccine were expedited and testing facilitated, there were still the issues of mass production and the country's capacity to afford and implement hundreds of millions of vaccines.

In the midst of this, hydroxychloroquine dropped

from the sky and into President Trump's mouth. The president took every opportunity he could to explain to Americans that hydroxychloroquine was a very effective cure for this disease. He said he spoke to doctors and patients who had been treated and everyone agreed it was the "miracle drug." The president's media mouthpieces immediately amplified the chant. Watching Fox News on TV, one would be convinced that hydroxychloroquine could immediately cure COVID, even the common cold, and increase weight loss, testosterone, and hair growth. Hydroxychloroquine was the silver bullet.

But the medical community was skeptical. Hydroxychloroquine had been on the market before and was used to treat malaria. Bona fide medical professionals raised questions about the risks and doubted its effectiveness to treat COVID. But the president and his supporters were 100 percent convinced. As usual, the president needed a villain, and he suggested that political forces were conspiring to keep the COVID virus alive to hurt him and his reelection and were therefore trying to discredit hydroxychloroquine. The president was so successful in communicating his message there was a run on the drug. Pharmacies and suppliers couldn't keep up. Patients who normally use hydroxychloroquine to treat illnesses such as lupus couldn't get it because the demand was so high from doctors prescribing it for their patients. New York had to pass a regulation limiting prescriptions for hydroxychloroquine to fourteen days so there was a supply for people who normally relied on it.

At the same time, the president and the FDA wanted to expedite testing for the drug. Because New York had the highest number of cases, it was the obvious and best location to do it. Hydroxychloroquine's potential was the one topic that Trump repeatedly raised in every conversation I had with him for weeks.

Hospitals in New York began participating in a standard testing regiment with FDA protocols to see if the drug actually worked. The test took about five weeks, but the president was eager to get the results and communicated total certainty on what they would find. I had said publicly that I didn't know whether hydroxychloroquine was effective for treating COVID. I'm not a doctor, scientist, or pharmacist. Obviously, everyone would love a cure and if it's hydroxychloroquine, or any other drug, that would be great.

Sometimes we see in others what we see in ourselves. Or we think other people are motivated the same way we are motivated. Trump and the White House assumed the Democrats, myself included, would not want hydroxychloroquine to work because we feared that the president would get credit for it. And if COVID was resolved, it would be good for the president. However absurd, I had heard this from enough Trump supporters to know that they were sincere. They believed Democrats would sabotage hydroxychloroquine for political purposes. How sick is that? People are dying, billions of dollars are being spent, how could anyone put politics above a cure? Maybe the White House could.

I had been working very hard to keep our COVID efforts in New York nonpartisan, and I had even gone on Sean Hannity's show to reach out to all New Yorkers, because if you're not on Fox News, you're missing the best platform to talk to conservatives in the state. To be clear, Hannity was perfectly cordial with me. Because I had no national agenda, I wasn't a threat.

However, hydroxychloroquine became the line in the sand for Fox; Hannity talked about it all the time. Dr. Oz was talking about it. But there was an undercurrent of doctors saying, "We're not sure it works, and we think it may be causing harm." And if you were against hydroxychloroquine or even unsure about it, you were the enemy.

The White House was growing increasingly eager for the test results. State government had nothing to do with the timing of the tests, because it was all done by hospitals, with the data to go to the FDA for review, but that didn't stop them from pressing to get the test results done faster.

Mark Meadows, the White House chief of staff, called me. It was highly unusual for him to call me. When we did meet, he had a general air of negativity around him. When I picked up the phone, Meadows said that they wanted the results from the tests on hydroxychloroquine. I told him, as I told the president, that the tests were being done by the hospitals and when they were complete they would be sent to the FDA. I didn't know how long they took, but no one had any interest in causing undue delay. Meadows then communicated to me that the federal government was about to send out funding for hospitals and strongly implied that if the tests weren't completed, New York wouldn't receive any funding.

Now, I am a New Yorker, I am not a shrinking violet, and I am accustomed to dealing with all sorts of personalities. I have no problem dealing with tough guys—whether they are genuine tough guys, or really scared guys trying to act tough, or guys who think they need to act tough to impress me. I don't mind exaggeration or expletives, but I draw the line at extortion. It is incredible to me that the chief of staff to the president of the United States would ever link the production of drug tests to federal government health-care funding. Government Ethics 101 tells you that's a no-no. Meadows might not have had any federal executive experience, but he was a congressman and as such should've known that quid pro quos are no-**bueno**.

I wondered if Meadows wanted the results because he was assuming they would be positive or if he already knew what they were. I assumed that the results must be positive or he would not have been as aggressive in wanting their release. I told Meadows that the state Department of Health would transfer the test results to the FDA as soon as they received them and that to threaten me with not funding the hospitals in my state was not a good tactic to take and would not prove productive for him.

Then I spoke to Dr. Howard Zucker and asked him when the hospitals would finish the tests. Dr. Zucker said he didn't know, that he had nothing to do with the tests, but that as soon as they were ready, the hospitals would send the results to the FDA. I asked Dr. Zucker to let the FDA know that as soon as the results were ready, they would receive them.

At last, the results came in, and they were negative. Hydroxychloroquine is not effective in treating COVID, and the results actually raised possible health risks. At the same time, a number of doctors were publicly speaking out against hydroxychloroquine and the risks of using it. Remarkably, in June the FDA itself would conclude that hydroxychloroquine was of no beneficial effect and was in fact dangerous. This is just after President Trump announced that he was personally taking hydroxychloroquine as a preventative for COVID infection.

I have two theories about what motivated the president and his minions. First, it was about money. Maybe someone had stock in a drug company related to hydroxychloroquine, or there was some financial scheme by which someone would financially benefit. The second theory is in some ways more troubling. The president was desperate to end this nightmare of coronavirus that was disrupting his reelection by disturbing the economy, and he desperately wanted to believe that there was a simple solution: There was one pill to make it all go away. Literally.

———

"This is a war, and let's act that way, and let's
act that way now."

A LITTLE BOOST ONCE IN A WHILE WAS
helpful, and one of the great symbols of
hope in this crisis was the recovery of Lawrence
Garbuz, known as patient zero from New Rochelle.
He had been quite sick, and the doctors did not
expect him to make it. He had been put on a ventilator, and approximately 80 percent of people who
are put on ventilators never come off. But he had
survived and was out of the hospital. This was a
reason to be hopeful.

But so many others were dying. Early on, I had
set a goal that no one would die simply due to
the fact that they did not receive our best medical
attention. COVID would kill people. I knew that,
and it was hard to come to terms with. But no life
should be lost because of our lack of organization,
resources, or talent. I kept going back to images
of people dying in Italian hospital corridors. There,

infected individuals, including young people, were dying not from coronavirus alone but from lack of access to health-care services—lack of a ventilator, lack of medical attention. I refused to let that happen here.

Meanwhile, I had received some more hope from a surprising source. In early March, Bill Clinton called me to touch base and see how I was doing. It meant a great deal to me that he took the time. He had been in the hot seat many times, as attorney general and governor of Arkansas and, obviously, as president. He knew what it was like to make hard decisions and live with the consequences. We had spent eight years working together, during which he had been enormously kind to me. I was one of the youngest cabinet secretaries in history, and he had taken a big chance on me and he had also taken the time to counsel and advise me. I still appreciate it to this day. Bill Clinton is an extraordinary politician, and his ability to connect with people—to put his own self aside and actually appreciate where another person is coming from and respond on that level—is a true skill. He has a personal touch unlike anyone I have met.

When we worked together, one of his objectives was to "reduce the New York in me." New Yorkers are high-strung and can come off as intense. President Clinton took me on many presidential trips with him and would spend time talking to me on Air Force One about the event we had just attended, the people there, my observations and his. I remember one conversation early on when he suggested that I reach out to the House and Senate members on the HUD authorizing and appropriations committees to develop a relationship with them. He made the point it would be much more effective to visit them in their home districts than in their Washington offices. Visiting them in the district was a sign of respect and also showed constituents that their representation made a difference on the local level.

HUD had a broad portfolio and was active in every district in the nation, so I could certainly find something that HUD was doing to justify the trip. The president simply said I should "go visit" them. I am a very literal person, so I wanted to make sure that I understood what he meant by "go visit."

"What do you think I should be talking with them about?" I asked him.

The president repeated, "Just go visit."

As a New Yorker, I didn't understand the concept of just visiting. I was goal oriented. Everything had to have a purpose.

"Andrew, there is no purpose; the only purpose is to visit," the president said.

But I couldn't take a hint. "But what do I want to accomplish?"

"Nothing," answered the president. "Just visit."

Eventually I understood. There did not always have to be an agenda. The personal connection was

Declaring "New York State on PAUSE," with secretary to the governor Melissa DeRosa, budget director Robert Mujica, and president of SUNY Empire State College Dr. Jim Malatras, on March 20, 2020.

Kansas farmer Dennis Ruhnke wrote to Governor Cuomo saying he had five N95 masks. His wife had only one lung, so he was keeping four masks, but he sent one for a New Yorker, along with a handwritten letter.

march 6, 2020
2020

Dear Mr. Cuomo,

I seriously doubt that you will ever read this letter As I know you are busy Beyond belief with the disaster that HAs befallen our country. We currently (As of MARCH 26, 2020) are a nation in crisis. Of that there is no doubt. Your Approach has Bonspot on correct. I commend you for that & for especially for telling the truth, something that has been sorely lacking As of late.

I am a retired farmer hunkered down in N.E. Kansas with my wife who has But one lung and occasional problems with her remaining lung. She also has diabetes. We are in our 70's now & Frankly I am Afraid for her.

Enclosed find a solitary N-95 mask left over from my farming days. It has never Been used. If you could, would you please give this mask to a nurse or doctor in your city. I have kept four masks for my immediate family. Please keep on doing what you do so well, which is to lead —

Sincerely, Dennis & Sharon Ruhnke

Delivering a press briefing commending members of the National Guard, March 27, 2020, at the Jacob K. Javits Convention Center.

Unveiling the "Self-Portrait of America," a wall of masks sent from citizens across the country, April 29, 2020.

Corning Tower in Albany was lit "NY Tough" in honor of health-care professionals and essential workers, April 23, 2020.

A desolate Grand Central Terminal during the early Monday evening "rush hour" on May 11, 2020.

Governor Cuomo demonstrating the three-step disinfectant process of a New York City 7-line subway train car on May 2, 2020.

Waving goodbye, April 12, 2020, after returning ventilators to the Pathways Nursing Home, where residents and staff made an unsolicited donation to New York State.

After seventy-five days, this is what sleep looks like. The governor and his daughter Michaela on their way back to Albany on May 15, 2020.

To encourage New Yorkers to get tested for the coronavirus, Governor Cuomo took a test via nasal swab during his daily briefing on national television, May 17, 2020.

Taking the helicopter to New York City, May 26, 2020, to re-open the New York Stock Exchange, which was shuttered on March 23.

Signing police reform legislation in the aftermath of the murder of George Floyd, joined by the Reverend Al Sharpton; Dr. Hazel N. Dukes, president of the NAACP State Conference; Valerie Bell, mother of Sean Bell; Gwen Carr, mother of Eric Garner; state senate majority leader Andrea Stewart-Cousins; and state assembly Speaker Carl Heastie, on June 12, 2020.

Preparing for the final daily briefing, on June 19, 2020, which the governor would give from behind his desk, the same one used by FDR.

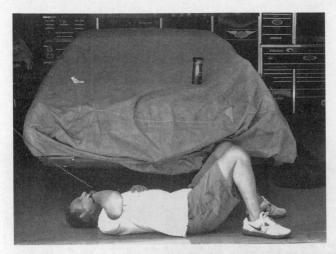

Day 112, the first day after the final daily briefing.

The governor's mother, Matilda Cuomo, with her favorite son and Chris.

At home with Michaela, Cara, and Mariah—and Captain.

simply for the sake of the personal connection. This lesson has served me very well in later life. I would recall it when I was working through my briefings.

President Clinton and I had another encounter that sticks with me. As HUD secretary, I was going to receive the Man of the Year Award from the Detroit NAACP. I often received these awards, which were really based on an organization's desire to have a featured speaker. But HUD had been very aggressive on antidiscrimination work: We sued the Ku Klux Klan, and we dramatically advanced fair housing and home ownership opportunities for Black Americans.

President Clinton called me a few days before the event to congratulate me. I didn't think it was a big deal, and I was taken aback that he would have the time to call.

"It's the largest indoor sit-down dinner in the country with several thousand attendees," he said. "I'm proud of you. I'd like to come along. You should bring Kerry. We'll go on Air Force One."

"Mr. President, I'm really flattered, but that's not necessary."

He insisted, and a few days later we were on Air Force One going to Detroit, and sure enough it was the largest dinner I had ever attended. The president spoke, and the crowd loved him. I spoke, but obviously no one was really that interested after hearing from the president.

I had heard the advance people telling the

president there was a shortcut to exit behind the stage so that he would not get caught by the crowd. I thought that was the plan. However, when it came time to leave, rather than exiting the stage through the back, the president walked right toward the crowd. Several thousand people surged the rope line to shake his hand. He must have stood there for two and a half hours shaking hands and taking pictures. I think he shook hands with everybody in the room. We got back on Air Force One at about one o'clock in the morning.

I knew President Clinton could've just walked out the back of the hotel and saved hours, so I asked him why he stayed back. He made two points. First, he said this was a big thing for the people at the dinner and they deserved it. They would have a picture with the president, and it would be treasured. He also said, "Andrew, that's the job. We are elected by the people to serve the people, and we must always take the time to honor and respect them and show them gratitude and humility."

It wasn't as if the president had to win over anyone in that room; they all loved him before he showed up. They loved him even more after he showed up and spoke. Two hours of handshaking didn't get him one additional fan or vote. He had them all. But he did it anyway. I've never forgotten that message, and I truly appreciate the human and emotional connection with the people I serve.

One afternoon I was speaking with a young state

assemblyman, and he asked me how I got people to connect with me during briefings. I said it can be simply stated. If you want people to open up to you, you open up to them first. Open your heart; show your emotion, your truth, your vulnerability, your humanity. I told my kids all their lives, "Give love, get love," but you have to "give" it first. No one wants to go first. It risks rejection. But it's the only way.

The assemblyman then asked me, as he was just starting out, what advice I could give him. I had been in a reflective mood, so I gave him more than he expected. I said that government is actually a more substantive trade than many young people now appreciate. It's not about just having an opinion or identifying a wrong that needs to be righted. Every student in a college-level political science course can do that. You must understand the issue from all dimensions, understand the complexities and the consequences. Too many opinions now are only "tweet deep." You then need to know how to make change: how to get it done from the legislative perspective, but even more, how the change would then be implemented. How do you make it happen and how do you make it happen with no unintended consequences? Raising problems without effecting solutions is pointless, if not counterproductive. I said, look at the extraordinary baseball players: They are "complete players." You must be a power hitter who can also bunt. A fielder who can also run bases. In government you must be a strong advocate but also know how to manage, execute, compromise, and forge consensus. Criticism is easy. Construction is hard.

More than two decades later, President Clinton and I talked about the pressure and the consequences of my situation, and then he passed on a piece of information. He knew a lot of people in big pharma through his work to bring necessary drugs to Africa for many years. He told me that people whom he respected suggested that remdesivir was a drug that might be helpful against coronavirus and that our Department of Health should check it out.

After the call, I phoned Dr. Zucker and told him what the president had said. Zucker had also heard about remdesivir and agreed it might be helpful. He said he would call the FDA and ask what they thought. I followed up a few days later, and he told me that the FDA was reviewing studies.

Fast-forward approximately three and a half months. The HHS secretary, Alex Azar, says on national TV during the last week of June that the administration will be buying a drug that they recently discovered and that showed promise. What was the name of the drug? Remdesivir. All those weeks wasted obsessing over hydroxychloroquine, and there was an existing drug that actually worked which they knew about months before.

MARCH 31 | 9,298 NEW CASES | 10,929 HOSPITALIZED | 332 DEATHS

———

"The main battle is at the apex; we're still going up the mountain."

WE WERE STILL TWO TO FOUR WEEKS FROM the apex of this mountain we were climbing, and we were all tired. A month of bad news, our lifestyles disrupted, and nobody knew when it was going to get better, not even the president, who was harping on reopening the country by Easter, less than two weeks away.

The nation was realizing the disparity in the infection rate between lower-income communities and higher-income communities. Luckily, in New York the disparity was much less than other states across the nation. We were testing more people than any state in the country, even more per capita than China and South Korea. New York City had an infection rate of about 19 percent. The infection rate among the Black community and the Latino community was about 23 percent; in some states there was a nearly 50 percent differential.

We wanted to ensure that every New Yorker was getting all the help they needed. We were increasing testing and services in Black and brown communities and made special efforts in public housing. Our greatest challenge was in New York City's crowded public housing. In these areas special teams were going door to door to offer people testing and information on social distancing, masks, and precautions.

The high-infection areas were what we called hot-spot zip codes. The highest infection rate hot spots had an infection rate of approximately 50 percent. Corona, Queens, which is served by Elmhurst Hospital, was one of those hot spots. Elmhurst made national news when it was overwhelmed with patients and suffered a severe shortage of supplies. It was an eye-opener on several levels. Elmhurst is a community that comprises many new immigrants and low-income people. It is a community that did not have as much access to health care and had many underlying illnesses. It was also a community suffering from a housing shortage, with many new immigrants living in tight quarters.

Elmhurst is a public hospital as opposed to a private hospital. In downstate New York, there are approximately one hundred hospitals with about ninety "privately run" and eleven "public" hospitals operated by the City of New York. While we had understood that it would be a challenge to get the private hospitals to work together, we didn't know that the eleven public hospitals, all owned by New York City, were not already coordinated as one system either. If Elmhurst was overwhelmed, why didn't it coordinate with the other ten hospitals in the same system to shift patients, resources, and staff as necessary?

As usual when one deals with a bureaucracy, there were no good answers. Bureaucracy takes comfort in the status quo, relying on an almost arrogant belief that there is an inherent wisdom in the current system. It's usually quite the opposite. For me, the health-care system was a single chain; if one link breaks anywhere in the system, the whole chain is broken.

In fairness, this was an unprecedented crisis, and the old model simply couldn't deal with it. While our concept of one coordinated statewide hospital system was a good one, the shift would be more traumatic and difficult than anyone anticipated. COVID was exposing many existing problems. Fundamental ones like a divided country and dysfunctional government, social inequities in health care and education, but also the failure of basic operating systems.

I started speaking to the hospital executives again because I had to educate myself as to exactly how they operated.

What was becoming clear was that for all the talk of a "public health system," this nation was wholly unprepared for an emergency. How could that be after all the warnings we'd had with Ebola, swine flu, MERS, and SARS? Who knows? But that's where we were.

It was no time for recriminations; we had to deal with the situation. Winston Churchill came to mind. Imagine how frustrated he was in the early years of the war when he was fighting Germany and he couldn't get the United States to join forces against the obvious common threat. He was on his own, and he improvised. He needed to cross the English Channel to rescue the soldiers at Dunkirk. I'm sure he wanted to complain about the fact that the government didn't have enough ships, but there was no time for that. He scrambled and put together a "citizen navy" to form a flotilla of private craft to cross the channel and rescue hundreds of thousands. There is an old saying that you go to war with the army you have, not the army you want.

The breadth and depth of our need was clear. We would have to create an emergency public health system out of whole cloth. We were told by all the experts that we would need between 110,000 and 140,000 hospital beds, and we had only 53,000. If we didn't accomplish that goal, we would repeat the experience in Italy, where the hospital system was overwhelmed. That couldn't happen here. I understood fully that it was an impossible task, but we had to do the best we could.

We had sketched out the concepts. All hospitals

increasing capacity 50 percent, building thousands of emergency beds and coordinating a unified, cooperative hospital system. But this was a massive and revolutionary undertaking. It would normally take years to implement. The hospital industry is a $100 billion industry in New York with 415,000 employees. You don't turn it inside out overnight. That was our goal. We had the concept, but we had to do it!

For a plan to work, we would need specific operating procedures and leave nothing to the imagination. As I had learned too many times before, it's not enough to have a good idea; you have to know how to implement the idea. If you want to make a change, you must know exactly what you want to do and how to do it.

The Northwell hospital system, New York's largest, was run by Michael Dowling. Luckily, Michael had been a friend for thirty years and was the top health-care professional for my father during his twelve-year administration. As a former government official and now hospital administrator, Michael understood the system from both perspectives. If Northwell bought into a new model, other institutions would follow. We spent many hours talking through the details, addressing all the questions, and leaving nothing to chance. We knew what we needed to do; now we needed to do it.

I called a dozen of my staff into the Red Room. We had to move beyond conceptualization to implementation. We sat—socially distanced—around a square table. The chamber operations team, led by Reid Sims—who has been a dedicated and loyal member of my staff since I was elected governor—can turn the Red Room from a press conference setup to a TV studio to a meeting room in a matter of minutes. I am not sure how they do it so quickly and efficiently, but they do.

I explained to my team gathered in the Red Room my view of the situation: Testing was up; we were now doing more than twenty thousand tests per day. PPE and ventilators were being pursued. Staff was signing up by the thousands on our portal to volunteer. And thousands of new beds were coming online as hospitals increased capacity and new emergency facilities such as the Javits Center opened. As we barreled toward what was projected to be our apex, the problems at Elmhurst showed that it was going to be all about management. The Elmhurst Hospital debacle made that point. I wanted it all done centrally, in one room—no space for miscommunication or errors. Getting it right was a matter of life and death. Many of my most senior staff were wearing two hats at this time; the state budget was due at midnight that night! Melissa, Robert, Beth, and Dana Carotenuto Rico (my adept and tireless legislative director) were simultaneously addressing the COVID crisis while negotiating the final pieces of the budget bill. Rob is an extraordinary talent on the budget and finance. I trust his judgment and it took a major burden off my shoulders. I laid out my vision for a hospital capacity coordination center—a central nerve center where any hospital in the state could call 24/7 to request patient transfers, staff support, PPE, ventilators, or any other need. The operation would be guided by real-time data reporting, and if the center saw a hospital reaching capacity, it would proactively reach out to help support patient movement to a hospital with more capacity.

We called the plan "Surge & Flex." Not the most artful name, but it was descriptive. We would have to operate the individual hospitals as if they were one health-care system and work to manage the surge of patients and the increased demand. Patient load would increase exponentially, but the surge needed to be balanced throughout the system. As patients came in, we would monitor the numbers and direct them to hospitals that had vacancies and capacity. If patients needed to be moved from one facility to another, we would provide transportation.

The system would also have a "flex" capacity. No hospital had significant inventory of ventilators and PPE. We would flex resources as necessary among the hospitals and develop a central supply of materials. All hospitals throughout the state would work together in purchasing supplies. Rather than having separate hospitals competing against one another, we would cooperate.

The flex concept would also apply to staff. If one

hospital had a shortage, we would identify staff from other hospitals who could be moved. This would all be coordinated through a daily reporting system where each hospital reported its capacity, vacancy rate, ICU bed availability, PPE, ventilators, and so forth. Every night there would be a coordinating call run by the state with all the hospitals in that region which would allocate and adjust the load across the system. This would be an extraordinary and unprecedented management exercise, but it had to be implemented tomorrow. Like everything else, it seemed, what was impossible yesterday was a necessity today.

We set up a meeting at the Javits Center with all the major downstate hospital administrators to go through our new Surge & Flex plan. It was a large group, and Javits had the space for a socially distanced meeting. This physical setting at the Javits Center drove home the urgency of our situation, without my saying a word. The seemingly endless row of hospital beds and sea of green uniforms took your breath away. They were frightened. We went through the details, and everyone was shocked and dubious, but they were on board to try.

Of course, we received concerning news right after the meeting. Par for the course. One of the hospital executives who was there, Lee Perlman, from the Greater New York Hospital Association, tested positive the next day. I spent time at the meeting in proximity to Lee, as had many of the other hospital executives.

It would be one thing if I got sick. I understood the risk; more troubling would be if it spread to my senior team and the others at that meeting, which included all the key hospital administrators who were running the entire system. Lee's infection reminded all of us of the power of the virus and how quickly our situation could get even worse.

THE NEXT PERSON CLOSE to me to contract COVID was very close: my brother, Christopher. He spoke openly about battling the virus on his nightly show: the teeth-rattling chills, how he lost more than ten pounds. What people were seeing in our exchanges wasn't much different from how we were in private. I was nervous for Chris; he's my little brother, and I've always been there for him. He was staying at home with his three kids and wife, confined to the basement, and he couldn't see anyone else. It felt unnatural for me not to be able to see him and help him. But that was the curse of COVID.

Chris is relatively young and healthy and not in a vulnerable category, but COVID is frightening nonetheless. He was fortunate to have the best doctors available and all the help he needed. Dr. Fauci also spoke to him. Dr. Fauci is from Brooklyn. I knew him from the 1980s when he worked on the HIV/AIDS crisis. I was talking to him a couple of times a week as it was. He was the best mind on the science.

Chris's broadcasts and my briefings were the most comprehensive and intimate communications people were receiving about this crisis, and now he was giving people a front-row seat to the disease's devastating symptoms—even for those who were young and healthy before. Chris recovered after about two weeks, so people saw someone battle the virus from start to finish. They also watched me experiencing it with Chris, so they knew once again that I understood the crisis on a deeply personal level. They were right.

"If we don't stop the spread, then it's going to
burn down our country."

NONE OF MY TASKS EVER SEEMED TO BE finished. They just kept going. It was hard for me to deal with. I am a "closer." I find comfort in completion. The doctors kept telling me hospital beds without ventilators would be virtually useless. We would need about forty thousand ventilators at a minimum, at the projected apex. That would at least give every ICU bed a ventilator. We had about four thousand to start, and ordered about seventeen thousand, of which about three thousand had arrived, for a total of seven thousand on hand, and the search for more was a daily undertaking.

China remained a major supplier of ventilators. Who could help in China? I contacted Bob Rubin, former secretary of the Treasury, chairman emeritus of the Council on Foreign Relations, and a colleague from the Clinton administration. His partner Blair Effron is an old friend and a wise, trusted investment banker. They were pursuing every contact they had. I also spoke to Elizabeth Jennings at the Asia Society, who has extensive contacts and is indefatigable. They were great and had many good ideas that we pursued together for weeks. In this exercise of manic networking, a gentleman named Jack Ma came forward to help. Mr. Ma founded Alibaba, known as the Amazon of China. The president of his company was a great guy from New York, Michael Evans. Joining together with Joe Tsai, the executive vice chairman of Alibaba, and his wife, Clara, successful Chinese entrepreneurs and owners of the Nets basketball team, they arranged to donate two thousand ventilators. This was welcome news and a big deal. I spoke with him and thanked him very much, and we announced the gift publicly.

Much to my surprise, shortly thereafter President Trump took credit for the gift, saying that his "friend" Joe Tsai gave the ventilators essentially to him. In all the conversations I had with the Tsais, Trump's name had never come up. I think in the president's mind, the gift highlighted the federal failure, and he couldn't bear the idea that he wasn't included. In any event, when the press asked me if the president was involved, I just never responded. The president's ego was fragile, and it wasn't worth the risk of angering him.

In the midst of this, the state of Oregon and its governor, Kate Brown, announced they would donate 140 ventilators to New York, an act that displayed that we are all in this together. Now, if only the federal government had that perspective, leadership, and credibility to bring such a message to the American people, imagine how much better we would be. What if there had been a national effort, with states working together to help other states in need and implement a national Surge & Flex program? It was infuriating that every state needed to scramble for equipment, staff, and material when we knew the timetable for each state's critical need would be different. We would lose lives; that was unavoidable. But not doing the best job that we could was unacceptable.

———

"It's been a long month."

I WOKE UP FEELING AS IF I HADN'T SLEPT A wink. I went into the bathroom, looked in the mirror, and saw my father's face, that face of lines and crevices. Some call it character, but to me it just looked like old age. For fifty-five years of my life, I was always "the son," and the son is perpetually young. In my mind I was still in my thirties. How could this be?

I asked Michaela later that day, "Do I look older to you?"

"Oh, no, Dad, you just look a little tired." That's Michaela, so sweet that sugar wouldn't melt in her mouth.

I asked Cara the same question later when we were alone.

She said, "Yes, Dad, you look older, but maybe when this is over and things are normal, you will look better." That's Cara, kind but realistic, even if it's hard.

I felt that every death from COVID took a little piece of me. I believed we did everything we could to save every life, but it didn't give me peace. A bus driver died from COVID. He was an "essential worker." I determined that buses had to operate. He went to work because I said he should. If he stayed home, maybe he would be alive. I was committed to beating this thing, but it was harder and more debilitating than I had even imagined.

I still very much wanted to do the briefings every day. It was my way of being present and saying to people that I knew every day was a struggle for them and I respected and appreciated that reality and I was living it with them. But every morning when I first opened my eyes, I lay there and thought, **"Maybe I could skip today. Let me sleep in just once and catch my breath. And I will be better for it tomorrow."**

I would review in my mind the many reasons to give in to that urge:

I was too tired and I would convey the wrong tone.

I could not deal with the stupid press questions today.

The team needed a break and skipping one day would be good for them.

But the sense of obligation and commitment to the relationship I had formed with the public was paramount. It was personal. I was reading their emails, taking their phone calls. I knew people relied on me. They never quit on me, and I would never quit on them. My instinct was that consistency was important. People needed to comply with these new rules every day, and I wanted to be there for them every day. Some days I was just exhausted. I tried to keep my tone factual and calm. Other days I just didn't have the strength to control my emotions, and they were apparent. Some days I was so exhausted that I was in a daze.

These were not only long and exhausting days; the information was so extreme and extraordinary I was actually finding it hard to compute. If I had not been in the room hearing for myself, I don't think I would've believed it.

Many times, I just had to get away from it, at least to the extent possible. I didn't want to seem distressed for my team or family. That would alarm them. I would take my dog, Captain, on long walks just to restore my sense of reality and try to clear my head. But even on a walk with the dog, everything seemed strange. There were fewer people on the streets, stores closed, people who were out were social distancing, but at least the walks presented the semblance of normalcy. There were still trees and buildings and familiar landmarks. The entire world had not gone mad, yet.

NEW YORK CITY WAS a surreal place at the height of the pandemic. The streets were largely empty of cars and people; storefronts and offices were shuttered and dark. But the quiet was punctured by the constant blare of sirens as emergency vehicles answered COVID calls, one after another after another. Sirens were the new sound of the city. EMS workers who might handle four or five calls in a day were handling dozens. As the death rate spiked into the hundreds every day, many more than the city's morgues and funeral homes could handle, we had to call in refrigerator trucks to store the overflow of bodies. The last time New Yorkers saw refrigerator trucks to store the dead was after 9/11, and this dwarfed that in numbers. 9/11 was horrific and traumatic and this was worse. It was just incredible to me. People's loved ones went into the hospital and died, and they were never seen again. The closure that comes with the ritual of a funeral was no longer possible. We had to bring in funeral directors from out of state, waiving the licensing requirements. I had to sign an executive order that allowed for expedited cremations and electronic signatures for orders to dispose of a family member's remains, and the crematoriums were allowed to operate twenty-four hours a day. For hundreds of COVID victims whose families couldn't afford burial, or were simply unclaimed for any number of reasons, a mass grave on Hart Island, a public cemetery off the Bronx, was their final resting place. It was heartbreaking at a level I had never imagined.

———

WE HAD LOST SIX hundred people overnight—
a staggering amount. A reporter asked me at the
briefing if people would get numb to the number
of deaths. I was shocked by the question. For me it
has been the opposite. The death toll was a constant
weight on my chest and made it hard to breathe.
An ironic coincidence given the primary symptoms
of the invisible beast we were battling. Every day I
had conversations with family members, hospital
staff, and union representatives asking them to
be strong and helpful. I understood my role and
obligation, but I didn't wish my role on my worst
enemy.

Scientists were telling me that we might be
approaching the apex of the curve, the point where
it starts to flatten. But I didn't even believe them
anymore. It was all projections based on extrapo-
lations and assumptions. How high up does the
incline take us? Once we hit the apex, how long
does it last? How fast is the decline on the other
side? No one knew. For all the geniuses and experts,
no one could tell me anything definitive.

Every day in my briefing I listed the number
of hospitalizations and deaths. Every day it went
up. Every day there was a bar on a chart in the
PowerPoint presentation that represented the daily
toll. And every day the bar went up a little bit higher
than the day before. When you connected the tops

of the bars, that was the curve: a sloped line going up. I would stare at the chart every day, and I would see a climb up a mountain. Each day was another step up. No one knew how high the mountain was and how many steps it would take to reach the summit. In fact, we knew that the summit had not even been determined; it would be determined by the actions we took right now. We would reach the summit when we created the summit. We would create the summit with the closedown and social distancing. We were defining the mountain as we climbed it.

I had to talk myself through it. Every mountain has a peak, right? Even Denali has a peak. Ours had to be somewhere. We just couldn't give up. And when we reached the summit, we would plant the flag and start the descent. And the descent would be easier because the way down is always easier than the way up. We just had to make it to the top. Every day, even though it was a hard day, was one step closer. Maybe today is the day!

We were still having trouble getting people to understand how important social distancing was. I didn't blame them; it was a new concept, frightening and difficult. The problem was, by the time they realized its importance, it might be too late. I had tried to communicate it every way possible. I increased the fine for violations to $1,000. Local governments were supposed to be enforcing the rule but were lax. I had spoken to them about stepping up enforcement compliance, but it was very unpopular on the local level. Some local officials stepped up, but most didn't. The lack of compliance was worse among young people. The crowds that had turned out to watch the USNS **Comfort** arrive in New York Harbor were a portrait in irony.

There was nothing left for me to do but keep beating the drum, raise the fine, and hope that with cases going up, deaths going up, and hospitalizations going up, people would get the message.

And then there was a new problem. The number of unemployed people in New York State was skyrocketing as shuttered businesses laid off or furloughed workers. The federal government passed a new unemployment law to be administered by the states, including "Pandemic Unemployment Assistance" for gig economy workers, the self-employed, and those specifically laid off as a result of the pandemic. The new benefits required individuals to fill out multiple applications, and necessitated that we obtain certain specific information from enrollees and then certify continued unemployment status for every applicant every week. The New York State Department of Labor administers unemployment insurance and had become totally swamped with the number of people requesting assistance. As of this writing, New York State has now paid over $38 billion in unemployment benefits to more than 3.3 million New Yorkers—compared to just

$2.1 billion paid in all of 2019. That's more than sixteen years' worth of benefits paid in just over four months.

The press was harping on the number of people who were understandably frustrated that they hadn't yet gotten any unemployment aid. These are the same reporters who will be the first to criticize when it turns out the state rushed payments and that certain people received money who were not technically eligible.

My team was doing everything they could. We brought in Google to launch a streamlined un-employment application and reboot the website. We brought in over three thousand additional people to handle the incoming requests, contracted with outside call centers, and reassigned person-nel from other state agencies to help manage the influx. Pre-pandemic, it took two to three weeks to process payments—the deluge of incoming caused a backup, and the public was understandably pan-icked; so many New Yorkers live check to check, and people in New York City paid rents that could swallow more than half of a worker's income before they could even think about food and utilities. There was very little patience and lots of anxiety.

I told my team to strip out all the bureaucracy but not become lax on the mandated federal certifications. I have seen too many times when government "waste, fraud, and abuse" becomes an all-too-easy refrain when a mistake is made. My team worked very hard to accomplish both goals, and while nothing is ever perfect—especially in an emergency—as of this writing, we were successful in preventing over $1 billion in fraudulent unemployment claims, protecting taxpayer money and upholding the integrity of the system.

———

"This is not an act of God that we're looking

at; it's an act of what society actually does."

S OME GOOD NEWS: THE NEW YORK STATE lab had developed its own test for antibodies. It was a new weapon in the arsenal. There were now two types of tests: diagnostic and antibody. Diagnostic tests detect whether a person is positive or negative at the time of the test. The antibody test tells you whether the person has had the virus in the past. Experts at this time said they believed that once a person was infected, they could not be reinfected. This was promising, if not entirely con-clusive. It suggested that the presence of antibodies could identify workers who could immediately return to the workplace safely.

The antibody test could also help determine how the virus was spreading and where. It could target the spread by demographics and geography. To me, data was the key. We were flying blind for so long, looking at vague projection models with so many caveats they were virtually meaningless. Maybe, just maybe, now we would have actual facts that we could study and that wouldn't change. I was also worried about protections for our essential workers, and this test could now give us specific data as to the infection rates among different work groups.

"EMOTIONALLY OVERWHELMING" IS A concept that I now fully appreciate. It is the culmination and bombardment of a number of intense and some-times conflicting emotions. The fear and exhaustion were constant. The intensity was also a constant. But I also had a growing frustration at the "unforced" errors. We will make mistakes no matter how good we are at what we do. There will be unknowns and miscalculations. But unilateral, unnecessary, unforced errors are incredibly infuriating for me to accept.

The COVID virus was starting to spread across the country. The federal government was still in full denial and minimization mode, but they had also persuaded a number of states to follow their political posture. This was an unforced error. Every health expert and scientist who researched COVID said the same thing: COVID will spread. This country made that horrendous blunder once already when the virus spread undetected from China to Europe to New York. We watched the spread across countries, and we saw the pain. I was watching it spread from New York City to Long Island and then upstate. We know it will spread within states and among states. We know that if some states allow it to spread, it will infect us all. It is a proven fact. Why is the nation making these unnecessary, damaging mistakes?

———

"Every number is a face."

THERE HAD BEEN A SERIES OF NATIONAL polls that had tested different officials' credibility and popularity during the COVID crisis. The most credible and popular had always been Dr. Anthony Fauci. He communicated with sincerity, and he was not a politician. There was also the suggestion that he had been more loyal to science than to Trump. I spoke to Dr. Fauci regularly and he was a great support.

Right below Fauci was me. This came as a huge surprise. I knew the briefings had attracted a large national audience, but it had been a relatively short time—it only felt long! The briefings were generating a lot of social media. While everyone was locked in their homes, they spent a lot of time on their computers. One moment that lightened everybody's mood was Randy Rainbow's parody of the song "Sandy" from **Grease,** now renamed "Andy." I don't know if it was Randy who coined "Cuomosexual," and to this day I'm not really sure what it means, but I think it's a good thing.

Trump was still not rated favorably at all. His popularity had been falling from past polls. People didn't believe him and didn't think he knew what he was talking about—a bad combination. It was remarkable that my polling was as high as it was, because I had been making a lot of difficult decisions and this had been my first exposure to a national audience on any significant scale. I am also a known Democrat from a northeastern state, which immediately brings a certain negative baggage. It still amazes and heartens me that people just wanted the truth, competence, and confidence from their leaders.

I'd always admired Winston Churchill as a great leader, and he's served as an inspiration throughout the crisis. He communicated with people and urged them to action. He also delivered. He made the mechanism of government produce, made it effective on the details. An army was assembled and fought a war.

I never forgot this Churchill truism: Either you deliver or you don't. While I spent a great deal of time working on my relationship with the people, I put as much energy into the management of government. It's all about the details and achieving results, especially when it's life or death, making the bureaucracy work. I understand why some state governments and the federal government ran from the challenge. It's really hard.

———

"None of us has done this before."

W E BELIEVED WE HAD HIT THE PEAK.
Today was the highest number of deaths we
had, but the number of occupied ICU beds and the
number of new hospitalizations were down from
the day before. The number of deaths couldn't keep
growing if fewer people were entering hospitals.

Were we finally seeing a break? If so, the question
would now become, how long would we be on the
"plateau"? The plateau is where the number stabi-
lizes but does not yet begin to drop. The follow-up
question was, how steep is the drop? Meaning, how
quickly would the number of new people entering
the hospital system slow?

Trump was fully focused on "reopening" the
country, although he had to give up on his Easter
plan, because that had come and gone. It was clear
he believed his reelection would hinge solely on
the economy. While the economy is normally a
sound predictor of an incumbent's reelection, it

is not definitive. And what's ironic is that a strong response to the COVID crisis could have all but guaranteed Trump's reelection. If Trump had any ability to understand the responsibility of government and the responsibility of leadership, he would have seized the moment. If he had led the country through COVID, he could have been one of the greatest national leaders in a generation. Trump just had to recognize the reality and lead. He had to see the situation through the eyes of the public rather than through his own narcissistic lens. But then that is the difference between Trump and a great leader. Asking him not to act in his self-interest is like asking a skunk not to smell.

I WAS READING BOOKS about war. I wanted a distraction and to read about a time that was worse than the time we were in. But I was also curious about how military leaders could make decisions that they knew would cost lives—situations where even if you won the battle, you knew there could be hundreds of thousands of casualties. All great military leaders manage to do it. General Dwight Eisenhower was told days prior to the D-Day invasion of Normandy that as many as three quarters of his troops might be killed. There was no battle or victory to be had without the loss of life. They celebrated the victory and mourned the dead. But how could they rationalize that their decisions cost soldiers their lives? Was every victory really that important? What calculus did they apply?

I realized that my situation was so much easier than a military leader's. I was doing everything I could to save every life possible, but still people would die and it would be on my watch. Maybe there was something else I could've done. Maybe there was a better drug to use. Maybe if more people would've worn a mask we could have avoided more infections. Maybe I should have had fewer essential workers report to work. The questions went on and on and on and on. During the day I was too busy to torture myself, but at night I would lie in bed and scroll through the reel of questions. I had discussed every decision before I made it with every expert I could find. There was no decision made in haste or without exhaustive conversation. But that didn't mean every decision was right.

As a general rule, I am very conscious of asking for constructive criticism. I even ask for destructive criticism. People don't like to deliver bad news. They especially don't like to deliver bad news to people in power. You have to ask for it and invite it and make sure they know that you won't shoot the messenger. I compliment people who give me the harshest criticism. People don't like to deliver criticism, because people don't like to hear it themselves. We run from our weaknesses and try to deny them, even to ourselves. But if we don't acknowledge them, there will be no improvement.

There's no doubt that the long-term relationship with my team provided grounding and a source of comfort. As did my family and my daughters. But for all the input and collegiality, the responsibility still lies with you, right or wrong. You make the final decision. For all the love you receive from family, they can't shoulder the burden for you. With all the expert advice, no one else really sees the entire chessboard. As close as people are to you, they still can't feel the pressure you feel.

When I would lie in bed at night replaying all the scenarios, I found an exercise that actually helped me. My father had written a book called **Why Lincoln Matters: Today More Than Ever**. It took Lincoln's principles and applied them to current-day issues. I found the book more illustrative of my father than of Lincoln. My father believed that if you hold your principles dear, you can just apply them to different fact patterns. I knew my father better than anyone did, except maybe my mother, and I knew his principles better than anyone. So I would lie in bed and have a conversation with my father. It wasn't a dream conversation; it was just an exercise. I would list a fact pattern and ask him what he thought. And then I would provide his analysis: He would break down the facts into the relevant components and then analyze each group of facts by the applicable principles—legal, constitutional, ethical, moral, and pragmatic.

Omnipresent with my father was the principle of

responsibility. You ran for office and asked people for the job, and they vested you with authority. Respect your authority and do not demur. Don't make excuses. Step up; do not step away. Trust the people; don't think that you are smarter than they are. Tell them the truth, and they will do the right thing. My father very much believed in the collective conscience: that there was goodness in people, if you could engage them. He would say give it your all. Don't relax. Don't go easy on yourself. Don't think you need a break. Don't feel sorry for yourself. He would repeat what he called the Churchill quotation: "Never give up, never give up, never ever give up." I would then tell him that wasn't really a Churchill quotation, and he would say yes it was, and I could not prove that it wasn't a Churchill quotation, and even if it wasn't a Churchill quotation, it was something that Churchill would have said.

After I went through the exercise, if my reasoning and decisions completed the exercise successfully, it would bring me some level of peace. It also highlighted my shortcomings from the previous day and showed me what I needed to focus on and improve for the next. It also made me feel as if I were not alone.

APRIL 14 | 7,177 NEW CASES | 18,697 HOSPITALIZED | 778 DEATHS

"We don't have a king in this country; we didn't want a king."

IT HAD BEEN SIX WEEKS SINCE NEW YORK had had its first case, and we had made more progress than any of the experts believed that we could. New York State had started to turn the corner. We had reached the apex of the virus's impact, having plateaued at the end of March, when we saw the death toll spike. We had defied all the projections saying we would need 110,000 to 140,000 hospital beds. We "flattened the curve" faster than any expert believed possible.

They did not believe that we could put such dramatic policies in place as quickly as we did. Nor did they believe that even if the government put the policies in place that people would accept them and their compliance would be as high as it was. Now I was concerned that our position was still tenuous, and searched for ways to harden New Yorkers' resolve. There would still be many more long weeks of staying home. Also, someone else had another agenda in mind.

For the president, the six weeks the country had spent on lockdown was not about the overwhelmed hospitals, the urgency of building up insufficient stockpiles of supplies, or bringing testing to scale, nor was it about the immeasurable human toll. He had little appetite for the role the federal government was supposed to play in a national crisis. The carnage of a virus no one could predict or control was little more than an inconvenience to him. And with every passing day, with an unemployment number that was rising faster than the death toll, the president was done waiting. He wanted to "liberate" the economy.

While it was obnoxious, it was also irresponsible and illegal. Governors across the country were still responsible for all the tough decisions on COVID, and we were on our own. Our tristate coalition of New York, New Jersey, and Connecticut expanded when we invited the governors of other contiguous states to join us. We would band together to make regional decisions in the face of a national leadership vacuum. I also rejected and resented Trump's "liberate" the economy message because I was saying the exact opposite: Stay home and reopen smartly.

It didn't take long for word to reach Washington. The president, desperate to take control of a situation he had relinquished total authority over months earlier, weighed in with two consecutive tweets:

For the purpose of creating conflict and confusion, some in the Fake News Media are saying that it is the Governors decision to open up the states, not that of the President of the United States & the Federal Government. Let it be fully understood that this is incorrect . . . It is the decision of the President, and for many good reasons. With that being said, the Administration and I are working closely with the Governors, and this will continue. A decision by me, in conjunction with the Governors and input from others, will be made shortly!

The president didn't like my message on a "phased, smart reopening" and didn't like my northeastern coalition. But it was his doing. He absented himself. He created the void I had to fill.

Trump doubled down. He started tweeting, "LIBERATE MINNESOTA!" "LIBERATE MICHIGAN!" "LIBERATE VIRGINIA."

During one of his daily briefings, he said, "When somebody is the president of the United States, the authority is total."

I was eating dinner with my daughters and a few members of my executive staff while I watched, and I remember dropping my fork when he said it. I couldn't believe my ears. He had "total authority"? He abdicated responsibility. He wanted nothing to do with the hard closedown decisions. Did the president actually believe he legally had total authority over the states' reopening?

Did he have even a cursory understanding of our nation's history? Of the Constitution? Of the Tenth Amendment? Either he was completely ignorant of the law, or he had decided—in the middle of a national crisis—to lie to the American people, or he was setting up a major constitutional battle.

I started furiously writing down notes and called my special counsel, Beth Garvey. Beth was whip smart and knew constitutional law backward and forward; I knew she would have this information at her fingertips.

"I need the language on the Tenth Amendment and the case law on public health authority," I said, "exactly where states' rights end and the federal government's authority begins."

I called Dani Lever, my talented director of communications, to set up whatever press interviews she could.

The president had to be stopped. His assertions could not go unchallenged, and his version of the facts couldn't be allowed to take root. We didn't need this confusion now. Within fifteen minutes, I was live by phone with Erin Burnett on CNN, from my living room couch.

Erin recapped what Trump had declared: "He specifically said the president of the United States calls the shots and he has total authority to decide over New York or any other state. Do you agree?"

I laid out the facts: "Well, I don't agree, Erin . . . I don't agree with the president's legal analysis. The president doesn't have total authority. We don't have a king. We have an elected president. That's what our founding fathers did when they wrote the Constitution, and the Constitution clearly says the powers that are not specifically listed for the federal government are reserved to the states, and the balance between federal and state authority was central to the Constitution."

One cable news appearance wasn't enough. I needed to repeat the facts. And fast. Five minutes later, I was on MSNBC, further asserting my case.

It was unclear if the president was going to back down. I had to continue the pushback with a steady drumbeat. The next morning I had my press office book me with whoever would take me. I did the full lineup: MSNBC's **Morning Joe,** CNN's **New Day, CBS This Morning,** NBC's **Today Show,** and ABC's **Good Morning America.** Show after show I kept banging away, quoting the Constitution and laying out the facts to the public: A president isn't a king, the Constitution governed absolutely, the states had rights, and despite all assertions to the contrary Trump did not, in fact, have "total authority" over the reopening of any individual state.

I wanted someone in the White House to hear my response and read the law so they could tell the president he was wrong and he would lose in court.

At 10:07 A.M. as I huddled in the conference

room with the team going over numbers and final-
izing the day's PowerPoint presentation for the
briefing, Melissa walked in. "The president just
responded to you." She proceeded to read the tweet
aloud:

> Cuomo's been calling daily, even hourly,
> begging for everything, most of which should
> have been the state's responsibility, such as new
> hospitals, beds, ventilators, etc. I got it all done
> for him, and everyone else, and now he seems
> to want Independence! That won't happen!

I refused to take the bait. I knew that if we fully
engaged in hostilities, there would be no going back.
No matter how offensive and ridiculous his position, I needed to preserve a functional relationship
for the state. At the same time, I wanted to make
it clear to the people and businesses in my state
that we were not reopening yet. We had enough
confusion with local elected officials making illegal
pronouncements on opening schools, businesses,
and parks. We couldn't have more confusion coming from the federal side. People needed to know
definitively if they were supposed to send their children to school or if they were supposed to show up
for work the next day. Mixed messages would only
confirm skepticism about government and erode
the confidence I was trying to build. I believed the
White House staff was telling Trump that he was

wrong on the law, because Trump was really coming unglued.

Trump tweeted later: "Tell the Democrat Governors that 'Mutiny On The Bounty' was one of my all time favorite movies. A good old fashioned mutiny every now and then is an exciting and invigorating thing to watch, especially when the mutineers need so much from the Captain. Too easy!"

Trump was right: It was too easy. Trump's tweet damned Trump. In **Mutiny on the Bounty,** a 1962 classic, Captain Bligh actually loses the fight to maintain control over his crew, and the first lieutenant, played by Marlon Brando, mounts a successful rebellion to oust him.

But this exchange was at a new level. Trump was watching my briefing and tweeting during my briefing. The reporters saw the tweets and asked me to respond. It was reality TV meets government in real time. I thought it was bad form for the president to tweet at me while I was in the midst of a briefing. He was taking a cheap shot at a time when he knew I could not respond. And I didn't even want to fight. I was trying to state my position but not destroy the relationship. With Trump, the only goal for me was how I could get him to help New York.

So that's what I said in response. I said in a press conference, "I'm not going to fight." I also said, "He is right, I did call and say I needed federal assistance.

I did call and say I needed possible overflow beds. He is right that he did move very quickly to get us the Javits and the USNS **Comfort**. I said that. Repeatedly. I praised him for his actions and he was right there too."

But I also drove home that this was a shift in the president's position. He had left the economic closings to the governors, yet he wanted to now direct the reopening of the states. There were dozens of questions to be answered before we were ready to reopen. We would need masks and precautions in place. I raised the issue of the states having to compete for the procurement of PPE and that it would be better for the federal government to take over nationwide procurement. I said that we needed testing to be in place to guide the reopening and that we needed federal assistance to increase our testing capacity.

The reporters knew that Trump's tweet was nasty and personal and they were working hard to get me to respond in kind. In truth, they also knew that I was capable of taking the bait. I can be impolitic in telling the truth and my capacity to accept BS has diminished. But here the stakes were too high. I made my point clear that I could not just reopen the economy without precautions and that the president had no legal authority to demand it. But I didn't want to get into a political food fight.

"It takes two to tango," I said. It takes two to get into a fight; it takes two people to get into litigation.

I wasn't interested in fighting with the president, and I couldn't be more clear in that. I wasn't going to allow anything bad to happen to the people I represent. The president was wrong on the law. Point made. I'm sure the White House lawyers were scrambling and knew that on the law I was right and that I would win in a litigation. I was also sure the White House political advisers were counseling that they wanted to make COVID a "blue state" problem and establish that Democratic governors mishandled it. They wanted the red-versus-blue fight. I also assumed the White House would need to reconcile their lawyers' advice versus the political advice. They wanted to fight with Democratic governors, but this fight they would lose. What would they decide?

Within about twenty-four hours, the president changed his tune and said he would allow the governors to authorize their own reopening plans. While his "authorizing each individual governor, of each individual state," was still a glaring mischaracterization of his constitutional authority, we had arrived at the debate's obvious and legal conclusion. Just like that, Donald Trump had completed another full presidential pirouette.

APRIL 15 | 11,571 NEW CASES | 18,335 HOSPITALIZED | 752 DEATHS

———

"Don't tell me that we can't do it, because I know that we can."

B Y NOW I WAS CONVINCED THAT MASKS were more effective than the experts initially said. It took me some time to realize that many of the "experts" didn't know what they were talking about. But every time I watched an "expert" on TV pontificating, I wanted to yell, "Why didn't you know the virus left China and went to Europe last year!" What a glaring mistake. A part of me thought they were all full of beans. The U.S. surgeon general, Jerome Adams, had tweeted on February 29: "Seriously people—STOP BUYING MASKS! They are NOT effective in preventing general public from catching #Coronavirus, but if healthcare providers can't get them to care for sick patients, it puts them and our communities at risk!"

Because of that, I was concerned it could cause public backlash when I mandated that all New Yorkers wear masks. I was the first governor in the nation to do it, and I wasn't sure what to expect in terms of compliance. This was a significant action, and I risked losing public support. I was aware that if I ever issued an executive order that was dismissed, we would run the risk of losing control of the situation. However, once again, I felt that the people were with me.

Reopening the economy in and of itself would be complicated and contingent on public compliance. If you reopen too quickly, you can increase the viral transmission, which makes more people too sick to work and actually sets back economic progress. If you reopen too slowly, you will have an anxious public violating government orders, increasing the viral spread and slowing the economy as well. Once you lose public support for government action, it's all over. Once the public knows it can violate the mask order and the government can't do anything about it, it becomes socially acceptable and all is lost.

When I said we were past the plateau, people understandably heard that as good news. It was. But people were also looking for any excuse to resume life as normal. I wanted people to know that we were making progress but that they couldn't let down their guard. I had been saying, "We are not out of the woods."

But people hear what they want to hear, and I was worried that if compliance dropped, the virus spread would increase. Flattening the curve didn't mean the virus went away; it just meant the rate of transmission had been reduced by the change in behavior. It would be a serious mistake if people prematurely relaxed.

Trump was working hard to politicize the situation, framing it in terms of a fight between Republicans wanting to get back to work and Democrats who were against business and didn't appreciate economics. Trump's conspiracy theory in this case was that the Democrats wanted to hurt the economy, to in turn hurt his reelection chances.

At the same time, my state economy was hemorrhaging billions of dollars. Small businesses were going bankrupt by the day. Workers were eager to get back to work. Mental health issues, domestic violence, and substance abuse were all on the increase during this stressful time while people were stuck at home. Michaela had been studying the social and educational dynamics for children and we had been discussing the consequences of children being at home and out of school for extended periods, which was complicated by the trauma and fear of COVID. There is no doubt that further child development issues will be created by this situation. Despite all this, Trump wanted to inject politics into the narrative. It was reprehensible, but it was also reality.

Trump supporters were starting a "Liberate New York" movement with Facebook and Twitter accounts that promoted rallies against my executive orders. Trump denied the political connection, but the organizers of Liberate New York were the same people who ran the Trump campaign in New York. Subtlety was not his trademark. The protests were at the capitol and in front of the governor's mansion, so I had to hear their chants all day.

I had been doing everything I could to keep a functional relationship with Trump to maximize federal efforts for our state. People close to the president and White House officials had repeatedly told me that the way to get Trump to respond was to publicly praise him and his efforts. Thus I consistently expressed my gratitude and appreciation. While I found it personally repugnant, it was a valid sentiment to the extent that the president provided for New York. I said from day one, if the president helped New York, I had no problem acknowledging the effort. To the extent Democrats in my state objected to my expression of gratitude, I was willing to incur that political damage. The president did send the Army Corps of Engineers to help set up the Javits Center. He did send the USNS **Comfort**. They had sent us ventilators, and they did help us procure PPE. I expressed gratitude on multiple occasions. But it wasn't enough for Trump. He wanted total praise and no criticism. I couldn't do that.

Plus, these isolated instances of logistical assistance paled in comparison to the federal government's many actions that actually exacerbated the damage from COVID. The federal government's supplies were far less than what we needed. Also, our entire situation was caused by the federal government's negligence that allowed the virus to arrive in New York from Europe in the first place. But Trump couldn't hear the truth.

THE NEXT NIGHT, I was sitting at the dining room table having dinner with my girls. The TV was on in the other room when all of a sudden my image appeared at Trump's COVID briefing press conference on video playing on a large screen. The screen showed a clip of me at my briefing praising the president for the Army Corps of Engineers' help at the Javits Center. But there were technical difficulties with the video, and it stopped prematurely. Trump then recited the remainder of what I said from memory; he knew every word.

My girls were stunned. To say they don't like the president is an understatement. We had a long conversation about why I would say anything nice about the president. I had to explain that there is a difference between politics and government and that I don't have the luxury of operating through my own political or personal lens when it comes to doing my job as governor. I had to work with people whom I personally don't agree with if it is in the best interest of the state. They were not buying it, and I understood why. I wish it were that simple.

In that moment, Trump had gotten what he wanted, a video of me praising him. The senior Democratic governor was thanking him for his efforts during COVID. That was his campaign ad. It was cheap, and tawdry, and dishonorable. He knew that I had more credibility than he did and it was a total act of desperation. He had failed on COVID, and he was trying to construct an alternate reality.

If you listen to President Trump, he will tell you what he needs. He doesn't hide his neurosis. He said about me in a White House press briefing on April 4: "We have given the governor of New York more than anybody has ever been given in a long time. And I think he's happy, but . . . I watched what he said today, and it was fine. I wouldn't say gracious, it wasn't gracious, it was okay.

"I'll tell you who's been nice, Mayor de Blasio," Trump said in a tone of surprise. "He understands what we've given him."

A psychiatrist could have a field day.

First, on the facts: Trump "gave us" very little. The federal government, through its congressionally approved budget, routinely gives billions in aid to New York. This is a function of law. Trump did more to hurt us than to help us. Any fair federal government would not have stopped billions in funding for the subway, stopped congestion pricing, or refused funding to repair its own Hudson tunnels, and wouldn't steal $14 billion through the SALT scam. Trump didn't know facts or didn't want to be bothered by them. The Obama administration gave us $5 billion to build a new Tappan Zee bridge. They gave us $8 billion for Medicaid reform. And none of this was during a historic pandemic. When I was at HUD, we would fund billions for natural disasters. After Superstorm Sandy, New York received $60 billion to rebuild. If you added up the PPE, ventilators, and military assistance, Trump's aid to New York during COVID didn't amount to $1 billion in supplies.

In the scope of things, it was chump change, or should I say "Trump change." He says de Blasio was nice. How delusional. De Blasio decimates him regularly.

But the idea that I should be "gracious" for Trump doing the bare minimum to meet the federal government's responsibility was bizarre. It wasn't his money, it was tax dollars, and it wasn't his largesse we were asking for, it was for him to fulfill his basic constitutional duty. But with Trump, everything was always political and personal. It was all transactional. He gave me money, so I should be "gracious," meaning I should say nice things that he could use in his campaign videos. It was a proxy for political support. He would make Tammany Hall blush. "I give you government money and you agree to give me political support." No political support, no government money. It was a reality show of an unsophisticated politician's criminal enterprise.

In June, Trump would give Governor Murphy

of New Jersey $2 billion for a New Jersey bridge. Ironically, the bridge was an element of the Hudson River tunnel replacement program that Trump consistently refused to fund. I asked the White House why they would do that, since the tunnels were the priority and the bridge replacement without the tunnels was virtually pointless. They said the funding for the bridge was in repayment to Governor Murphy because he was "gracious" and always said many positive things about Trump, and that's what Trump needed.

Murphy's comments will be in a campaign ad, I am sure. I told them I had said New York was "grateful" for the things they did do for New York, such as the Javits Center and the USNS **Comfort**. They said yes, but I also said negative things, and they wanted only positive. I said frankly, I just can't do that.

I will be grateful for the things they do, but I must point out the needs they refuse to address, which I believed were basic federal responsibilities and were being withheld for political reasons. They were giving us crumbs, and I had to say New York needed more. This was not an acceptable stance.

My only remaining option was to go the other way. When Trump said he needed gratitude, he was exposing his insatiable need for affirmation. Going the other way meant openly criticizing him. If he needed affirmation, it meant he couldn't take criticism. My weapon was to criticize his failure and neglect. I did it often and loudly. He hated criticism and couldn't handle it, and this discomfort caused him to deliver more for New York than we would have otherwise received. A sick, disturbing, unethical federal posture, but in battle we pursue the strategy that wins.

"The beast will not destroy us."

I ALWAYS ENJOY IT WHEN A TECHNICAL EXPERT can simplify a complex topic so a "normal" person can understand it. I was talking to a WHO official who had been working in China on its reopening, and he was explaining the pros and cons of different reopening schedules. He then said to me, "Governor, think of it this way: When you are home sick with a virus, you want to get back to work quickly to make money. But if you get out of bed too fast and get back to work too soon, you will have a relapse and wind up back in bed longer. What would you have accomplished?" The analogy stuck with me and helped me communicate our situation to people.

Above all, the reopening had to be calibrated. We wanted to reopen as quickly as possible, but the question was how to define "as possible." The key was testing and tracing. I remained obsessively focused on testing. Testing could provide real facts, and facts could allow me to make a decision. Facts could also give people information and allow them to understand the basis of decisions. Facts are how I would defeat politics.

Anytime there was a function that needed to be performed by government, Trump instinctively withdrew. He had no knowledge of what government could or could not do. Trump's instinct was also to avoid liability by refusing to be responsible for any quantifiable or specific task. He was still bristling over the criticism that he did not have enough ventilators. He was not about to now become engaged in establishing or operating a true nationwide testing system, which would be necessary for reopening.

So Trump developed a new mantra: "Testing was up to the states." He was distancing himself as far as possible from this urgent challenge. His position was absurd. States had to handle the closedown and emergency operations. He wanted to handle the economic reopening, but states had to handle the testing to make reopening possible! The factual problem was the states couldn't perform the testing because the national manufacturers controlled the actual testing kits and chemical agents. And the federal government controlled the national manufacturers.

The lack of a national testing system was just another component in the revelations about our failure to have a national public health system. There is no "national testing system." There are private laboratories located across the nation that buy testing machines from different private companies that operate proprietary testing programs. Supplies are provided by specific manufacturers and can run only on that specific machine. In New York State we have 250 laboratories that purchase equipment from approximately ten large national manufacturers. Each national manufacturer then supplies that lab with materials needed to operate its machine. To increase testing capacity required each national manufacturer to provide more testing supplies for its specific equipment.

Once the 250 laboratories agreed to increase production on a 24/7 basis, the obstacle became their inability to secure the supplies from the national manufacturers. I called the national manufacturers. They told me their issue was the supply chain. They needed certain chemical reagents, and their main supplier was . . . wait for it . . . China. We needed the federal government to work with China and open up the supply chain.

The White House was frustrated with some states for not taking control of the testing function on the ground. They wanted the states to be more aggressive in setting up testing sites and marshaling local laboratories. They were not wrong: New York was unique in the way we had marshaled our private labs in our state to conduct our testing. Many states had not done enough with their own lab systems. New York had established eight hundred testing sites across the state and organized the 250 labs for maximum output. But we did not have the national manufacturers providing our labs with the necessary supplies to meet the capacity we had developed. We needed the federal government to intervene.

APRIL 21 | 4,178 NEW CASES |

16,044 HOSPITALIZED | 481 DEATHS

—

"Some of the most tragic situations
actually forged the character and
resolve of this nation."

THE BRIEFINGS WERE REALLY GOING WELL. They were informative and even entertaining at times. And while occasionally the press questions could create great theater, some were just nasty and uninformed. Sometimes I would ask Melissa to answer. She grew up immersed in politics and has a computer for a mind. She would undress the reporter when the question was based on incorrect assumptions, always methodical in her dissection. Melissa was involved in all aspects of the crisis so she, like me, saw the whole field of engagement. This helped me immensely because I relied on her as a sounding board and I knew her advice was smart and informed. Her instincts are better than mine. Melissa is the only other person who did every briefing, so she heard everything I heard. She never took a day off. Many women across the country wrote that they loved seeing her in action at the briefings. She is a tremendous advocate for women and girls and was a great role model during those stressful days.

THIS WAS ONE OF those days when developments necessitated a second briefing. The morning briefing was in Buffalo. I talked about how our curve was starting to plateau, although we were seeing variations region by region across the state. New York City, one of the densest cities on the globe, had one infection rate. Upstate, where many of the counties are rural, had different infection rates. Each region had its own need for testing. Watching the news with my daughters the previous night, I saw that Governor Larry Hogan of Maryland had purchased test kits from South Korea, and one of my kids turned to me and said, "Why didn't you think of that, Dad?" While I did momentarily feel chastened, it wasn't realistic or productive for fifty governors to go scrounging for testing all over the globe. Once again, I called on the federal government for help with the supplies we needed to get the testing done.

The president was telling his people to slow down testing because he didn't like the higher numbers of positive cases. If you reduce testing, he figured, the number of reported cases went down, and then you can reopen. It was a child's logic and the continuation of his policy of denial. He just wanted the good press of the economy coming back from reopening; he didn't care about the virus. He was constructing his political narrative that COVID was a Democratic problem and was not a problem for the Republican states. A few weeks later, Ron DeSantis of Florida would give a press conference with Mike Pence at his side affirming this narrative. He demanded an apology from the media for fearmongering, because his state of Florida was doing fine on COVID. (And in late July, **Vanity Fair** would publish an article saying that the White House believed there was no need for a national testing effort because they could just blame blue-state governors for their own problems. Also in late July, Florida's infection rate was exploding, then at nearly half a million confirmed COVID cases, with no end in sight.)

After the briefing that morning, I would head to the White House to make the case for why they should be doing more to help New York meet our testing goal. Up until that point, the president had demonstrated little interest in helping the states ramp up testing capacity, but I knew they controlled the supply chain and we couldn't get what we needed without them. It was a long shot, but life is options and I didn't have any. Melissa was opposed to the trip. She was convinced that the only reason they had agreed to the meeting— conspicuously scheduled for 4:00 P.M., an hour before when the president normally conducted his press conference—was to corner me into appearing at the president's daily briefing, and that we would return with nothing but a positive political press hit for the White House along with a promise for help that would never be fulfilled.

Nevertheless, I flew down with Jim Malatras and Gareth Rhodes for the meeting with Jared Kushner; Admiral Brett Giroir from HHS, who was their testing czar; Dr. Deborah Birx, the White House coronavirus response coordinator; and others to discuss how the states and the federal government could work together on testing. We showed up with a PowerPoint presentation complete with actual quotes from our labs, such as "We could run at full capacity but we don't have reagents." Boom, boom, boom, one slide after another.

Birx oversees a task force at Walter Reed that allocates the national manufacturers' reagents to the states, and as a result of that meeting, she opened up the allocation to us. Afterward, I was brought to the Oval Office to meet with the president. I said that we had a good meeting on testing and that I would advocate with other governors for the state-federal partnership that we had discussed. (I had also served as the vice chairman of the National Governors Association and in that capacity had dealt with both Democratic and Republican governors.)

The president, as usual, just wanted positive

public relations about his COVID response. We were joined in the Oval Office by Hope Hicks, who was setting up the president's COVID press briefing later that afternoon. And sure enough, as Melissa had predicted, during the meeting they asked me if I would join Trump at his press briefing to communicate how the federal government was helping on testing. The president also reiterated his claim that hydroxychloroquine was going to be the silver bullet and pushed again to accelerate the New York hospitals' testing of the drugs. Also in the Oval Office was Dan Scavino, who was the president's social media and Twitter maven. I asked Scavino whose idea it was to continually lambaste me in the president's tweets. I never got a clear answer. Jim Malatras would later say he felt the Oval Office visit was like going onto a TV set and playing a part, after which they would move on to the next scene. I had seen how the president had run the video using the positive statements I had made about him, and I was not going to be in the same situation twice. I politely demurred from joining the briefing. I restated my position that I would call it straight and when the federal government fulfilled its role I would say so, and if he abandoned his role I would say that also. For good measure, I also brought the president a bottle of our special New York State Clean hand sanitizer and left it on the Resolute Desk.

The situation was becoming more and more clear

in my mind. We needed him to do more than he wanted to do. The president didn't understand the federal-state relationship and the true capacity of an engaged federal government. He didn't see this as his problem. I was tempted to say to him that if the federal government was not responsible for a national crisis affecting all fifty states, what was it responsible for? What was the federal government's role if not the interests of the states? It was all absurd to me. But I had promised myself I would bite my tongue. The president had agreed that they would help us with the testing supply chain, and that would be an accomplishment for the state. I would hold him to it. It was also becoming increasingly clear to me that while I knew COVID would be a fifty-state problem, the White House still believed COVID would be only a blue-state problem. That was the disconnect.

Six days later, he would make a statement in the Rose Garden promising to help states with the reagents.

IN ADDITION TO DIAGNOSTIC TESTING, which tells you if a person is positive or negative at that moment, we had started antibody testing in early April all across the state, and the results were very interesting. Antibody testing tells you if the person had the virus in the past. Our April antibody survey showed that in New York City 19.9 percent of those tested had antibodies, meaning they were infected at one point in time. On Long Island, 11.4 percent; in upstate New York, 3 percent.

We also aggressively tested all the essential workers. I had never gotten over the philosophical issue of having the essential workers show up so that other people could stay home safe. I wanted to make sure they were okay. Every death of an essential worker resonated with me. Expert opinion and common sense assumed essential workers were exposed to greater risk. Testing would tell us. We decided to do thousands of antibody tests of essential workers to find out what was going on. We tested police officers, nurses, doctors, and transportation workers all across the state. If essential workers had a higher infection rate, we would know.

We did the police departments first, both state and local. The New York City Police Department had an infection rate of 10.5 percent. Amazingly, New York City itself had an infection rate of 19.9 percent. That meant the NYPD actually had a lower infection rate than the general population. How was that even possible? We tested nurses and doctors next. These were people who worked in emergency rooms and were obviously exposed to COVID-positive people in the most dangerous circumstances. The infection rate for New York City doctors and nurses was 12 percent. That was even lower than the infection rate in the general geographic area.

Two thoughts came to mind. First, what a relief. It was the best news that I had personally received since this began. Yes, I asked essential workers to step up to the plate, but by the grace of God they were at no more risk than people within their community. A major weight was lifted from my chest. Knowing the low infection rate of essential workers lifted the morale of my whole team. The second thought was, how could this even be possible? How could people working in an emergency room have a lower infection rate than the general population? It became my new obsession to find out.

The global experts were somewhat surprised, but they had also seen lower infection rates among health-care workers in other countries compared with the general population. The only explanation was that the PPE worked. Of the PPE, the face shields and gowns were helpful no doubt, but the masks were the most critical piece of equipment.

Early on, disease experts warned of surface transmission. We took significant precautions to minimize surface exposure. However, as time went on and the experts had more data, emphasis turned to airborne transmission. Medical professionals stressed that the masks were helpful to stop positive people from transmitting it in their breath. But some experts had been telling me that the masks might also help prevent the particles from being inhaled.

This antibody testing data confirmed their

theory. Many of the positive people coming into an emergency room didn't have masks. The health-care professionals did. The masks were stopping people from inhaling the virus. Health-care professionals were equipped with N95 masks. These are different from surgical masks. N95 is a designation referring to the size of the particulate matter stopped by the filter in the mask. N95s are the highest-level masks in general use. Interestingly, they are used not just by health-care professionals but for industry applications as well, including applying fertilizers, paints, and other potentially dangerous chemicals that could be airborne. The N95 mask has two straps, and it had to be molded to the nose, cheeks, and chin to make sure there were no air pockets. Any gaps would reduce their effectiveness.

The run on N95 masks was so significant that they were hard to get even for health-care workers. I would venture to say that health-care experts would have recommended everyone in the general public wear N95 masks if they were not afraid of worsening the scarcity. There is also an argument to be made that an N95 mask is overkill for a member of the general public. They are uncomfortable and hot. Pictures of the health-care workers who wear them sometimes show marks on their faces from the tightness of the masks. They originally cost about seventy cents per mask before the price gouging began. In an ideal world there would be enough supply for all Americans. Again, health-care professionals might disagree and say they should be prioritized for health-care workers.

Masks became a political statement. President Trump would not encourage mask wearing, nor would he wear a mask himself. To him, if you wore a mask, you were a Democrat. Remember, the White House narrative was that this was only a blue-state problem. There was also a machismo element to the president's message. If you wore a mask, you were weak. Real men didn't wear masks. I'm sure he didn't want to wear one because doing so would clearly demonstrate that COVID was a real problem, and that was the last thing Trump wanted to do.

The mask was also a visible manifestation of government action, and Trump would never vindicate government action. Also, it wasn't his idea. If it had been Trump's idea, he might very well have accepted it. He could have red masks embossed with "Make America Great Again."

New York was the first state to seriously advocate for masks, which made it a Democratic idea and so political paralysis set in immediately. It was frustrating to know that such a simple thing could make such a big difference but had been mired in this hyper-political environment. Everyone now had access to masks. Why wouldn't you wear one? It required so little, and you had so much to gain.

We did everything we could to publicize the benefit of masks. I wanted to make mask wearing "cool." My daughter Mariah led a PSA mask contest, and the winner's ad would run on television.

Mariah has my drive and functionality. She is purposeful and directed, creative and talented. She is a social media guru with a great public relations sense. She watches social media during the day and sends me texts alerting me to information I need to know and suggesting responses and strategies. I get a kick out of how protective Mariah is of me and how offended she becomes at hostile tweets or negative posts. I know how she feels because I felt the same way with my father. But the tweets only hurt me because they hurt Mariah.

We had celebrities like Chris Rock and Rosie Perez do PSAs for mask wearing. Morgan Freeman, the voice of God, did a PSA. I was especially interested in getting younger people to wear them. Social media and advertising could help there. A mask should be emblematic of intelligent social action. We tried to appeal to people's better angels: I wear a mask out of respect and caring for you, and you wear a mask out of respect and caring for me.

Overall the initiative worked very well. We estimated 97 percent of the population was complying with the mask order. We didn't mandate masks be worn all the time, only in public if you couldn't socially distance and if you were going to come within six feet of a person. I thought that was entirely reasonable. Even as the numbers grew worse and other states started to spike, it was incredible how few states mandated masks. Republican governors were in a difficult position because they didn't want to offend Trump. Trump was doing rallies with thousands of people, and few wore a mask. Herman Cain, a onetime presidential candidate and Trump supporter, would tragically die five weeks after attending one of those rallies maskless. I can only imagine the number of unnamed supporters who attended those rallies who met the same fate. In the midst of this, the White House was showing evidence of a split personality. Vice President Pence said people should wear a mask, and Trump's CDC and FDA commissioners said people should wear a mask. But the president would have none of it.

What was the conversation when Trump was with his health advisers? Did any one of them say, "Mr. President, you should be wearing a mask"? Or did the president say to them, "Don't tell people to wear a mask"? I find it inconceivable that such a situation could even exist.

I NEVER BLAMED the president for not having enough ventilators in the national stockpile. However, he took my comments factually stating that there was a national shortage as a personal attack. And I understood full well the difficulty in procuring ventilators in the midst of a global shortage. What I did not expect was that FEMA, the main federal operating agency that can help states, would offer assistance, only to make the situation worse by involving us in a scam.

When we contacted FEMA on the issue of ventilator procurement, they directed us to a company that would sell us ventilators for immediate delivery. FEMA did not offer to pay for the ventilators, but they would facilitate the procurement. We thanked them for their help and contracted with the company they recommended.

The price that the company was charging for ventilators was outrageous. Each ventilator would cost on average more than $59,000. The pre-pandemic price of a ventilator was $15,000. But we believed lives were on the line and understood we had few alternatives.

We agreed to the terms and signed an $86 million contract requiring a $69 million pre-payment with Yaron Oren-Pines's company for delivery of 1,450 ventilators. Detecting possible fraud, banks in the United States and China froze the funds. At the same time, Oren-Pines began to warn of delivery complications and failed to arrange required inspections. We moved to cancel the contract and recovered $59 million. Not a single ventilator was delivered. To date we are in the midst of legal action to recoup the remaining $10 million, and law enforcement is reviewing the matter for possible prosecution.

I have a top-flight team to protect every tax

dollar. We wear a lapel pin I designed that has three hallmark principles: Performance, Integrity, Pride. The integrity protection team includes my counsel, Kumiki Gibson, special counsel Judy Mogul, and inspector general Letizia Tagliafierro. Kumiki is a top-shelf Harvard lawyer whom I met when she was counsel to Vice President Al Gore. Judy is a former federal prosecutor who practiced privately and is as sharp as they come. Letizia is a former assistant district attorney who worked with me in the attorney general's office; as the state inspector general, she is the watchdog for the entire operation.

When people ask me why New York was so much more advanced than any other state in its fight against the virus, my answer is simple. Besides the advantage of 19.5 million New Yorkers who were New York tough, no other state government had the talent that we had. My team is in many ways more talented than I am. I enjoy surrounding myself with people who are smarter and better than I am. Some people get defensive when the people around them are stronger and smarter. I don't. I know my limitations and they are many. I know what I do well and I know my weaknesses. I want people on my team who complement one another and me. Melissa, Rob, and Stephanie really manage the whole operation. It gives me the freedom to focus on what I need to do without sacrificing a beat.

The juxtaposition between my team and the White House operation could not be more stark.

To further compound the federal incompetence, FEMA and the White House refused to honor an agreement made by the president himself. The customary arrangement is that a state reimburses FEMA for 25 percent of the total cost incurred by FEMA in assisting a state during an emergency. This 25 percent state allocation can be waived by the federal government, and it often is.

When we were at the White House on April 21, I was on my way out of the West Wing when I ran into Secretary of the Treasury Steve Mnuchin. Secretary Mnuchin is a New Yorker, and I had known him tangentially. As we were standing in the hallway near the Roosevelt Room, Mnuchin informed me that they were considering waiving the requirement that New York State pay the 25 percent share of the FEMA cost. This was a positive gesture by the federal government and was surely warranted, because New York had paid a much higher cost for the COVID virus than any other state.

"I just need the president to sign off," he said.

Jared Kushner was nearby, and Mnuchin suggested that we go back into the Oval Office to get the president's sign-off, which we did. They called the president back into the Oval Office to meet with us; Mnuchin explained the situation, and the president authorized the waiver. Secretary Mnuchin estimated this would save New York State approximately $300 million. The president told me that I should announce it publicly. We left the

White House, went to the airport, and flew back to New York. I was grateful for the assistance. It didn't make any sense that the state that endured the most pain and death had to pay because it endured the most pain and death. The reprieve made my trip worthwhile, and we agreed that we would publicly announce it immediately. That evening I did my briefing and among other news thanked the president for the waiver and the $300 million in savings for New York.

Several weeks later, I was in Albany when Robert Mujica, the budget director, came in with the FEMA agreement, which was requiring that we pay the 25 percent match. I told him it was a mistake and that he should contact FEMA. Several days later he came back and said that FEMA refused to waive the 25 percent. I called the FEMA administrator, Peter Gaynor, and he said he had no knowledge of the 25 percent waiver. I asked Gaynor if the president was authorized to make such decisions—because he had. I told Gaynor that when I was a cabinet secretary, the president did have authority to make such decisions and that the president's decisions usually mattered. I suggested Gaynor call the president and call me back. I told him if he wanted more information, he could google it by punching in "Trump Cuomo FEMA." I never heard back from Gaynor.

I then called the White House chief of staff, Mark Meadows, and told him of the disconnect, and he

said he would look into it. To this day, FEMA has
refused to grant a waiver that the president agreed
to. How do I explain it? I can't. It is either a level of
operational incompetence beyond my imagination
or just more smoke and mirrors. The White House
wanted positive publicity for helping New York,
and they received it when I made the announcement in my briefing, but there was no incentive to
follow through. Jim Malatras was right: It was all
a scene from a reality TV show. In any case, to me
it was the perfect metaphor of the federal government's role in this crisis.

———

"Make no mistake, this is a profound
moment in history."

GREAT PROFESSIONALS HAVE DEDICATED THEIR
lives to the field of public health. And there are
great institutions dedicated to educating the field.
However, it shocked me to see how little public
health operational capacity we actually have. I hope
the COVID crisis will turn what has been a largely
academic field into an operationally oriented profession to the scale necessary. Public health threats
are no longer theoretical; they now exist in the real
and practical world.

The systems we had to design on a moment's
notice must now be institutionalized. Beth Garvey,
my special counsel, and I spent hours writing the
state manual on quarantine back in March. Now
what I call the T&T twins—testing and tracing—
must be studied and implemented. Our initial
scramble was to assemble the testing programs,
but the tracing operation is what makes the testing

work to reduce the viral transmission rate. The concept is to debrief individuals who test positive to find out whom they have been in contact with in order to find out whom they might have infected. They call tracers "disease detectives." The function predates COVID; they were used in previous outbreaks such as Ebola. The CDC has an entire division of dedicated disease detectives who travel the world. The scale of the operation we would now need for COVID made it a much different undertaking.

There were only so many balls I could juggle, and my team was on the verge of collapse from exhaustion; they often worked fourteen-hour days under normal circumstances, and the past months had been anything but normal. Larry Schwartz was a former top aide to me. I called Larry and asked him to come back and help. I hated doing it because I knew that if I asked, he couldn't say no; he was that good a friend. I'd known him for thirty years. I told him that he could stay with me in the mansion and that we would "hang out" and have fun. Larry laughed: He knew hanging out was not in the cards for either of us.

Larry came to Albany and met my dog, Captain. Before COVID, it was just me and Captain. There were people at the mansion whom Captain interacted with. Captain loves Carol Radke, who has worked at the mansion since before my father was governor. The entire crew at the mansion had to adjust to a full house during COVID and took extra special care of my girls. Carol takes good care of me but better care of Captain. Captain and I were the pack members. I was the boss, and he was not the boss. That was the social order. It was simple. Captain is a Northern Inuit, and the order of the pack is important to him.

Then the three girls arrived and were in the house all the time: meals, mornings, nights. Captain's world changed. This disrupted his perception of the pack and his place in the pack.

Now Larry was added to the pack. And Larry was another male. Larry appeared afraid of Captain, and Captain adopted a somewhat hostile posture toward Larry. Larry worked late and would not return to the mansion, from the capitol, until midnight or 1:00 A.M. By that time, I was usually upstairs. The conundrum was that Captain was still downstairs, and Larry and Captain had a number of encounters. I would set up blockades to allow Larry free passage without encountering Captain, but never with much success. Captain weighs about a hundred pounds and is quite resourceful. I could hear the commotion from my bedroom.

Altercations with Larry aside, Captain's personality changed dramatically with the girls at home. Before the girls came, Captain was a "dog's dog." He was energetic and loved to be outside. He would chase squirrels and rabbits, although never catching them. He would bark when strangers came to the house. He had a cool detachment about him. There's an Italian Renaissance concept called **sprezzatura:** a grace and aloofness that is most appealing. He exuded strength and confidence in his very presence.

But then the girls smothered Captain with kisses, hugs, sweetness, and constant cooing. Captain has become a tender, loving couch potato. Michaela is the main cause of Captain's personality transformation. She has a hypnotic charisma. Now Captain doesn't want to go outside, and he won't give a squirrel a second look. All he does is walk over to the girls and put his head on their laps so they can whisper sweet nothings in his ear.

Don't get me wrong, I enjoy the kinder, sweeter, gentler Captain. But I tell the girls they broke him. They say, no, they fixed him.

Meanwhile, Larry coming back to Albany was a significant asset. He took over the contact tracing portfolio, working with Mike Bloomberg, the former mayor of New York City, and his Bloomberg Philanthropies along with the Johns Hopkins Bloomberg School of Public Health, to establish a unified system in New York. We developed a contact tracing system for every county to use, and a training program for the thousands of new contact tracers. We established a benchmark minimum number of contact tracers every region of the state would need. We established a formula requiring

30 per 100,000 residents, but the formula allowed adjustment to the required number of tracers if the infection rate changed.

With Mayor Bloomberg's help, over the next weeks New York developed the most sophisticated tracing program in the country, and we were soon in a position to offer the training online to any state that needed it. The tracing program is run by the state but operated by local governments. Statewide we have about fifteen thousand tracers working as of August 2020. It has allowed us to reduce the infection rate, identify originators of the virus, and attack hot spots before they become dangerous.

Every morning, either at the mansion or in my office in the state capitol, I would go over charts with new positive cases, analyzed by region, per county, and sometimes per zip code. Having this data was invaluable. It informed our reopening strategy. One day in mid-June, our zip code data would show an uptick in central New York, specifically Oswego and Cayuga Counties. The Oswego County Health Department had traced three new positive COVID-19 cases to an apple-packaging plant in the county. Over the next days, the New York State Department of Health and the local health department sent staff to test all employees and close the plant to conduct a deep clean. The team set up a free testing site at an apartment complex where a number of the employees and their families lived. The effort was successful; an initial three cases led to eighty-two total positive cases tied to the cluster, and the local and state health departments' quick action ensured the cluster didn't grow or spread into the broader community.

APRIL 24 | 8,130 NEW CASES | 14,258 HOSPITALIZED | 422 DEATHS

———

"An outbreak anywhere is an
outbreak everywhere."

(A. J. PARKINSON)

PEOPLE WERE WATCHING THE BRIEFINGS not only across the country but across the world. I was deluged with phone calls, emails, texts, and letters from every state in the nation and countries I have never even visited. It was remarkable and touching. Across the country, people were expressing their support for New York in any way they could. People sent baked goods, poems, prayers.

I received literally thousands of masks from across the country. Some masks were handmade. Some were incredible works of art. Many were sent with beautiful letters and cards. It was a daily boost to me, like a B_{12} shot for the soul. I asked my staff to put all the masks up on a large board in the front of the press conference room so we could unveil it during one of our briefings. We did that. It was huge and magnificent. We called it "Self-

Portrait of America." It showed we are not alone. We are a mosaic of people from different places, with different strengths, but there is so much beauty in our unity.

I never stopped being touched by how supportive people were. I mentioned to someone that I was a fan of the Fonz from **Happy Days,** and next thing I know, Henry Winkler called. Hillary Clinton called to check in and see if there was anything she could do to help. Robert Redford wrote to say they were watching me out in Utah. Winston Churchill's granddaughter, the artist Edwina Sandys, inscribed a copy of her book about her grandfather, **Winston Churchill: A Passion for Painting:** "In great admiration for the inspirational leadership and efficiency you are radiating in this 'Your finest hour!' "

Citizens from all walks of life reached out in the tens of thousands, through emails, calls, Instagram messages, all asking, "How can I help?" I did a briefing from a hospital in Syracuse on April 28. When I drove up and parked, there was a semicircle of at least four hundred nurses and doctors, all holding signs and cheering. I walked by, staying a safe fifteen feet away, waving, taking in this incredible energy. It was moments like that, and they happened all over the state, that made me realize all New Yorkers were in this together. It gave me great strength to go on.

One letter I received touched me so much that I actually teared up while reading it at my desk. I later read it at a briefing. A farmer in Kansas wrote saying he had watched our daily briefings, saw what was happening in New York, and was compelled to help. He said he had five leftover N95 masks from his farming days. His wife had only one lung, so he was keeping four masks, but he sent one mask for a doctor or nurse in New York. Wow. I read the letter at the briefing and never gave his full name, but a reporter somehow tracked down the farmer and wrote an article about it. After the article appeared, the governor of Kansas called the farmer, Dennis Ruhnke, to thank him, and that generated more press. Ultimately, the head of Kansas State University contacted the farmer. It turned out the farmer never graduated because he left college to care for his mother and the family farm after his father died. Kansas State gave him his degree, and he spoke at the commencement. How beautiful in the midst of such agony. I called Mr. Ruhnke to congratulate him and his humility overwhelmed me. He was so grateful for all the kindness that had been shown to him, and I don't think he fully appreciated the kindness he himself had shown. He was doing what he assumed was the right response to the circumstance, and that is what made it so special.

—

"Life is going to be different."

THE USNS **COMFORT** SAILED OUT OF NEW York Harbor a month after it arrived. The ship cared for about two hundred patients. The right-wing press was mocking us because it had barely been used. This was a perfect snapshot of the bizarre and incongruous situation. The truth is this: I had never asked for the USNS **Comfort**. I had never thought of asking for a hospital ship. I asked for the Javits Center to be built, and I was the first one to suggest to the president the use of the Army Corps of Engineers. Sending the USNS **Comfort** was the president's idea. He sent two ships—the USNS **Comfort** to the East Coast and the USNS **Mercy** to the West Coast. Why? Because they were the ultimate photo opportunity. Large white ships emblazoned with a red cross in the middle, designed to be visible for miles. The president is a market-ing man. He anticipated the media feeding frenzy watching the **Comfort** sail into New York Harbor.

It would be a tremendous visual display of the president's assistance. The president was so excited about it that he actually left the White House to go to Norfolk, Virginia, to bring the press to see the **Comfort** off. One ship for the East Coast, one ship for the West Coast, they were the two most impactful press releases that the White House has ever issued.

Furthermore, all our efforts on providing emergency field beds whether on the **Comfort** or in the Javits Center were preparations for the worst-case scenario. Any intelligent strategy says "prepare for the worst and hope for the best." All experts and the president's own projection models said we would need additional beds beyond our current hospital capacity. By these models, even with the **Comfort**, the Javits Center, and all other emergency beds we provided, we were still tens of thousands of beds short of the maximum need. We never reached the maximum need because New Yorkers did a better job of "flattening the curve" than any experts had predicted. It was a tremendous success. Any informed person would have said, "Thank God we didn't need the **Comfort**!" If the president was smarter on the issue, he should have claimed success in flattening the curve and reducing the need because that was the substantive success. The CDC projections, the Peter Navarro memo, Dr. Birx's projections, all pointed to a need for 110,000 to 140,000 hospital beds. We flattened the curve such that our hospital need never went beyond 18,875. That was an accomplishment beyond anyone's wildest predictions.

The irony is that the states that followed Trump's guidelines would also end up beating projections—in the opposite direction—and the administration would have to constantly revise their projections upward. The numbers were irrefutable. How could Americans continue down this road? How did we not see the cliff?

APRIL 30 | 4,681 NEW CASES |

11,598 HOSPITALIZED | 306 DEATHS

———

"Nobody ever said it was going to be easy.
But nobody ever said it was going to be
this hard, either."

NEW YORK CITY POSED MANY UNIQUE complications for reopening. The density and crowding was an aggravating factor in the spread of the virus, and public transportation in New York makes it extraordinarily difficult to socially distance. But a significant challenge for us was figuring out how to keep people who use subways and buses safe. The initial information from the experts was that the virus could live on a surface for up to two days, depending on the surface. Stainless steel was supposed to be one of the surfaces that allowed the virus to be the most viable for the longest period of time, and the interiors of buses and subway cars are largely stainless steel.

Cleaning the New York City subway system has been one of the city's great challenges for the past hundred years. The system is one of the largest on the globe and the only system that operates 24/7. Over the past thirty years the subway system had become a permanent facility for the homeless. I had worked on the issue of homelessness since my twenties, and I have been continually frustrated by society's gross failure to handle this issue. Once again we see the typical formula for failure in our society: political paralysis and government incompetence. Oh, but you say, you are the governor, why didn't you fix it? Good question. Sometimes even the governor can't fix it.

In New York City, homelessness is handled by City Hall and the NYPD. The mayor's refusal to remove the homeless from the subways was making the problem worse instead of better. The subways were filthy and filled with homeless people. This is the dynamic not just in New York City but in urban areas all across the country. Homeless encampments have become urban fixtures. Why a so-called homeless advocate would support keeping human beings in subhuman conditions has always been perplexing to me. Why politicians would accept this position as "progressive" is also beyond me. Nonetheless, the advocates support the right of the homeless to live in the subways, and the mayor refused to have the NYPD remove them. The MTA and New York City have spent tens of millions of dollars on grants for nonprofits to "outreach" to the homeless with virtually no success. Now enter the COVID crisis.

This wasn't doing the homeless any favors, letting them stay on trains in the middle of a global health pandemic with no masks. In addition, crime was rising even as ridership had dropped 90 percent.

The subway system needed to operate throughout the COVID crisis because essential workers needed it to get to work. Essential workers—police, firefighters, health-care workers—were still using the system to get to their essential jobs, without which society would have collapsed. We were committed to doing everything we could to keep them safe. I still had not gotten over the responsibility I felt for calling out the "essential workers." They were risking their lives and some had died. I would do everything in my power to keep them safe. That was my obligation to them. That meant that the subways had to be disinfected every night, which is something that hadn't been done since the system began. It was almost a laughable concept.

First, I had to figure out if cleaning at this scale was even possible. MTA officials told me it was impossible because the system runs twenty-four hours a day and there are six thousand subway cars and they are filled with the homeless. We'd have to disinfect the entire interior of every car—every rail, every pole, every door, wherever a hand could touch or a cough or sneeze could land, wherever droplets could land. We'd also have to disinfect the stations, the handrails, everything that people could be touching.

I personally spoke to a number of commercial cleaners about the application and safety of different chemicals. Some vendors suggested the use of ultraviolet light. Others proposed a new technology that could be sprayed on a surface to kill viruses for up to thirty days. While some of the technologies were experimental, I was convinced it could be done. To even try to accomplish this goal, we would need to do two things. First, stop the trains from running for several hours in the middle of the night to allow them to be cleaned. Second, homeless individuals and all their belongings would have to be out of every car and every station in the system.

This was going to be a monumental challenge. The homeless advocates would be outraged, city officials would balk, and the police and MTA workers would need to perform at a higher level than ever. But there was really no alternative because we couldn't have people on the trains unless we knew they were safe. I moved forward, and the MTA and I identified the right cleaning contractors and chemicals. I told city officials I was doing this and if they wanted to oppose it, that would be their prerogative, but that I was confident the people of New York City would support me.

If we put out a plan and discussed it for weeks, it would get bogged down in political controversy. Once an issue becomes politically complicated in New York City, it slows, stalls, and then dies. Moreover, the essential workers were riding the subway every day and we needed to ensure it was safe—immediately. I told the MTA to just do it and blame me. And if the mayor wouldn't allow the NYPD to cooperate, I would send in the state police to facilitate the plan. If the homeless advocates wanted to attack me, so be it. I was more than comfortable with my record supporting the homeless. I had worked to help the homeless all my adult life and all across the nation. I also believed getting the homeless off the trains and into shelters where they could receive the services they actually needed was the best way to help them.

We pushed the plan forward, and on April 30, Mayor de Blasio decided to support it and joined me for the daily briefing when I announced we were going to shut down the system for four hours every night between 1:00 A.M. and 5:00 A.M. when ridership was at the lowest, and we'd offer buses or for-hire vans to provide transport to any essential workers who needed to travel during this time. The entire system would be disinfected every twenty-four hours.

Our subway cleaning plan went into operation, and surprise, surprise, it delivered as promised. Every subway car and bus is disinfected every twenty-four hours, and the subway system is cleaner and safer than it has ever been. It took the COVID crisis to clean the New York City subway system and to really help the homeless. Pat Foye, the MTA chairman, and Sarah Feinberg, the MTA president, did a really great job.

It was an important lesson for me and for New Yorkers. We can still do big, bold things; we just have to dare to try. Any New Yorker will tell you that the conditions of the trains, subway cars, and subway stations have been unacceptable for many decades. The plight of the homeless in the subway was a daily reminder of urban deterioration and human suffering. Most New Yorkers had given up. It made no sense, but it seemed impossible to change. The idea of disinfecting the system was almost ludicrous. If you couldn't clean the system, how could it now be disinfected? No one believed it was possible. They were wrong. Nothing is impossible. You just have to be willing to try.

MAY 1 | 3,942 NEW CASES |
10,993 HOSPITALIZED | 289 DEATHS

"Our past actions changed the path's trajectory.
Our present actions will determine the future
trajectory. You tell me what we do today; I will
tell you the number of people sick tomorrow."

NEW YORK'S CASES WERE DROPPING WHILE many other states were still in denial, embracing the president's rhetoric rather than following the facts and science. The president's "liberate" supporters were demonstrating across the nation and across New York State. Everyone wanted out of the house, and everyone wanted to get back to work.

I have learned something as I have gotten older: Ultimately, the truth wins out. I was more impatient as a young man and wanted to cut to the chase immediately. But sometimes situations have to unfold. The president's denial strategy was being exposed for the fraud it was even if his most devoted apostles were still with him. While the president had some early political success in selling his message of "liberation," the virus was unimpressed and took its course. The president's message was totally counter to science, and it was only a matter of time before the virus won.

Trump was very good at playing to emotion. Indeed, he became president by playing to people's fear. He knew that he could increase political pressure on those politicians who were slower to reopen their states. It was a full-court press from the White House and all of Trump's allies. They claimed they had polling information saying the public wanted to reopen immediately. I had no doubt that might be true. Of course people wanted to reopen immediately—so did I—but that didn't mean it was right.

Trump sells the product most easily purchased by the largest number of people. In this case, "Let's get back to life now" was essentially his slogan. However, it was also shortsighted and wrong. By now it was clear to me that a reckless reopening would increase the spread of the virus, which in the medium and long term would actually hurt the economy. Trump was playing a very irresponsible strategy of short-term gain for long-term pain. I didn't even think that the gain would last until the election in November. But that was his calculus. And Americans would die on his gamble.

There was never a choice between public health and economic progress. The path forward always had to prioritize both. A plan that focused only on public health or only on economic progress was doomed to fail. And reopening only to see the virus increase would devastate the financial markets and further cause stock market decline. But I felt as if I were talking to myself. Everyone wanted to hear that we could reopen quickly. I wouldn't say it or do it even if I risked losing public support. I believed this was a situation that would be judged by the history books rather than pundits. We had been to hell and back, and I was not willing to jeopardize our progress or dishonor the lives lost.

SO MANY UNDERLYING PROBLEMS had been exposed by COVID. Some of them would have to be solved immediately, or else they would inevitably recur. The PPE shortage was understandable only if one accepted that our government and health-care system were incompetent. Why didn't our nation have the capacity to manufacture PPE as a matter of national security? Public health is a matter of national security.

I said publicly that the country should learn these lessons immediately and develop American industries that could provide all the materials lacking during COVID. With no response from the federal government, I announced that New York, New Jersey, Connecticut, Pennsylvania, Delaware, Rhode Island, and Massachusetts would work together to develop a regional supply chain for PPE and medical equipment. Within our states we needed to have companies that could provide the necessities. Together we could form a purchasing coalition to support their development. COVID would come back for a second wave or some other virus would develop, and we needed to be in a better position than we were this time, and we had to start now.

It never made sense to me that New York's own health-care system didn't have a better supply. The hospital administrators said that they didn't like to stockpile equipment or inventory as a general rule. I understood their point, but we now realized we needed a buffer. At my direction, the New York State Department of Health issued an order requiring all hospitals to have a ninety-day supply of PPE and nursing homes to have a sixty-day supply that they could access. We would not go through this again.

Necessity can also be the mother of invention, as the saying goes. Educators had been discussing remote learning for a long time. The technology has been available, but the bureaucracy has been slow to move and the status quo is protected. Higher education has made more progress on remote learning. A professor of international distinction can teach a course in the United Kingdom that can be broadcast to students around the world. Why couldn't we have that for New York's nearly three million K–12 students? I understand the advantage of the in-class experience, but it doesn't have to be one or the other. There is a benefit of having access to other opportunities offered by technology. Think of students at rural or disadvantaged high schools that might not be able to offer AP courses; remote learning would give those students access to more course offerings, which would improve their chances at the college level and improve their work opportunities later in life.

COVID forced an abrupt and imperfect transformation to remote learning. Wealthier school districts had more success in the conversion, while school districts with lower-income families had more difficulty. Remote learning requires internet access and computers at home, which people in public housing or rural areas might not have. We worked to put the infrastructure in place, including remote wireless hubs in certain communities.

I spoke to Bill Gates, who had been working in this area, about the opportunity presented by the COVID disruption. Gates agreed to work with New York through his foundation to help us develop a blueprint to "reimagine education" in the new normal.

Beyond the immediate crisis, I wanted to know how you could take the blueprint devised in these days of crisis and make it permanent and actually strengthen the system going forward so, like the subway system, we don't just fall back to the old ways post-COVID. The future is still a question mark for now; we have issued guidance for school districts to follow if and when they reopen, because we have rural and urban communities with very different needs and populations.

—

"I wish I could be with you, but I can't be
because I love you."

Mother's day during covid was a
particularly lonely time for families. Afraid
to hug or even be in the same space as a loved one
who was elderly or in a vulnerable population
meant over two months of unnatural solitude. We
were saying "I love you" to one another by staying
away, but the long, lonely days of isolation caused
depression and angst.

The most painful aspect of the COVID crisis has
been its devastating effect on our elderly in nursing homes. The first COVID case in the United
States that really caught people's attention was the
nursing home near Seattle, Washington. Ever
since, nursing homes across the nation have suffered
tremendous hardship and loss; as of this writing,
more than 41 percent of this nation's COVID
deaths have happened in nursing homes.

Understanding the threat, on March 13, we

were taking every precaution that we could think of. Even before New York had a single COVID death, we banned visitors from going into nursing homes for fear that they might be transmitting the virus, and we required PPE, temperature checks, and cohorting of residents with COVID. Despite this, as was the case in every state in this nation, New York's nursing homes were not spared from COVID's wrath.

By early spring, Republicans needed an offense to distract from the narrative of their botched federal response—and they needed it badly. So they decided to attack Democratic governors and blame them for nursing home deaths. On April 25, conservative columnist Michael Goodwin published a piece in Rupert Murdoch's **New York Post** aimed at New York with the headline: "State Lacked Common Sense in Nursing Homes Coronavirus Approach." It was an orchestrated strategy and a Fox News drumbeat. It wasn't just me—Phil Murphy in New Jersey, Gretchen Whitmer in Michigan, Gavin Newsom in California, and Tom Wolf in Pennsylvania were all in the Republican crosshairs on nursing homes. As the states with the most deaths were Democratic states, the Trump forces saw us as an easy target. Moreover, their entire COVID strategy was political: This was a Democratic state problem mishandled by Democratic governors.

The entire episode was truly despicable. Imagine having lost a loved one in a nursing home. You are already questioning yourself about whether you should have removed them and then you hear their life was lost because of a government blunder. I have talked to many people who have lost loved ones in nursing homes, and I could see the agony on their faces and hear it in their voices. It's not so much that they were looking to blame anyone, they just needed to know what happened.

Unfortunately, although I tried, I never successfully communicated the facts on this situation. The Trump forces had a simple line: "Thousands died in nursing homes." It was true. But they needed to add a conspiracy, which was that they died because of a bad state policy that "mandated and directed" that the nursing homes accept COVID-positive people, and these COVID-positive people were the cause of the spread of the disease in the nursing homes.

It was a lie.

New York State never demanded or directed that any nursing home accept a COVID-positive patient. The Federal Centers for Medicare & Medicaid Services guidance was that a nursing home should continue to accept patients from hospitals where COVID-19 was present, and not discriminate against a COVID-positive person. The state followed the guidance, stating that nursing homes should not reject a patient "solely on the basis" of COVID status. It also applied to hospitals. We couldn't have a situation in which elderly patients who had been treated in hospitals ended up on the street because their nursing homes refused to take them back. Nor could we have a situation in which hospitals refused to take a COVID-positive person.

The context here is very important. Early on in the crisis, our main fear was that the hospitals would be overwhelmed, and collapse. All health professionals agreed that if that situation developed, we would need to free up hospital beds for people with critical needs. As it turned out, our success-ful efforts to reduce the viral transmission rate and create additional beds meant we were never in that dire situation. The state always had additional beds available all across the state. Therefore, the critics' premise that we "forced" nursing homes to take COVID-positive people is patently false and illogi-cal because we always had alternative available beds throughout the state. We never "needed" nursing home beds.

Also, the critics misstate the law and policy. No law or policy would have ever required a nursing home to take any COVID-positive person. The policy was that nursing homes couldn't discrimi-nate, not that they had to accept. That makes all the difference in the world. In fact, in New York law, it is clear that a nursing home can "only accept" a patient that it is prepared and equipped to treat given the needs of the other patients in its facility.

The law clearly states that while nursing homes cannot discriminate, they also cannot accept any patient that they cannot properly care for—in this instance, that specifically meant nursing homes had to be able to separate residents into cohorts of positive, negative, and unknown and needed separate staffing teams to deal with COVID-positive residents and nonpositive residents. They had an obligation to keep the other residents safe from the virus. If they couldn't do that, then they could not accept a COVID-positive person and they were legally obligated to decline that person's admission. In fact, many nursing homes in New York did just that, opting not to accept COVID patients. Factor into this the reality that nursing homes get paid for every person they treat, so they have financial issues. The law therefore dictates that every nursing home must have the capacity to effectively treat every patient as a safeguard to financial interest.

The facts totally defeated the Republican claim. Interestingly, this was not even a New York–specific issue. Quite the opposite. New York was number forty-six out of fifty in the nation when it came to percentage of deaths in nursing homes. There were only four states with a lower percentage of nursing home deaths, and New York had a much worse situation to manage. But this was all politics. No one wanted to hear the facts.

In early July, the New York State Department of Health did a full review of nursing homes in the state, and what it showed was that the virus came into nursing homes as the workforce got infected—mainly through asymptomatic spread.

Twenty thousand nursing home workers were COVID-positive in March and April, and who knows how many there might have been who were COVID-positive in January and February, before we were doing testing. In the geographic regions where the infection rate was higher, more staff got infected and brought the virus into facilities. It is also possible that visits early on from family and friends brought the virus into facilities before they were banned. The rate of infection and deaths in nursing homes correlated with that of the broader regional community—a phenomenon that played out in every single state across the country and in nations around the world.

On May 10, as soon as we had the capacity, we mandated testing twice a week for staff of nursing homes. Any infected staff were identified and not allowed into the facility. The nursing home operators were very unhappy with the regulation, but I wanted to make sure we did everything we could. Ironically, the same Republican politicians who seized on the order not to discriminate against COVID patients were also the loudest critics of the staff testing mandate.

Political attacks aside, the situation in nursing homes has kept me up at night from the beginning. I have spoken with governors across the country, international and medical experts, nursing home operators, and family who lost loved ones. I am continually thinking it through because in my mind we are always preparing for the next time, and I believe there will be a next time. I wonder what we could have done differently and can do differently in the future.

Here is the conundrum. The virus was here earlier than we knew and therefore was spreading among the nursing home workers before we were aware. There is nothing New York could have done about that. I don't know even today that New York can do anything besides push the federal government to build an effective CDC and global alert system. The federal government was also wrong about asymptomatic spread. Again, all New York can do is push for a competent federal health agency. But even once we knew that the virus was here and the nursing home workforce was probably getting infected, what could we do? The ideal scenario would be to test every nursing home employee before they go to work every day. But there are 158,000 nursing home employees. New York did not have enough testing capacity, even at our height, when we were doing 70,000 daily tests, to accomplish this feat. A more modest goal would be to test workers once a week. Even this was not achievable when COVID first came to New York, because the statewide testing capacity was only about five thousand per week, and again, there were 158,000 nursing home workers. Once our testing capacity increased, we mandated testing every nursing home worker once a week. We would do that again in the future.

However, even this is imperfect. Some workers can get infected and bring in the virus between weekly tests. It could slow the number of infected people entering nursing homes, but it wouldn't prevent the virus from entering entirely.

We also could have stopped family visitation earlier. Again, we didn't know the virus had come to New York, or that there was asymptomatic spread. We stopped visitation on March 13. But even going forward, if at the first sign of a virus we stop all family visitation, that would be a harsh, dual-edged sword. I hear many recriminations about stopping people in nursing homes from having visits from their loved ones.

Theoretically, we could test all visitors and workers daily going into nursing homes. Again, theoretically, that could be applied to hospitals, group homes, and so on. But that would require a testing capacity that as of this writing is impossible to achieve. It would require serious federal participation.

The ideal scenario would be to hermetically seal off nursing homes. The closest model to this was done by a nursing home in France, where some workers volunteered to live in the facility and not go back to their own homes. They essentially quarantined in the facility. This is extraordinary: staff living in the facility for months and not seeing their families. This would have to be combined with no outside visitors. Theoretically, it would be the safest procedure but I don't know that it is practical or replicable on a large scale. Legally, I could not force 158,000 workers to stay on site. If that is what we need in the future, we would need to be clear and hire workers willing to do that. We should then also consider that for hospitals, group homes, et cetera. It would be ideal but virtually impossible to implement.

I believe we need the best federal health experts to review international data and determine a national nursing home and congregate facility protocol to be implemented at the first sign of an outbreak. The key would be large-scale testing capacity, which only the federal government could provide.

Wisdom comes back to the same point: We control what we can, but we must accept that we cannot control everything.

As of this writing, six months after everything New York experienced, COVID is now devastating nursing homes in Florida, where nursing home patients and staff account for approximately 45 percent of all deaths in the state. To explain the increase in deaths, Governor DeSantis's secretary of the Agency for Health Care Administration (AHCA) said, "Infected, asymptomatic health workers themselves are carrying the virus and transmitting to their own patients." (That is what happened in New York five months ago without the notice Florida had.) On July 15, the AHCA issued Emergency Rule 59AER20-6, allowing

nursing homes with healthy residents to accept
COVID-positive patients. Following the order, it
was reported that "many long-term care facilities
throughout Florida quietly, quickly, and deliberately began bringing COVID-19-positive patients
into places where healthy residents live." COVID
patients are being transferred from hospitals into
Florida nursing homes with the express blessing
of the DeSantis administration. Florida was having the problem we prepared for but which we
avoided. Their hospitals were over capacity, and
they had no choice but to send seniors back to
nursing homes. They did not reduce the viral
transmission rate the way New York State did,
nor did they build the alternative additional beds
we did. For New York, it was a worst-case-scenario
plan that never materialized. For Florida, it was
reality. Unsurprisingly, neither Donald Trump nor
Fox News maligns Republican governor DeSantis
for actually doing what they incorrectly accused
New York of doing.

———

"We have been smart through this, and we have to continue to be smart."

THE BUDGET IN THE FEDERAL GOVERNMENT is not real. The numbers don't add up, but then again they don't have to. The federal government can print money, so theoretically it can solve any financial issue by turning on the printing press in the basement. States don't have a printing press; however, I do have an old Xerox copier in the basement. A state must pass a balanced budget. By July, the COVID crisis had already caused a $14 billion budget shortfall in New York because of reduced tax revenue. That was an impossible number for me to deal with. If there was ever a day that it was not top of mind for me, I was joined at the daily briefings by my budget director, Robert Mujica, who made it his business to remind me.

We had to reopen, and we had to reopen smart. While every expert talked about an economic reopening plan that included testing and a data-driven approach, no such coherent methodology existed. No state had successfully done it yet. There was no template or blueprint. I assembled my team and said that I wanted to develop the most science-based reopening plan in the country.

I wanted the reopening plan to track specific metrics like infection rate, hospital capacity, and testing and tracing rates. I wanted two specific data thresholds: first, a series of metrics that had to be met—showing the virus is under control— that would be required before a region could begin reopening; second, a series of metrics that would monitor the reopening and allow us to slow down if the virus spread began to increase.

To illustrate this approach, I made a PowerPoint slide that had gauges on a pipe, each measuring a specific metric, such as hospital capacity and infection rate, and a valve at the end to illustrate the pace of the reopening. If the gauges showed upticks in hospitalizations or infections, the valve would be tightened. And vice versa.

First, we started with the ten regions of New York State and set seven metrics that each region needed to meet before starting to reopen: (1) decline in total hospitalizations; (2) decline in deaths; (3) decline in number of new hospitalizations; (4) sufficient hospital bed capacity; (5) sufficient ICU bed capacity; (6) sufficient diagnostic testing capacity; and (7) sufficient contact tracing capacity.

Second, we set four phases to the reopening,

starting with low-risk, more essential businesses and gradually moving to higher-risk, less essential businesses. Phase 1 would allow low-risk businesses within construction and manufacturing and agriculture. Phase 2 would allow some nonessential businesses including retail (but not malls) as well as outdoor dining and takeout—with strict rules in place. Phase 3 allowed for restaurants and personal care services, like hair salons, to reopen—again, with strict rules about mask wearing, testing, and social distancing. Phase 4, which we wouldn't get to until midsummer, allowed for professional sports without fans, and, importantly, schools could reopen, but this would be a complicated and ongoing discussion in every district in the state.

Each phase would be separated by two weeks, which was the period of time needed to determine if the virus spread increased due to the increased activity, to detect such a spread, and to see if there was any effect on the hospital system. Each region would continue to need a certain number of tests to be performed on a daily and weekly basis. We recruited a team of global experts, including Dr. Michael Osterholm from the University of Minnesota and Dr. Samir Bhatt from Imperial College in the U.K., who, before giving a region the green light to move from one phase to the next, would review our data and then advise whether it was safe to continue the reopening of that region of the state. Counties within each of the ten regions would work together, and regional control rooms would be responsible for coordinating hospitals, testing, contact tracing, compliance enforcement, business, education, and data collection.

I said we needed to do "a reopening book" to distribute to local governments across the state. A "book" had no specific definition, but in my office it meant more than a discussion, more than a memo, more than a twenty-page paper, and that meant it would take a lot of effort. I spent hours working on drafts with the team. The result was our **NY Forward: A Guide to Reopening New York & Building Back Better**. It was a 156-page book complete with charts and graphs, just like my daily PowerPoints in the briefings. We printed five hundred copies to distribute; I wanted people to be able to hold it in their hands, not just click on a link, although they could do that too.

Additionally, I insisted on posting all these metrics and the daily data online with an easily readable dashboard so that every New Yorker and local elected official could understand them and see the impact of the reopening on the virus transmission. This way, if we had to slow down the reopening, we would all be operating from the same set of facts. I would also review the data daily at the press briefing. We would announce any troublesome occurrences in the data in real time so the people of that region would know what was going on. If we all have the same information, then we are all on the same journey. Governor, mayor, local supervisor, business leaders, newspaper reporters, small business owner—if we all knew the same things at the same time, we could openly discuss all decisions before they were made. That was the ideal relationship between citizens and their government: a relationship of trust and credibility.

I don't know how many people actually read **NY Forward**. It might not have been a best seller; that wasn't the point. It existed. It was not a theory or a slogan. It was sound government policy built on facts.

I had said at a briefing the week before that "how New York reopens is not an emotional question, it's not a political question, it's not an anecdotal question, it's not a gut instinct question. Follow the facts and follow the data." We now had a sound plan that implemented that vision. I was confident that we were right and we would do it our way: damn the torpedoes and damn the politics. New York would reopen smartly.

We started on May 15 opening phase 1 in much of upstate New York, followed four days later by western New York, then the capital region, then the Hudson valley, and then Long Island. Much of the state would already be in phase 2 before New York City was in phase 1 because its infection rate had been so high and because of its uniquely high population density and crowding. It would take several weeks to get to phase 4 across the state, and even then we'd be watching the numbers daily and vigilantly for hot spots and flare-ups.

MAY 17 | 1,889 NEW CASES | 5,897 HOSPITALIZED | 139 DEATHS

—

"Getting a test is easy. Even a governor
can do it!"

OPERATIONS, OPERATIONS, OPERATIONS. ALL THE
plans and all the briefings depended on being
able to deliver. Even in government, the bottom
line is still the bottom line. Can you do what you
said you would do? Can you perform?

To me, this was a basic credibility issue, both
personally and politically. As a leader, I needed to
be able to accomplish what I proposed. I either
produced or I failed. I was either another empty-
suit, windbag politician or I was an effective leader.

It is a provable proposition and it should be
proven. Accountability matters. If you don't want
to be accountable, you shouldn't be in a government position. The people pay your salary. What
did they get in return?

Operational capacity is also a metric for political
validity. If we want politics to get beyond the empty
rhetoric and "advocacy in action" betrayal, then

government must be able to make an actual difference. If government can't make a difference for one
reason or another, then stop deceiving people. At
some point, politicians have to stop making excuses
and accept responsibility.

An official is elected to make a difference. Either
they can or they can't. During COVID, this became
true on steroids. The timeline is short, progress or
failure is evident, and the consequences could not
be more dramatic.

While I spent a great deal of time working on
my relationship with the people in briefings, communication, and follow-up, I put as much energy
into the management of government. It's all about
the details and making the bureaucracy work.

From the beginning, we understood that setting
up a testing system would be the top priority. The
federal government had no interest in enacting a
national testing strategy, and without testing we
were flying blind. After my first conversations with
the Department of Health and my own team, I
knew how hard it would be to bring testing to mass
scale in just weeks—but there were no options but
to tackle it head-on.

To set up a testing organization required several
large steps, some of which I have already described.
But to review, first, the laboratories in the state capable
of the highest production needed to be brought up to
speed and equipped. The state lab at Wadsworth, the
Northwell Health system lab, the Mount Sinai lab,

the NYU Langone lab, the University of Rochester Medical Center lab, the Columbia-Presbyterian lab—with the right equipment operating seven days per week, these facilities could conduct several thousand tests per day.

The second step was to somehow mobilize the state's smaller private laboratories into one system. New York State licenses about three hundred private labs to do clinical diagnostic testing. Each lab had to be brought online and incorporated into the system. We had to find out what equipment they had, what equipment they needed, and what supplies and reagents were needed, and we had to work with them to create a seven-day-a-week operation. As of this writing, about 250 of these labs conduct testing each day for New York State—an increase of 249 from when the FDA gave the state approval to test on February 29!

Third, we contacted the major out-of-state "reference" labs, which were national labs that did businesses across the country, such as LabCorp and Quest. These labs had enormous capacity—more than 100,000 tests per day—but were relied on by all fifty states.

Fourth, we had to locate and construct public testing sites where people would actually go to have the test taken—normally a nasal swab. Proximity was important, as were the practical logistics of a suitable site to manage the COVID challenges—long waiting lines where people congregate could end up resulting in more viral spread.

We took a multifaceted approach. We set up outdoor drive-through testing sites all across the state, using the National Guard to erect temporary tent structures, and brought in health-care providers to do the tests. For urban communities where fewer residents had cars, we set up mostly outdoor walk-in sites, but we made them appointment-only to avoid lines where the virus could spread. In addition, we partnered with Northwell Health and SOMOS Community Care to set up additional testing sites in hot-spot zip codes, including at churches and community centers, where people would feel comfortable coming to get their noses swabbed. I also signed an executive order to allow pharmacies to become test sites. Tom Feeney, a competent and hardworking staff member who is an expert at advance planning and operations, was instrumental in this effort; in July, as part of the New York delegation, he traveled to states such as Florida, Georgia, and Texas to help them set up testing sites. When all was said and done, we had more than 850 sites across the state where New Yorkers could go get a test.

Fifth, we had to convince people to go to take tests. By May 17, we had both a good and a bad problem. The good problem was that while we were doing about forty thousand tests per day, our labs and testing sites were running under capacity. The bad problem was that New Yorkers didn't want to get tested. People were not showing up to appointments, and many still thought testing was scarce—and possibly painful! We needed to be creative. We used advertising campaigns to communicate how important testing was. We also had to ease the fear of testing. Everyone wanted to know if it would hurt.

I had the idea of getting tested at a briefing to show the public how fast and easy and painless it was. It was a good idea in concept. I had taken the test before, and having a long swab put in your nose isn't pleasant. It can make your eyes tear and make you cough or sneeze. Normally you have a few minutes to recover afterward, and normally you don't have a camera in your face broadcasting it on live TV.

My team said that if I did the test on TV and had a bad reaction, it would set the progress made on testing back months. I told them I was sure that I could do it. Really, I wasn't so sure. The day of the test, I was about to go out to the briefing and I met the nurse who was going to perform the test. She seemed a little tense and was not accustomed to performing tests on national TV, for obvious reasons.

We chitchatted, and I was trying to put her at ease with my cool-dude-in-a-loose-mood banter. At one point I said something about "just taking a nasal swab." She shook her head and was adamant in saying that it wasn't just a nasal swab—it had to reach the inner cavity to get the best sample possible. I was disquieted. I went to the briefing and after a few minutes called up the nurse to take the test. I made a couple of bad jokes and asked her to start the test. This nurse had a swab that looked like it was a foot long. She put that swab into my nose in slow motion. It felt like she was inserting it for a good five minutes. I could see the swab going in, as it was just a couple of inches from my eyes. I could also see that the swab was not going up but apparently straight back on a horizontal trajectory. I thought nasal passages went up, not back. I had no idea where she was putting that swab, but it seemed she was aiming for the back of my head.

I knew I could not flinch, nor could I say anything. If it weren't for the television camera, I would have recoiled, shouted obscenities, and run from the room. But I didn't. I smiled and impressed myself with my self-control. After the briefing I asked the health commissioner, Dr. Zucker, why the nurse thought it was necessary to pierce my skull with the swab. Dr. Zucker said the nurse wanted to ensure that I got an adequate sample so I got an accurate result. I was speechless.

In any event, it worked. We expanded the list of who could get a test that day to all front-line workers as well as any of the employees returning to the workplace as part of our phased reopening. We launched a website where any New Yorker could type in their zip code and find a testing site near them. With the testing sites in all corners of the state, my pronouncement that it was "painless," and our elimination of cost sharing, the public had no good reason not to take the test—and thousands more New Yorkers each day signed up for appointments.

MAY 29 | 1,551 NEW CASES | 3,781 HOSPITALIZED | 67 DEATHS

———

"Life is not about going back. Nobody goes back. We go forward."

THE KILLING HAD HAPPENED OVER MEMORIAL Day weekend, but it took a few days until the video was widely circulated. As had become our daily ritual, my team was assembled in the living room of the Governor's Mansion, eating breakfast while going through the day's numbers and PowerPoint in preparation for the morning briefing. CNN was on the television in the background when we saw the video for the first time. It was devastating to watch. The entire team stopped as the images played over and over again. We were shocked. This was murder.

Shortly after, we traveled to Iona College in Westchester County. The major announcement that day was that New York City—the once global epicenter of the pandemic—was finally set to begin to reopen and enter phase 1 on June 8. In our COVID crisis, this was a monumental day. Mayor de Blasio joined us on Zoom for the announcement. But a new crisis had emerged, and protests that began in earnest in Minneapolis were taking hold in cities nationwide.

I addressed the murder of George Floyd head-on. I said at this briefing, "I stand with the protesters." I've been a prosecutor, I was attorney general of New York, and if that were my case, I'd think something criminal had occurred.

But the bigger issue was that what happened to George Floyd in Minneapolis was hardly an isolated incident. This was another chapter in the book of injustice and inequality in America. "Thoughts and prayers" wouldn't cut it.

George Floyd's murder fit into a continuum of cases and situations that have been going on for centuries. Within the last thirty years alone, this nation witnessed the brutal assault of Rodney King in 1991. And the killings of Amadou Diallo in 1999, Sean Bell in 2006, Oscar Grant in 2009, Eric Garner, Michael Brown, and Laquan McDonald in 2014. Freddie Gray in 2015. Antwon Rose in 2018. Ahmaud Arbery and Breonna Taylor in 2020. It was about the same situation happening again and again and again and again. We were seeing the same injustice and no meaningful governmental response.

After years of injustice and inaction, George Floyd's death would be the tipping point in this country. After centuries of systemic racism compounded by three and a half years of Trump—

children in cages at the southern border, white nationalists in Charlottesville, the attacks on synagogues, and dog-whistle racism—the country said, No more. You can hammer a wedge into a crack in a boulder, and hammer and hammer and hammer, and eventually that boulder is going to shatter.

JUNE 1 | 941 NEW CASES | 3,331 HOSPITALIZED | 54 DEATHS

———

"You want to change society? You want to end the tale of two cities? You want to make it one America? You can do that. Just the way you knocked coronavirus on its rear end. People united can do anything. We showed that."

THERE ARE VERY FEW THINGS PRESIDENT Trump can do to surprise me at this point. But even for him, he hit a new low. The protests over George Floyd's murder were happening all across the country and in Washington, D.C. I was watching the nightly news at home with the girls when we saw what he had done. Trump called out the military to put down peaceful protests near the White House to execute an ill-advised and inauthentic photo op. The move was entirely predictable. It was also another grave mistake.

The George Floyd murder and the Black Lives Matter protests that grew in the wake of it, like the COVID crisis, brought partisan, racial, religious, economic, and demographic divisions front and center. It was a moment of national reckoning, and the moment cried out for national leadership. Any leader with a modicum of decency and awareness would have known what to do. In the sea of division, bring calm. When the ship of state is pitching to and fro, the captain furls the sails and steadies it.

But not Captain Trump. When Trump sees division, he seeks to aggravate it. Calling in the military was another cheap appeal to his base, and it infuriated the protesters. What Trump didn't appreciate was how repulsed and offended the majority of decent Americans were at witnessing the George Floyd murder.

Trump was incapable of seeing the Floyd murder for what it was: un-American. America doesn't knock someone to the ground and then step on the person. Americans don't gang up and kick a man when he's down. Seeing four uniformed police officers holding down and suffocating a man to death stung the American conscience. But Trump missed it. The great irony is that Trump was obsessively consumed with winning his own reelection, but he was also blinded by his obsession. The George Floyd murder, like the COVID crisis, was a moment when Trump could have stepped up to lead this nation and actually helped his reelection.

Instead, he used the military to push the protesters away from the White House. It was broadcast live, and it was ugly. But then it got even worse. Attorney General Bill Barr appeared in the midst of this chaos as the military were teargassing and forcing back the peaceful demonstrators. The next scene on TV showed the president walking out of the White House to the church next door for a photo opportunity, holding up a Bible and telling Americans that he would ensure order. It was a truly disturbing sight. Watching the president, the military, and Attorney General Barr, I imagined a military dictator taking control of a country.

I made a wager with my daughters that night. I often like to say to them, "I will bet you $10," as a way to get their attention and excite their competitive edge. I said, "I see the future. Donald Trump is going to lose the election in November and then claim voter fraud is the reason he lost, claiming that mail-in ballots were fraudulent and that the Post Office mishandled the mailings. Attorney General Barr will bring the lawsuit on behalf of the United States, and it will go to the Supreme Court. Trump will believe that the Supreme Court will side with him because he will have the support of his Court appointments. He will believe that it will be a repeat of **Bush v. Gore**."

I went further. "But Trump will be wrong. The Supreme Court will rule against Trump because his position cannot be supported under the law and he misjudges the basic integrity of the Supreme Court, even his own appointees."

I explained my rationale to my daughters. Even though Trump was first elected because of this country's division, most Americans would not think their president would be the cause for further division. A majority of Americans were not comfortable seeing their president create racial tension and aggravate unrest. Now they would not vote to deliberately increase the tension. Americans also knew that the federal government's denial and incompetence on COVID caused more Americans to die.

The attorney general will bring the lawsuit, I said, because he is first and foremost a political Trump ally. Trump had already subtly signaled the grounds for his lawsuit by stating that he opposed mail-in ballots (which would be used more widely in November because of COVID), alleging that they were vehicles for Democratic fraud.

The girls listened. And seemed intrigued. None of them would take the wager. Today, I would put up a lot more money.

I SUPPORTED THE PROTESTERS, and it was my hope that Mr. Floyd's killing and its aftermath would present a moment in which this nation actually learned and grew and progressed—this time by enacting real change. George Floyd could not be just another name on that long, long list.

The protests presented new complications in the time of COVID, because they were massive gatherings. Thankfully, they were held outdoors and most protesters wore masks, but ironically, many of the police did not. And local governments were still being timid in enforcing the mask order. The protests ignited opposition to the police department, and I think the local politicians were afraid to aggressively enforce any laws at this moment. There was no doubt that the circumstances posed a great risk, but the virus's presence in New York was already at a very low point before the protests began. I signed an executive order that allowed all protesters to be eligible for a COVID test and encouraged them to take it. Hopefully, if our data was right, the presence of the virus might have been so low there was not a great risk of spread. We would know soon enough.

Trump still wouldn't wear a mask, and he continued to make it a purely political issue. He said health officials had taken different positions on masks, and he was correct there. But it was clear now from all the research that masks work. I also signed an executive order allowing a private business to deny admission to a person who didn't wear a mask. Wearing a mask is so simple and makes such a big difference.

Despite all of our progress, it was clear that now we were facing two parallel crises: COVID and the unrest after the murder of George Floyd. A public health crisis and a social crisis, and they both demanded action.

JUNE 2 | 1,329 NEW CASES | 3,121 HOSPITALIZED | 58 DEATHS

———

"Rightful outrage."

I LOVE TO BE ON THE WATER, THE OCEAN IN particular. Its vastness and power simultaneously relax and excite me. I've taken small boats from Washington, D.C., to New York and around Cape Cod, Nantucket, and Martha's Vineyard. Some of my adventures have been quite foolhardy. There is nothing quite as intimidating as being in a storm at night in a small boat and looking at a wave you know could crush you in an instant.

That morning, after being briefed by my team on the violence and mass looting that occurred the night before in New York City, I was reminded of a scene from **The Perfect Storm**. In that movie, George Clooney plays the captain of a fishing boat. No, I do not think I am George Clooney; I am a realist. The captain decides to try to sail through a terrible storm to get back to dock to sell his fish. After fighting the storm for what seems like an eternity, the captain decides that he can't make it through and turns around to head out to calmer water on the other side. There comes a point where he has to concede he's in trouble. "She's not going to let us out," he says of the storm. In that moment on that day, that's how I felt.

Just weeks earlier, New York City was the global hot spot for COVID. Now, after so much progress controlling the virus and days before the reopening started, the city was descending into chaos. It started with people throwing bricks at NYPD cars. The next day the looting began. I supported the protests, but these were not protesters; they were criminals. The looting was nakedly opportunistic. The streets were empty, and while the police worked to manage the protests, looters smashed glass doors and ransacked businesses small and large, from mom-and-pop stores in the Bronx to the iconic Macy's flagship store in Herald Square. Watching the criminal activity and chaos was like a kick in the stomach. I feared what it meant for our economic reopening and our work to control COVID—just as we'd started to see the light at the end of the tunnel.

While New York City had it the worst, the violence and rioting spread to other cities in the state: Buffalo, Rochester, and Albany, where people burned down the Capital City Rescue Mission, which provides food and services to the homeless.

The looting could not go unanswered. We had been through too much and made so much progress, I would not let these criminals threaten all that we had accomplished. Mayor de Blasio didn't have enough of his police force deployed to control what was happening. Mayors in other cities around the state had requested assistance from the state police, but Mayor de Blasio did not. And the violence and destruction continued. I issued an ultimatum: Either he had to empower the police force to do their job, deploying all available personnel, or, I said, "my option is to displace the mayor of New York City and bring in the National Guard as the governor in a state of emergency and basically take over." That night, the full NYPD was out in full force. Peaceful protests continued, and looting began to dramatically subside.

"We've gotten to a place where people think talking is enough. Talking is not enough. Being angry is not enough. Being emotional is not enough. How do you transition that to action and change and results? And that's what we're doing here today."

A T THE BRIEFING WITH ME THAT DAY I HAD several extra-special guests: Eric Garner's mother, Gwen Carr; Sean Bell's mother, Valerie Bell; my second mother for many years and president of the NAACP, Hazel Dukes; and the Reverend Al Sharpton. I was also joined by senate majority leader Andrea Stewart-Cousins and assembly Speaker Carl Heastie. Gwen Carr and Valerie Bell were two women who had lost their sons to police violence. Because of COVID, we had to limit who could be present in the room, so these two mothers were there representing every mother who lost her child to police violence.

From the start, I said I stand with the Black Lives

Matter protesters, who continued to march since the death of George Floyd. But I had been unequivocal that we needed to translate protests into meaningful action. And New York acted most quickly, with the legislature enacting a nation-leading police reform law that I had proposed: the "Say Their Name" Reform agenda. It included a choke-hold ban, transparency measures, and other important law enforcement reforms. In addition, I signed an executive order that put forward a clear plan to fundamentally restructure the police-community relationship across New York State. It required all five hundred police departments in New York State to work with local governments to come up with a restructuring plan by April 1, 2021, or they would lose state funding. It was the most aggressive legal action taken in the nation, and l was proud to sign this package of bills into law with the legislative leaders, Al Sharpton, Hazel Dukes, and the two mothers by my side.

As the Reverend Al Sharpton has said, we need demonstration, legislation, and reconciliation. You hold demonstrations to generate public support; you pass legislation to make change; and only then can you proceed to reconciliation. At the end of the day, the politicians don't lead; the people do. New York State had seen and heard the people, and it was a moment for fundamental change to the system.

When it was Reverend Sharpton's turn to speak

that day, he said, "Twenty years ago, when I called a march in Washington on the anniversary of the March on Washington and Coretta Scott King presided over that march—the widow of Martin Luther King—the only member of President Clinton's cabinet that would come to the march was Andrew Cuomo, and he stood with me when I was much fatter and much more controversial."

I have known Al Sharpton all of my adult life.

We first met when the legendary columnist Jack Newfield at **The Village Voice** (back when the **Voice** was really something) took Sharpton and me out to lunch at this little Italian restaurant in lower Manhattan. He said, "You guys are going to be around for a long time; you should get to know each other."

As we're taking our seats, Newfield said, "This is the restaurant that inspired Billy Joel's 'A bottle of red, a bottle of white.' "

Sharpton and I were both in our twenties, and to us Newfield seemed like an old man. He was probably forty. Sharpton thought he was a wise guy, and I thought I was a wise guy. We looked at each other like "Sure it is. What a line of crap." This couldn't possibly be the restaurant.

Thirty years later, Billy Joel invited me to his birthday party. It was in the back room of a little Italian restaurant called Il Cortile. When I walked in, I said, "This place looks familiar. I don't know why." The owner comes up to me and says, "You were here before, with Al Sharpton and Jack Newfield."

I had a great laugh with Sharpton about it when I told him. And Newfield was right when he introduced us; we'd been around a long time.

Thinking back on the forty years since Sharpton and I met at the restaurant that day, I felt it was fitting that we were together on this historic occasion when New York took a giant step toward addressing racial injustice.

JUNE 15 | 620 NEW CASES | 1,608 HOSPITALIZED | 25 DEATHS

———

"When we were talking about a curve—
I never saw a curve. I saw a mountain. That's
what I saw. I saw a mountain that we had to
scale and we didn't know where the top was."

IT SEEMS THAT EVERY DAY I TELL PEOPLE not to get cocky about this pandemic, and every day they get cockier. Sometimes I had the same level of success communicating in the briefings that I have communicating at home with my daughters: Everyone thinks they know better. The growing accomplishments in our war against COVID were causing people to get more confident. After months of home quarantine, people were desperate to get out of the house. The warm weather and small apartments increased their desire for freedom. There were scenes from across New York of large congregations in front of bars, in parks, and on street corners. The prime responsibility of local governments during the pandemic was to enforce compliance of the reopening rules. The state workforce did not have enough police or health officials to cover the entire state if the local governments did not do their job.

Upstate had just moved into phase 3, while downstate areas outside New York City were in phase 2. Restaurants and bars were supposed to allow takeout alcohol and outdoor dining, but it was clear from pictures and videos that the rules were being violated across the state. I had dozens of conversations with local officials pushing them to enforce the rules, but they just yessed me to death on the phone and then did nothing. Why did they cave to the fear of local politics when they knew the consequences? I said to them: If the virus spread goes up, we will have to roll back the reopening in your region, and then people will blame the local politicians as well as me and that is a worse situation than making them comply with the law.

But they either didn't want to get it or couldn't get it. They were being "politicians." I remember an incident when I was a teenager and my father was serving as the secretary of state in Governor Hugh Carey's administration. We were in a delicatessen picking up some food and chatting with some people in the store when someone referred to my father as a "politician." My father really got his back up, as if the man had called him a son of a bitch. When we got back in the car, I made the mistake of pushing the point.

"Dad, you **are** a politician."

He got crazed again.

"How can you be a part of a system that you despise?"

It's not logical and it is counterintuitive, but I understand it now. I am part of the system because I want to change the system; you need to be part of the system to be most effective in changing it. But don't ever suggest that I am part of the failure in the system. In my father's worldview, "politicians" are responsible for the failure in the system. "Politicians" are politically motivated individuals without professionalism or integrity. They say what people want to hear without doing what needs to be done. I consider myself a counter-politician. That may sound like a nuanced difference, but to me it's all the difference in the world.

"Wake up, America!"

I N THIS CRISIS I THOUGHT WE HAD SEEN IT
all and faced every possible issue imaginable, but
in New York City the problems were compounding rapidly. In addition to continuing protests and
tensions with the NYPD, the city was experiencing a rising crime rate. The decline of the city was
palpable.

We had a similar situation post-9/11. Many
people felt being in the city itself was dangerous.
The fear was that the city would always be a terrorist target. It took months for people to return
to downtown Manhattan, the site of the former
twin towers. But this was even worse. People who
had alternatives left the city. We had closed down
businesses, and large congregations would not
be allowed for some time. The assets of living in
the city include the great restaurants, museums,
Broadway shows, events, and conventions. Without
them, many people decided they would move

out to Long Island or up to the Hudson valley or east to Connecticut and wait to see what happened. Depending on how the situation develops, they might never return.

We had seen people with means flee disaster areas before. In Hurricane Katrina, the people who could have fled New Orleans were gone by the time the hurricane hit. The people who were left behind were largely people without alternatives or resources. Often the people who needed to be rescued from rooftops were people in public housing. During COVID, the New Yorkers who fled were wealthy. They had second homes or had the disposable income to rent them now. Getting them back post-COVID would be one challenge. Getting them back post-COVID with no restaurants and no theater or other entertainment, and with increased crime and widespread dysfunction, would be an even more difficult proposition.

This was a dangerous situation. Wealthy New Yorkers are the overwhelming majority of the city's tax base. About 1 percent of people pay nearly 50 percent of the taxes. If they did not move back, there would be serious economic consequences. If they adapted to working from home, the residential and commercial real estate markets would suffer. If they did not frequent the retail stores, the business environment would continue to suffer.

There's no silver bullet. I said we were going to

accelerate the Reimagine New York Commission to revitalize the economy. We'll start with some large public works that show a different future, a brighter future for New York, to give the private sector some confidence that New York City has a long-term survivability and viability.

MY RELATIONSHIP WITH THE New York City mayor had always been problematic, to use a word. The New York City tabloids loved the drama and never really covered the substance of our relationship. First, there's always a tension between the mayor and the governor. It goes back to Rockefeller and Mayor Lindsay, my father and Ed Koch, Pataki and Mayor Giuliani. It is almost inherent in the relationship. It is like the natural distrust with in-laws. New York City mayors have always bristled at their lack of authority and autonomy. Almost all major actions require state approval. The state is responsible for all major financial decisions: public transportation, tax increases, education. The city is the creature of state law, and state law governs. The mayor really has exclusive control only of fire, sanitation, and police. This is true with every city in the state, but New York City mayors have always found it more annoying because New York City is an enormous international city. I understand the tension because I, as governor, am subject to

the federal government and its superseding jurisdiction, as well as the political whims of President
Trump, and that is truly infuriating.

My relationship with Mayor Bill de Blasio is even
more complicated. I've known him for many years,
and we were personal friends. One of de Blasio's
first jobs was working for me at the Department
of Housing and Urban Development when I was
secretary and he was a regional representative for
New York. But now there are real issues between us.
It isn't personal; it's philosophical, as they say.

At sixty-two years old, I am watching the clock,
and I know that Democrats have to score more
points, more quickly, if we are to win the game,
and I am more convinced that we must win the
game if America is to survive. After a lifetime in
the crusade and frustrated with our lack of progress
and the insanity and pain of a Trump administration, I am out of patience. And I think this country
is out of patience. So for me, the philosophical
question now is, how do we win?

My priority is to make sure Democrats are doing
everything we need to do to be successful and to
minimize our own vulnerabilities. My philosophical
issue is with Democrats who make promises and too
often fail to perform and set back our progress. We
need a dramatic reboot, and it must start with blunt
honesty and a clear philosophy. I now call myself
a progressive Democrat. That's because nobody
uses the word "liberal" anymore, because "liberal"

became a dirty word, so the Democratic Party chose a new label.

But what does the term "progressive" mean? "Progressive" is not a new label. It goes back to the early 1900s. FDR and Al Smith ran as progressives. In modern usage, the term "progressive" is vague and also overused. So I distinguish between "real progressives" and "faux progressives." A real progressive advocates, achieves, and implements intelligent change on an expedited basis. Real progressives advocate for principles that are feasible, constructive, and intelligent. To be a successful real progressive official, you need to actually achieve progress: accomplishments matter. You can't just say you are a black belt in karate. You have to achieve it. My definition of "faux progressives" is officials who believe being a progressive is merely a function of advocacy and posturing. Faux-progressive officials advocate but never accomplish. Faux progressives frustrate the public by raising false expectations and by failing to improve matters. Faux progressives actually hinder the progressive movement and aid the conservative movement by reinforcing public cynicism that government change never happens and positive results are never the outcome. Conservatives win when government fails to make positive change.

Let me explain. Most Americans would agree with progressive aspirations. They agreed with FDR's and JFK's and Mario Cuomo's visions.

But they would also agree with the conservatives' emphasis on reality, feasibility, and practicality. This tension leaves the American people essentially saying, "Yes, I would like to do these good things, but I have doubts about whether government can actually achieve them."

My model of real progressivism is to affirm the aspiration and prove it can be achieved—to show government can work to realize the aspirational goals we seek:

> Government can pass a law allowing same-sex couples to marry without interfering with anyone else's individual rights.
> Government can raise the minimum wage without hurting the economy for anyone else.
> Government can build affordable housing without destroying the neighborhood.
> Government can take on large construction projects and complete them on time and on budget.
> Government can build bridges and airports and roads and convention centers.
> Government can achieve our aspirations both in theory and in practice.

I believe once progressives demonstrate that capacity, they will vindicate the optimism of the American people, and the potential to do good will be unlimited. But they must address the skepticism that conservatives have firmly planted in the American psyche. Progressives must show government can work to improve their lives.

Every day conservatives say, "No we can't," and every day I say, "Yes we can."

On a principled level I resent people who enter government without either the intention or the capacity to make it work and do good things. For me, people who affirm the conservatives' argument are aiding the opposition. I have little patience for people who disrespect the profession. It's much the same way that a professional ballplayer disrespects another player who gets caught gambling on his own game. Or a police officer disrespects a cop who violates someone's civil rights. Or a finance professional disrespects a broker who is found to do insider trading. Or a clergy member disrespects another clergy member who abuses his position. When government officials disrespect their office, it affirms the negative stereotype that I and so many others have been working to overcome.

Every example of dysfunction, corruption, or incompetence sets back the entire movement. It makes the conservatives' argument.

Every Democratic mistake fuels the conservative cause. Every failed program and over-budget construction project fuels the conservative agenda. Every unrealistic or unintelligent proposal fuels the conservative agenda. Democrats have already given conservatives too much ammunition. Failed government and unrealized proposals only feed public skepticism.

Democrats who see government as merely a public relations position, or a pulpit for political pronouncements, or who are either unwilling or unable to actually get the job done have been a long-term liability for the progressive movement. If people want to be celebrities, they should go into show business. If people want to be advocates, they should join an advocacy organization. Progressives in government must be dedicated to achieving progress; otherwise they are really only bolstering the conservative cause. Too many progressives today fail to realize or focus on the fact that we must prove government can work to be successful and vindicate our cause. The burden of proof is on us. It is mastering the art form of effective government service. Some progressives now engaged in politics or government think they can just act the part. They can't.

When I was about eleven years old, a couple of my friends in the neighborhood said that they were forming a band and that I should come over and check them out. I went to see them in the neighbor's garage and sure enough there was a drum set, guitars, and a microphone stand. The band then turned on a record player, picked up the instruments, and played along with the song. Except they didn't really play. The record player was playing the music. The band was just lip-synching along and the guitars and drums were props. After this went on for a while, I said to my friend, "That's great, but I think a band has to be able to make music without the record player." He looked surprised and confused. I don't know if they missed the point or believed they were going to work up to it, or were ahead of their time as the next Milli Vanilli. In either event, I didn't care to join. That's how I feel when I see some now engaged in the political arena. It's not about holding an instrument or singing with the music. You have to know how to perform.

I applaud elected officials who know how to play the instrument, accomplish the goal, and affirm government capacity. Look at Mayor Keisha Lance Bottoms of Atlanta. She showed the nation brave, principled, competent leadership. She inspired. Likewise, I applaud Joe Biden. He is an honorable man who has dedicated his life to public service and constantly leads people to do better and be better. His career has produced positive change that builds public confidence.

The political contest in this country between Democrats and Republicans or, more clearly, between progressives and conservatives comes down to a simple proposition: "Who do the American people believe?"

People who call themselves progressives must be examples of why Americans should trust us. Their service must be honorable and productive. They must be willing and able to make the hard choices to effect change and deliver results. Not just to advocate, but to actually achieve. Not to talk, but to act. They must make things better. If they fail to do that for one reason or another, they set the progressive cause back and give Americans more of a reason to distrust us. An unanticipated result of the COVID pandemic is that it can be a transformational moment in politics. Not since the Great Depression has government been as relevant to domestic issues. Government has gone from an abstract concept to a practical day-to-day essential. It impacts everyone every day, for better or worse. The veil of political theory has been lifted and the reality of government capacity has been exposed. Government leaders have been scrutinized and the level of their competence has been revealed. People know who was up to the job and who wasn't. They know who stepped up and who fell down. It is an opportunity for progressives because it establishes our main point: Government matters and leadership matters. Progressives cannot miss this opportunity to rise to the public's expectations. Government must deliver; it is actions, not words. Leaders must lead, and they must respond to the crisis. In this moment, progressives can change politics for the next fifty years the way the ultimate progressive, FDR, changed the political trajectory after the Depression. The stakes are just too high to fail. That is my philosophy and that is the plain truth.

———

"We learned that our better angels are stronger
than our demons and sometimes we just need
to listen for them. Over the past 111 days,
we heard them and it was beautiful.
Let's keep listening together."

I HAD BEEN DOING BRIEFINGS EVERY DAY FOR
110 days. We had been reopening for over one
month, and the infection rate not only held constant but actually dropped. None of the experts
had predicted that. We had accomplished the goal
and actually achieved what all the experts told us
was impossible. Remember where we were. All
the models said we would need between 110,000
and 140,000 hospital beds on any given day at our
apex. We went from 53,000 hospital beds to a total
capacity of close to 90,000. They said we needed
to do everything we could to "bend the curve" and
reduce the transmission rate but that even with our
best efforts they did not believe we could get the
need below 110,000 beds. They did not believe

that we could institute social distancing practices, close down all aspects of public life, and cause individual behavior change to any large degree. They said to me many times that even if the government announced the policies, they did not believe people would comply to a sufficient extent to reduce the transmission rate any lower or any faster. New Yorkers proved them all wrong. Not only did we not hit 110,000 hospital beds, we never went above 19,000. It was incredible.

It's not that they underestimated New Yorkers alone, but they assumed the pattern of behavior would be what they were seeing across the country. They assumed the lack of government credibility and the fragmented body politic that has been evident in this country over the past several years would continue. They didn't expect people to rise to the occasion the way New Yorkers did. They didn't foresee the possibility of a unified population, empowered, informed, and educated, forging a strong sense of community. But that's what happened.

We had been up the mountain, traversed the plateau, and survived the slow decline. We had gone through hell, and we were on the other side. The numbers were as low as they would go. All the scientists and health officials said that we would never get to zero COVID deaths. The goal was to get the infection rate down to about 1 percent and maintain it during the phased reopening. We had done that.

That day, I would give my last daily briefing and do it direct to camera from behind the governor's desk on the second floor of the state capitol—the same desk that FDR and my father had used.

As I stood there, reflecting back on the past 111 days, a line from George Washington's Farewell Address came to mind: "Though in reviewing the incidents of my administration I am unconscious of intentional error, I am nevertheless too sensible of my defects not to think it probable that I may have committed many errors." In the span of time, with retrospection, facts and information may suggest there are things that we should have done differently. But I hope that New Yorkers know that I worked my hardest and I tried my best.

I addressed the people of New York and others across the world, simply saying, "Over the past three months, we have done the impossible." And they had.

I was ending the daily briefings because the immediate job at hand was done, and I wanted the people to know it. I wanted to communicate the confidence and sense of accomplishment they should rightly feel. There would be future challenges, and they could handle them. I wanted to signal a reduction in the anxiety, but not complacency. Also because the briefings were about the truth, I truthfully didn't have enough new information to justify their time on a daily basis. I said I would do the briefings in the future on an as-needed basis, which was probably a couple of times a week. If the situation changed and the facts changed, I would change.

People ask me what I did after the daily briefings ended. The answer is, the same thing I did before the briefings. For me the intensity was only slightly less. Operating at a high level is in my nature, and then there's really no time to relax when you're the governor. And we had to begin the rebuilding in full force while at the same time stay vigilant. COVID isn't done with us as a nation, because we haven't learned the lesson of COVID yet. It will continue beating this country until we understand the true cause of our vulnerability and strengthen it.

I believe New Yorkers were provided with the truth. They trusted the information they were given. They knew the challenge could only be mastered if they did it together, and they did. On day 111 it was over. It was time to catch our breath. We could sit back and reflect on what we had accomplished and mourn those we had lost. New Yorkers were proud, and they should have been. They were seeing the infection rate climb across the country and in countries around the world, and they knew they had done what we needed to do. They had saved lives—the lives of their neighbors, brothers, and sisters. They had gone from the worst infection rate in the nation to the lowest infection rate in the nation. For all the pain and loss, it was a beautiful moment in its own way. Yes, there would be challenges ahead—a growing national infection rate, young people not complying—and we would never really relax until the COVID vaccine was ready. But we had a new confidence in what we could accomplish together. We met a historic challenge. In some ways it wasn't the end but only the beginning.

THE AFTERMATH

——

A FTER DAY 111, I FINALLY HAD TIME TO catch up with my mother. Like all of us, this had been a very stressful time for her. The older we get, the more precious time becomes; we are painfully aware of how quickly it passes. Multiple months of disruption is a long time. My mother had been at my sisters' homes, but now she wanted to return to her home. She didn't want to debate it with me when I was in the middle of the briefings, but now she was clear and firm.

My mother and I arrived at an uneasy compromise that allows her to spend some time at her own home, without any home aides. Home health aides come and go and could bring the infection into her house. My parents bought their apartment in 1995 after my father lost his reelection. Now the apartment is basically a shrine to my father. My mother didn't change anything after his death. His desk, papers, books, are just the way he left them. His closet is still full. His razor is still on the sink. His office in the apartment is untouched, and it's almost eerie. The only thing that's missing is him. It's almost a perfect painting of "what was" but for my father's absence. If he reappeared in the painting, it would be exactly as he left it. I tried a couple of times to tell my mom to rearrange the space. I thought it might be better for her to move on. But I'm not sure that she wants to. My father is still very much present for her.

Their relationship was what I call a "real love" affair. It was not glamorized or idealized. It was hard and imperfect. They were very different in basic ways, and they both gave up much for each other and their children. I'm sure they both had their moments in which they questioned their decisions. I am sure they went through the what-if scenarios. What if they had made different decisions in life? What if they had chosen other options? "What could have been" is a question that we all confront. But they lived their lives where they were, and they lived them to the fullest with no regrets. They were fundamentally happy.

My mother had something that she wanted to share. She had watched all the briefings and been speaking with many people. All her friends through the years had called her. The people who worked with my father called and wrote to her. She had many thoughts and feelings that she had stored up for weeks until the time was right when we could have a real conversation. She had many specific points and questions that she wanted to talk through. My mother has been through a lot and learned much, and she wanted to share her opinions and thoughts. She had kept notes over the months, and she had pages of points that she wanted to make. But she had one main point that she wanted to convey. She wanted me to know how proud "we" were of what I had done. The "we" was she and my dad. My mother will still say "we" are happy or "we" want to give you this. She wanted me to know that they were both proud. Your father is proud, "so proud," she said repeatedly.

I do not have the right to speak for my father the way my mother does. After nearly sixty years of marriage she has that absolute right. That is what a lifetime of "real love" gives you. A lifetime of sharing everything. It is an intimacy from sharing life's indignities. A trust based on years of trials and tribulations. A loyalty earned by sharing losses. "Real love" gives you that right.

For all the complexity in life there are still essential elements that are so simple. Children want to make their parents proud. And parents need the vindication. It is the greatest gift a child can give a parent. I am glad that I gave her that gift. The fact that my children watched the entire situation unfold and were able to experience it with me was an unexpected treasure. There is a lifetime of wisdom in the past months. I'm sure they don't appreciate it all today, but I'm also sure that they will look back on these moments for the rest of their lives and learn from the mistakes but also cherish the good. When they think of the relationship between my mother and me, I hope they will smile. I truly hope they will. They should. It is a beautiful thing.

LET ME END WHERE I began. The COVID virus is not the extent of our problem. COVID merely exposed underlying weaknesses. America's vulnerability has been growing for years. Our national division and government incompetence allowed the COVID virus to ravage our country. The only way to stop the virus was for people to unify and work together. Our political, geographic, religious, racial, and economic schisms make unification challenging. The term for viral transmission is "community spread," and it is deeply ironic that the only way to stop "community spread" is by forging community.

For too many years government service has been a dying art. I primarily point to the federal government, but it is also true for some state and local governments. Government no longer performs. It doesn't build, solve, or improve. Our government has become an extension of our political campaigns. Rhetoric, platitudes, and positioning have become paramount. Our electoral process is for the most part no longer capable of selecting competent and qualified officials. We do not distinguish between those who merely advocate and those who actually accomplish.

COVID required government performance. Yet the shortcomings were obvious. Testing, tracing, and health-care capacity needed to be mobilized and operationalized quickly. And too many governments simply failed.

The two weaknesses exposed by COVID are not separate but rather symbiotic. National division and government incompetence feed and breed on each other. The less competent the government, the less progress is made, the more frustrated the public becomes and the more divided the nation. A divided nation leads to government paralysis, and the cycle continues.

In theory the formula is simple: quality leadership, government competence, and national unity. New York conquered the first wave, but now I fear a new wave possibly coming. It is off in the distance, but it is building. What is worse is that it is a man-made wave. Mother Nature cannot be blamed for this one.

By mid-June, New York's problem had become that visitors from other states were bringing the virus here. It was déjà vu all over again. Federal incompetence allowed the virus to arrive in New York from Europe in the first place, making New York a global hot spot. New York, on its own, designed and implemented a strategy to flatten the curve and reduce the transmission rate, and now here we are again with the virus coming in across our borders.

In late June, I joined with Governor Murphy of New Jersey and Governor Lamont of Connecticut to announce a fourteen-day quarantine for people coming from states with a high infection rate. The number of states on the list would grow to more than half the country, then more than two-thirds. If I had not lived the situation every day, I would not have believed what has happened. The new threat is that New Yorkers, who worked so hard to contain the spread and bend the curve, could now be infected by people coming from other states with soaring infection rates. Hadn't they seen what we went through? The refrigerated trucks to store the dead? Now those trucks are in Houston. Where else will they be needed? What does it take for people to open their eyes?

It was all so unnecessary. We all worked so hard to save lives.

We had the facts. There was nothing to debate. There were two theories that we tested in the laboratory of reality. The results were undeniable. Trump's theory was to deny the existence of the virus and, when that didn't work, act as if it were irrelevant and reopen the economy immediately. Our theory was that a virus requires a science-based solution and that a phased, data-driven reopening was smarter and better in the long term.

Both theories have been put to the test. States like Arizona, Florida, and Texas that followed Trump's demands to reopen quickly saw increased infection rates and needed to close their economies back down—reopening only to re-close. As a result, the financial markets were distressed with the volatility in these states. This stood in stark contrast to New York, where as of this writing 75 percent of our economy is open and our infection rate has been consistently 1 percent or below for nearly three months and among the lowest in the nation.

It is incomprehensible that people still support Trump's disproven theories. The states that most closely followed Trump's "guidance" were doing the worst. In Florida, Governor DeSantis was seeing an explosion of cases, and his hospital system was overwhelmed just two months after he demanded his apology. More than forty states were seeing the virus increase, and the federal health officials—Dr. Fauci, Dr. Birx, and the CDC director, Robert Redfield—warned that the situation would get worse. Trump wouldn't wear a mask or suggest the public should until mid-July.

There are important lessons to learn. When one looks back at how COVID arrived in the United States, it is a frightening and almost inconceivable series of failures and incompetence. It was a spectacular government catastrophe on one of its most vital activities: maintaining national security and public health. In retrospect, the failings are clear.

Where was this country's public health system charged with monitoring possible global diseases?

The federal Centers for Disease Control has the mission "to protect America from health, safety and security threats, both foreign and in the U.S." It failed.

The mission of the National Institutes of Health is to "seek fundamental knowledge about the nature and behavior of living systems and the application of that knowledge to enhance health, lengthen life, and reduce illness and disability." It failed.

The Department of Homeland Security's mission is "to safeguard the American people, our home-land, and our values with honor and integrity." It failed.

Our federal government, on all levels, has still not answered the basic question: "How did this happen?" To divert attention and responsibility from himself and the White House, the president blamed the World Health Organization. He has also added the conspiratorial element that the WHO was "too close" to China and implied that they were reluctant to criticize China and therefore didn't alert the nation to the coronavirus pandemic. The president often implies a conspiratorial element to fan Americans' fear and isolationism.

In truth, the WHO, which was created by the United Nations and is partially funded by the

United States (at least until Trump announced we were withdrawing in 2021), is charged with monitoring and mitigating worldwide diseases as they spread. The WHO might very well have been slow in realizing the way the virus spread. But to this day, we don't know what information the WHO gave our federal government and when. We don't have access to the federal communications with the WHO. We don't know from where Peter Navarro received the information that caused him to write the now infamous January 30 memo saying that one to two million Americans could die. We do know that the WHO publicly declared a global health emergency on January 30, 2020. While late January was sooner than the United States took action, it was still not soon enough.

The federal government didn't know the virus was in New York until it had been here for months. The consequences of that blunder cannot be underestimated. Rarely has a government failure had such immediate, significant, and quantifiable ramifications. You can count the consequences in number of lives lost and billions spent. You can count it in the number of unemployed Americans and bankruptcy claims. For New York State it was particularly devastating.

And now, the recent projection models show that due to the increased infection rate in the country, tens of thousands more Americans will die. As of this writing, the Institute for Health Metrics and

Evaluation model, the model the president follows, predicts that sixty-seven thousand more Americans will die because the nation did not adopt a mask mandate. This goes beyond government incompetence to government malfeasance and gross negligence. If a corporate CEO acted in the same manner as President Trump, he would be sued for breach of fiduciary duty by the families of the people who perished unnecessarily. In other words, he'd be fired.

The American people are smart, and they are paying attention. Even if there isn't legal accountability, there will be political accountability on Election Day.

THERE IS ONE IMPORTANT POINT that I want to make for the history books. People ask me all the time, "How did New York reverse the numbers?" or "How did New York turn it around?" The answer is clear and inarguable.

First, the results were solely produced by the people of the state of New York. This was an extraordinary example of social action. It was the actualization of the lofty concepts we talk about; it was democracy in action. It was a diverse group of people forging community. It was individual responsibility and a collective conscience.

The elusive concept of "the people" came to the forefront. It was the sum total of 19.5 million people's individual actions. The closedown procedures, social distancing practices, and individual precautions were all personal decisions that served the common good. The people had accurate information from a trusted source and acted quickly, responsibly, and collectively. My role was merely that of a public servant, an instrument of the collective. God bless the people of New York.

The second group are the "essential workers": the term that came to the forefront during this crisis. This battle was not won by the generals. Indeed, the federal generals pointed us in the wrong direction. We never received adequate federal reinforcements, and while we waged the war on the front lines, we were not even provided enough supplies. Nor was this battle won by those our society has deemed "leaders." There was no financial design or corporate solution; bankers, lawyers, developers, did not save the day.

The heroes who made this happen were the working families of New York. When we were in our moment of need, we called on the blue-collar New Yorkers to show up for everyone. We needed them to come to work and risk their health so that so many of us could stay safely at home. These are the people who have received the fewest rewards from society but from whom we now asked the most. These are the people who would have been most justified in refusing our call. They were not the rich and the well-off. They were not the highly paid. They have not been given anything more than they deserved. They had no obligation to risk their health and the health of their families. But they did it simply because "it was the right thing to do." But for some that is enough. For some that is everything.

These heroes are the people who live in places like Queens, where I grew up. These are the people working hard to better themselves and their families. These are parents concerned first and foremost with protecting their families, but who still showed up every day as nurses, National Guard members, train operators, bus drivers, hospital workers, police officers, grocery store employees, food delivery drivers. They are Puerto Ricans, Haitians, African Americans, Dominicans, Asians, Guatemalans. These are the immigrants who love America, who make America, and who will fight for it. These are the heroes of this battle. When COVID began, I felt it was unfair to call on them to carry such a heavy burden. I feared I would put them in harm's way. But we didn't have an option if society was to function. We needed food, hospitals, and electricity to stay alive.

All through this difficult endeavor there was never a moment when these people refused to show up or leveraged more benefits for themselves. At the beginning of a battle no one knows who will actually survive. Courage is determined by the willingness to enter the field. No one knew that when we started, the infection rate among our essential workers would be no higher than the general community infection rate. They have my undying admiration and the gratitude of every true New Yorker.

And in addition to the heroes here in New York, more than thirty thousand Americans signed up to come help us fight this battle.

THE GOVERNMENT IS ONLY as good as the people and as strong as a unified, mobilized society. The government is a societal reflection of our collective capacity. Throughout this crisis, I called for unity and optimism, and the people gave me that. In return, we gave them a government that was as good as they are. I said from day one that I couldn't do anything but what the people can do for themselves. I could give them facts, and I could be empowered by them, but I'm only their instrument. They are the ones who decided to listen to their better angels. They are the ones who decided to come together and support one another. They are the ones who decided to wear masks. They are the ones who decided to close down. They are the ones who agreed to socially distance. They are the ones who agreed to the phased reopening.

I tried to appeal to their best, and they manifested their best.

The virus was a perverse litmus test of what society

can do. How do you vanquish the invisible enemy?
You do it when you all stand up and decide you're
going to work together as a team. This state has more
tensions than most. If you'd asked the people of
New York before the pandemic arrived, they'd likely
tell you that ours is a fragmented, divided state. We
could have had an upstate-versus-downstate split,
or a Democrat-versus-Republican split, but that
didn't happen. We could have been derailed by
racial or religious tensions or any one of the fault
lines that exist across this country, but that didn't
happen. New Yorkers showed they were capable of
more goodness and more strength than they knew.
Only a strong body politic can overcome the virus,
and that's what happened in New York. It's in the
numbers, it's in the bending of the curve, it's in the
conquering of the mountain. It is the very definition of e pluribus unum—out of many, one.

As of this writing, New York's infection rate has
been at 1 percent or below for months, enabling us
to authorize the reopening of schools in the fall if
the infection rate stays low. The reality is, we don't
know what the fall will bring. I hope we will be able
to keep the virus under control but with travelers
bringing the virus here from out of state, the fall
flu season and colder weather, and the continual
federal denial, even if we remain New York Smart,
COVID can come back here and start spreading
again.

But even if we see a second wave in the fall due

to factors beyond our control, it is inarguable that New York's success is an antidote to Trump's message of nihilism. In the test of the two theories, the results are clear: New York tough, strong, united, disciplined, and loving defeated Trump's approach of division and fear and retaliation.

We have for two and a half centuries built the strongest nation on the globe. America's only threat is from within, from the growing division among us. People's frustration is turning to fear, and the fear is turning to anger, and the anger is turning to division. It is impossible to overstate how dangerous this is. I don't actually fault our federal government for causing the fear and frustration, but I fault them for a failure of leadership and government malfeasance. I fault them for deepening the division for their own political purpose. They didn't cause the darkness, but they have exploited it.

At the end of the day, we were right, and Trump was wrong. This isn't only a philosophical argument; it is quantifiable: Look at what New York managed to achieve and what Trump's denialism produced across the country. If you can do it here, you can do it anywhere—not because the song says so, but because we are a microcosm of everything that's happening in this country.

New York is living proof that in the end love wins.

A BLUEPRINT FOR GOING FORWARD

—

PROPOSED FEDERAL PROGRAM
TO ADDRESS COVID AND FUTURE
HEALTH CRISES

———

AS I SAID IN MAY WHEN WE BEGAN OUR reopening, the hard truth is that the COVID-19 pandemic has reshaped our nation and transformed our daily life. This statement was in recognition that to simply reopen to how things were before COVID-19 would be misguided—the world today is not the same world it was before the crisis began. I said that while COVID had brought unprecedented challenges, we must recognize the opportunity to "reimagine" and build back better than ever before. We must seize the moment to transform our health, education, and housing systems, our economy, and much more.

Most urgently, we need to reexamine and restructure our public health infrastructure to combat future pandemics and viral outbreaks, using the lessons we learned over the past months.

Below I detail eight priorities that I believe must be addressed as part of building back America's public health system better and stronger than ever before.

1. We must draw clear lines of responsibilities and authority between the various levels of government during a health crisis; the people must know who is in charge and when.
2. An early detection system of domestic and international public health threats is essential.
3. The leadership of public health organizations tasked to respond to future public health threats must be able to operate free from political interference.
4. Government's response to public health threats must be informed and guided by data.
5. The federal government must build a public health emergency operation team and program with the capacity to coordinate and respond to major health crises.
6. The country must have a health screening system as part of its border patrol control system.
7. State governments must reinvent the public health capacity.
8. Citizen action is essential.

1. We must draw clear lines of responsibilities and authority between the various levels of government during a health crisis; the people must know who is in charge and when.

During the pandemic, the federal government on several occasions created unnecessary public confusion—at a time when there was no room for error—by attempting to overstep its authority. The U.S. Constitution, specifically the Tenth Amendment, reserves broad authority for the states including over matters of public health. In a pandemic, the federal government should issue data-based uniform standards to give states the information and guidance they need to make decisions, such as closing businesses or schools. Once state government has set the rules, local governments must actively monitor and enforce compliance in their communities. This responsibility of the local governments is critical, because failure to ensure businesses and individuals are adhering to public health mandates and guidelines will result in viral spread.

Issuing data-based uniform standards and guidance is just one of the federal government's roles during a pandemic. It is also the federal government's responsibility to set national travel standards for both international and domestic flights during an emergency. When a pandemic is identified overseas, any delay in quickly stopping international travel activity can lead to rapid virus spread in the United States. As COVID demonstrated, federal inaction or delay in stopping international flights from hot spots overseas to the United States places states in a position where they are unable—both legally and practically—to control the virus from coming in. During a pandemic, the federal government must exercise its authority to conduct robust airport screenings of both domestic and international flights.

COVID demonstrated the need for states to redesign their public health care into a more coherent system and provide resources to modernize the system using technology. The federal government should provide states with the regulatory flexibility to innovate, because states are laboratories for nationwide change. For instance, in the new normal states must design a telemedicine program that is capable of providing patients with medical advice over the internet. Such a program will ensure the public has access to an array of health-care services in the midst of a public health emergency while helping keep people in their homes rather than having to enter hospital emergency rooms or local clinics where they might become infected or infect others. Likewise, states should strategically use their regulatory authority to expand private sector capacity during a pandemic. For example, states must enlist private local laboratories to assist in a public health emergency as a condition of their licensing.

2. An early detection system of domestic and international public health threats is essential.

The COVID crisis has illustrated with full force and fury that we are a global community, but we must also act locally. The COVID virus was discovered in late 2019 in China, but allowing it to travel for weeks without tracing or examination was a gross error with serious consequences that impacted New York State and, by extension, our entire nation and the world. A recent study by the Icahn School of Medicine at Mount Sinai found that the virus was already spreading in New York in early February 2020, well before New York's first official case on March 1, 2020. CDC reports in May and July confirmed the strain of the virus that spread in New York was from Europe, not China. The lack of an early detection system rendered New York effectively blind, because the erroneous information that the virus was still spreading from China led to the CDC's early decision to reserve the nation's limited testing capacity for travelers from China rather than Europe.

This initial error was compounded by the

premature and ultimately wrong conclusion that COVID was transmitted by symptomatic and not asymptomatic individuals, which exponentially multiplied the number of people infected. This false premise was accepted early in the United States, even though doctors in Europe had publicly pronounced the possibility of asymptomatic spread as soon as the virus was detected. This warning was largely ignored.

An early detection system of domestic and international public health threats is essential for helping states fully understand the complexity of the threats posed by global pandemics and appropriately prepare. As we now look back, the lack of early warning detection as well as inaction by the federal government was a profound and deadly problem. A national security matter of this magnitude should not be left to the capacity and accountability of any international organization like the WHO. The United States must build our own capacity to adequately detect and understand the next global health crisis. This requires data and clear information to enable our government to make informed decisions. The more quality information we have, the better we will be able to respond to crises.

3. The leadership of public health organizations tasked to respond to future public health threats must be

able to operate free from political interference.

COVID has shown us that political influence can have deadly consequences. While public health governance should have checks and balances, public health leaders—similar to other important positions in government—should be inoculated from political interference so they can express their expert advice without fear of political consequences. Public health leaders should require Senate confirmation and serve in term appointments so they are not subject to political interference by any president or federal administration.

Multiple media reports detail how during the COVID crisis Dr. Fauci, senior leadership at the CDC, and other federal health-care officials were censored by the Trump administration. The HHS secretary and the DHS secretary are presidential political appointees and too often appeared to be clearly charged with political spin over objective dissemination of information to the American people. In a public health emergency, it is paramount the public can trust the information they are receiving. If the American people are called on to take dramatic action, they will cooperate only to the extent they trust and respect the information and those providing it.

We do not need to create another bureaucracy,

but we must ensure the competence and integrity of the ones that exist. We must drastically and quickly reform how our federal agencies operate. The CDC is currently a subdivision within the Department of Health and Human Services. HHS is an agency run by political appointees of the president, many of whom have no experience in anything related to health or human services. The CDC should not be a subdivision of an agency directly controlled by the president. In the meantime, Congress should fully investigate whether the CDC did not have the expertise and capacity to detect COVID or if the agency was suppressed in its attempts to communicate the depth of the crisis to the American people by the White House.

As of this writing, we do not know what the CDC and NIH knew about COVID and when they knew it. We do not know what the WHO informed the White House of and when. We do not know the source of information to the White House in January 2020 that led Peter Navarro, a senior aide to the president, to write a memo suggesting apocalyptic consequences from COVID-19. We must demand answers to these basic questions to understand why such an early warning by a senior administration official was ignored at the highest level of the federal government.

President Trump has blamed the World Health Organization for the lack of timely detection of

COVID-19. However, the WHO did issue a global alert in late January—around the same time the president's own senior aide raised a serious warning. Why then didn't the United States act swiftly and deliberately to protect our citizens? An FDA press release on February 4 said, "At this time, federal health officials continue to believe that the threat to the general American population from this virus is relatively low."

To ensure the delivery of science-based, expert public health advice, steps must be taken to guarantee that the leadership of public health can do their jobs free from political interference.

4. Government's response to public health threats must be informed and guided by data.

During the COVID crisis, New York has collected and publicized more data than most other states, and the state's usage and reliance on data and metrics are something we have done extraordinarily well. Data allowed us to better manage the crisis, understand where to target resources and efforts, and identify and mitigate emerging areas of concern. From the earliest days in the crisis, New York required hospitals and other healthcare providers to submit detailed information daily on how many hospital beds were available, the number of ICU beds occupied, how many ventilators were in use and on hand, the amount of PPE available, the number of tests performed, and much more. We tracked how many patients were in hospitals, what communities they were from, and extensive socioeconomic information. In New York, we also collected individual data so we knew what was happening in each community down to the zip code level. This approach to data collection and attention to detail has supported our nation-leading contact tracing program.

The federal government should use New York's model and build a similar system, and it must be completed quickly. It should share the data that is collected with states, especially states that lack resources or technical capacity to develop their own robust systems. During the COVID-19 crisis, the federal government did not mandate data be collected or reported in any uniform way. Most states did not collect or publicize as detailed information as New York State. As a result, as of this writing, it remains impossible to do a true state-by-state analysis of what happened.

Data must be reliable and transparent to the public. As a starting point, it has to be free from political influence so that the people can have faith in the information they are receiving. Recent media reports have stated the White House is interfering with hospital data, asking hospitals to bypass the CDC and instead report information to HHS. Why would they make this change seven months into the pandemic? It raises seri-ous questions about the accuracy of information being collected, controlled, and released by the federal government.

5. The federal government must build a public health emergency operation team and program with the capacity to coordinate and respond to major health crises.

The Federal Emergency Management Agency was designed to assist in natural disasters such as hurricanes, floods, and fires, but it was wholly ill-suited to be helpful and responsive during the COVID crisis. Public health experts must be central to the response for their epidemiological expertise, but health agencies are largely regula-tory bodies and are not equipped with managing a crisis of the magnitude of COVID-19. In essence, public health experts in the federal government need the experience and expertise of emergency operational officials who can execute tasks like building large-scale testing capacity quickly.

A robust public health emergency operations team will be well suited to implement a national public health program that is responsible for building up the nation's health-care capacity to deal with future crises—an urgent need. It is obvious that the nation was unprepared to handle a viral outbreak on the scale of COVID-19. For instance, the federal government's own forecast in March estimated that the COVID virus would require between 2.4 million and 21 million hospital beds nationwide, yet the entire country has only 925,000 staffed hospital beds. One can argue that we should have been better prepared after H1N1 swine flu, SARS, Ebola, and other past public health challenges. Whatever the reason, it is clear we were not.

A public health capacity program must start with an early warning detection system as outlined above, but first and foremost it must focus on building a nationwide testing system. The United States has no capacity to quickly ramp up large-scale testing of our population. Other countries such as China and South Korea were much more successful in quickly determining the number of individuals infected with a virus and isolating them to stop the spread. In the United States, testing is a fragmented network of private labs with major national manufacturers selling different equipment and proprietary test kits and approximately seven thousand private laboratories and hospitals capable of conducting tests. It is imperative that the federal government design the necessary requirements to provide mass-scale, nationwide rapid testing—including for new and emerging viruses.

Likewise, the nation needs a contact tracing

operation to follow up on those who test positive and help limit viral spread. Like the testing
operation, it can be either federally operated or
federally designed and delegated to the states. In
New York, we set a tracing formula based on the
infection rate of regions within the state, and as of
this writing we currently have about seven thousand contact tracers. The program has helped
the state find and isolate COVID clusters before
the virus spreads more broadly in the community.

Staffing was also a challenge nationwide.
On the front lines of the crisis in hospitals and
other health-care facilities, nurses and physicians
would contract the virus or need a break because
of the severe fatigue of working long hours. Given
that COVID-19 is a national crisis and that future
viruses will likely be as well, the federal government should create a nationwide volunteer portal
where health-care professionals across America
can offer their services and states and local
health-care facilities can access as needed. Such
a system will avoid competition of scarce human
capital during an emergency.

The federal government must invest in isolation
and quarantine facilities, which must be readily
available to hold infected people who do not have
the ability to self-isolate. In dense and crowded
communities, like New York City, a person who
tested positive often did not have the ability to
self-isolate. We need a public health system that

can care for highly infectious individuals who don't require the acute care of a hospital but should not be sent to a nursing home or a rehabilitation center because such a facility may not be prepared to provide the level of care and isolation a contagious person requires. These convalescent facilities should be designed and identified by the states to be ready for an emergency, with operational and financial support provided by the federal government.

Further, the United States must maintain a real national stockpile of emergency medical equipment and supplies anticipating a future public health emergency. The reliance on China and other countries to supply us on a moment's notice with vital equipment is a national security risk. The federal government should identify necessary medical supplies and equipment that we may need in an emergency and incentivize private sector companies to increase their capacity to assist, both to build a stockpile now and to help with rapid production during a future emergency. Robust nationwide stockpiles were created under President Bill Clinton's administration, but recent reports found that the federal stockpile is currently "thin."

New York State distributed tens of millions of needed supplies during the COVID crisis, and many states undertook similar efforts. This is not normally a state responsibility, but it was a necessity; many health-care facilities were in short supply. To avoid this in the future, states must enact what New York has done: Develop baseline supply and equipment requirements for health-care facilities and mandate that they maintain the supplies necessary. At a minimum, states should require that individual hospitals have a ninety-day capacity of PPE and essential pharmaceuticals on hand during crisis situations. Then states should have an additional thirty days on hand. These supplies will then be supplemented by the federal effort.

6. The country must have a health screening system as part of its border patrol control system.

The original sin in this crisis was that the federal government failed to have an early detection system in place for COVID-19. The result was the virus had moved from Asia to Europe, where it began to spread. Then the federal Department of Homeland Security failed to control the spread from Europe to the United States, when it allowed millions of travelers to come to this nation on tens of thousands of flights throughout the month of February and until mid-March, many carrying the virus. This was confirmed in reports issued by

Mount Sinai as well as the CDC, which found that the virus came to New York mainly from Europe and was spreading here in early February. By the time the federal government instituted travel restrictions from Europe, it was too late.

Even after the travel bans were implemented, screening was almost nonexistent. A March 13, 2020, **New York Times** article, "Travelers from Coronavirus Hot Spots Say They Faced No Screening," reported, "As thousands of Americans flee from Europe and other centers of the coronavirus outbreak, many travelers are reporting no health screenings upon departure and few impediments at U.S. airports beyond a welcome home greeting." That must not happen again.

We need the federal government to develop a comprehensive screening system and protocol so viruses cannot enter our nation undetected. Ports of entry are a federal responsibility, and the national government must develop a screening process for the next virus. Customs and Border Protection is tasked with securing our country's borders, but they must also have public health screening safeguards in addition to verifying citizenship or checking for contraband. Let us not waste a crisis, and let's take this opportunity to retool Customs and Border Protection to expand its role and expertise.

7. State governments must reinvent the public health capacity.

In New York, we have one of the best health-care systems in the world with world-class physicians, nurses, and other health-care workers. But the COVID-19 situation demonstrated that we don't have one coherent health-care system, but rather a patchwork of different health-care institutions, both private and public, with varying capacities. The hospitals that faced the greatest stress during the crisis were the public municipal hospitals, yet nearby were other hospitals with more capacity and resources to help.

Under an innovative Surge & Flex program described in more detail later in this appendix, New York built and managed a centralized system where patients were transferred from one burdened hospital to a different one with more capacity—regardless of which system a hospital was part of. In the end, the state's program assisted in transferring approximately sixteen hundred patients from overwhelmed hospitals to hospitals with capacity. States should use their regulatory authority to institutionalize a similar program so various health-care institutions can be run as a single coherent system during an emergency.

Also under the Surge & Flex program, New York

helped health-care facilities with ample surplus share supplies and equipment with other facilities that were running low. This was an effective strategy that states should adopt and institutionalize.

8. Citizen action is essential.

We have learned once again that social action is the essence of political power and social change. All government action during COVID was dependent on individual action. The individual action forged the collective movement that protected society. People bent the curve in New York. In states where the virus spread, it was the people's actions that caused the spread. COVID illustrated clearly the strength and limitations of government as well as the power of individual action. Individual actions determine an individual's health. Individual social and political participation determines government action. Inform yourself, protect yourself, act responsibly, and participate in democracy. On a micro level, follow the individual rules of responsibility that I include in this appendix. On a macro level, participate, advocate, vote, protest, make social change. We did and we can. Be an American in the truest sense of the word.

COVID-19 HAS ILLUSTRATED this country's weakness and vulnerability. The only thing worse than having lost the lives of thousands of Americans would be for them to have died in vain. We must learn the lessons of this experience in order to do better. We owe it to the front-line workers who sacrificed so much and above all to those who lost their lives and the loved ones they left behind.

THE FOLLOWING ARE SUMMARIES of "game plan" protocols the state of New York implemented during COVID—one for testing, and the other for our Surge & Flex program. I hope these program details can be helpful to other states or to federal policy makers in the fight against COVID and in preparation for the next pandemic.

NEW YORK STATE SURGE & FLEX HEALTH COORDINATION SYSTEM

In early March, New York State's 213 private, public, and independent hospitals had approximately 53,000 total beds, of course many occupied by patients receiving care for non-COVID reasons. Starting early in the COVID crisis, to determine the effect of the virus on New York's hospital system, the State Department of Health required every hospital in the state to report daily how many beds in its facility were available, as well as how many were occupied, including by patients with COVID, those in the ICU, and patients requiring intubation.

Normally, these hospitals operate individually, competing with one another for patients, and rarely coordinating, particularly with hospitals outside of their "system." (Most hospitals are part of a network, such as Columbia-Presbyterian, Mount Sinai, Northwell, NYC Health + Hospitals [H&H], and the University of Rochester Medical Center). There has never been a single statewide public hospital system or even a coordinating entity to help these 213 individual facilities work together in times of crisis. The situation at Elmhurst hospital in Queens during the third week of March demonstrated that a new, innovative coordinating system would be needed to bring every hospital in the state under one true statewide public health system that effectively balanced patients, staff, supplies, and equipment across all facilities.

Elmhurst is a public hospital operated by the New York City Health + Hospitals system. Early in the fourth week of March, Elmhurst was overwhelmed with COVID patients experiencing serious symptoms—a startling situation that happened very quickly and was well documented in the media. However, at the time Elmhurst was under siege, there were only about 4,000 patients hospitalized with COVID-19 in the entire state—just one-fifth of what our eventual peak would be, at nearly 19,000. At the same time, the H&H system reported to New York State having 900 open hospital beds across the eleven hospitals in its network. Likewise, of the more than 21,000 total hospital beds in New York City, including all hospitals, more than 3,500 beds were vacant. Why were patients from Elmhurst not transferred to these nearby vacant beds? The situation at Elmhurst made clear that coordination between hospitals and hospital systems was just as important as—if not more important than—increasing hospital capacity.

Elmhurst revealed what was needed. The question was how to build and operationalize a real public health system overnight that could act quickly and have the logistical capability to ensure that no single hospital was overwhelmed or in need of additional staff or supplies while hospitals in the vicinity, or anywhere else in New York State, had vacant beds and available supplies, staff, or equipment. Unless such a system was in place, building new hospital capacity at the Javits Center and other temporary sites would be essentially meaningless and New York State would be unable to effectively care for even close to the number of patients that might require hospitalization at what experts believed would be our peak in late April.

A few days after the Elmhurst situation, New

York State launched what we called "Surge & Flex," an effort that effectively built one statewide, coordinated public hospital system. Surge & Flex included four key elements that are each detailed below: (1) building hospital capacity; (2) mobilizing additional staff; (3) balancing equipment and supply needs; and (4) establishing an operational command center to coordinate the entire system.

There is no question that Surge & Flex saved lives. Nearly 1,500 patient transfers between hospitals and hospital systems occurred as a result in just weeks. Millions of pieces of PPE were delivered to hospitals in need. A twenty-four-hour hotline in the command center helped address hundreds of logistical requests, managing ambulance transfers, staff travel and accommodations, and much more vital support. As a result, no other hospital was inundated to the extent that Elmhurst was during those days in late March, and New Yorkers in need of care had access to hospital beds, helping New York avoid the tragic collapse of the health-care system that we witnessed in Italy.

New York State has, via regulation and Department of Health guidance, institutionalized the Surge & Flex system that now gives the state the ability to quickly activate each component of the operation during a future wave of COVID cases or another public health emergency, and ensure hospitals know what is expected of them so they can properly prepare.

Four Elements of Surge & Flex

1. Increasing Hospital Capacity

In early March, epidemiological projections showed that New York needed between 110,000 and 140,000 hospital beds to meet the expected influx of COVID cases. This required New York State to effectively double the number of hospital beds available in the state's 213 hospitals. To increase this capacity, three steps were quickly taken. First, an executive order was issued for hospitals to postpone or cancel most elective procedures, freeing thousands of beds that would otherwise have been filled by patients seeking treatment for non-COVID and non-life-threatening conditions. Second, an additional executive order was issued that required all hospitals to increase their own capacity by at least 50 percent. This could be accomplished by adding a bed to single rooms, converting cafeterias and meeting rooms into patient care centers, and other measures. Third, the state deployed inspection teams to underutilized or vacant health-care and other facilities statewide in order to build temporary hospitals. These inspection teams also created detailed reports and plans to convert specific college dorms and hotels that were located near existing hospitals into temporary health-care facilities, if needed.

Remarkably, these three actions expanded

New York's hospital capacity from 53,000 beds to approximately 90,000 in just a matter of weeks.

2. Mobilizing Additional Staff

Additional hospital beds were of no use without additional staff—a particular challenge given that thousands of health-care workers were being infected by COVID. In early March, New York State issued a public call for retired health-care professionals from around the state and country to sign up to be relicensed. Further, the state asked medical and nursing school students, and related health professionals such as podiatrists, to also serve. The response was overwhelming— nearly 100,000 health-care professionals agreed to serve, including 30,000 from outside of New York State, willing to travel to what at the time was a global hot spot of COVID cases. To match these additional staff with hospitals in need, New York State built a world-class online portal that allowed hospitals and nursing homes, priori- tized by those with the highest need, to connect with these health-care workers and employ them at their facilities. New York State provided additional support, including human resources management, access to temporary housing, and transportation logistics to facilitate health-care facilities employing these volunteers. In addition, the state transferred health-care workers from underutilized hospitals upstate to hospitals in hard-hit communities downstate, and directed federal medical personnel to facilities most in need of additional staff.

3. Balancing Supplies and Equipment

Every state in the nation was faced with the challenge of quickly purchasing and deploying enormous amounts of health-care supplies and equipment, such as PPE, medications, and ventilators. This became particularly challenging given the nation's dependence on an international supply chain and the lack of federal coordination and leadership. While New York State secured tens of millions of pieces of PPE and thousands of additional ventilators, it was clear that even these efforts would not be sufficient to meet what might be required at the projected peak in late April. The Surge & Flex system took on this challenge. First, the Department of Health expanded the daily reporting requirements for hospitals to include not just bed occupancy and vacancies, but also detailed reports on each facility's individual stockpile of supplies and equipment. In essence, this data enabled the creation of a real statewide inventory of ventilators, medical drugs, PPE, and other supplies and equipment. An executive order was signed to ensure that New York State had the ability to properly distribute these items to hospitals in need—an exercise that was informed closely by data that demonstrated which hospitals were experiencing the most hardship and shortages of critical supplies and equipment. Further, a transportation logistics system was mobilized to help move this equipment around the state. It would be a tragedy for a patient in need of a ventilator to not receive one, while a hospital nearby had dozens of available ventilators. By the end of May, New York State had successfully allocated in excess of thirteen million pieces of PPE and other critical equipment and supplies.

4. Establishing an Operational Command Center

Standing up the Surge & Flex system in a matter of days was an operational challenge, and to ensure that the system worked seamlessly required a operational command center, staffed twenty-four hours a day, seven days a week, that could make each part work together in a coordinated manner.

The state created a Hospital Capacity Coordination Committee (HCCC) that served as a command center, comprising staff from the New York State Department of Health, senior officials from major hospital systems, and logistical experts from the New York National Guard. The HCCC operated 24/7 and was available to every hospital and health-care facility in New York State, accessible via a hotline that was answered at any time of day. With real-time data being displayed on large television monitors, members of the HCCC could see at a facility-by-facility level which hospitals were seeing influxes of new COVID patients and which facilities needed additional staff, equipment, or other support. Throughout the most challenging days of the COVID crisis, the HCCC was operational and helped facilitate thousands of patient transfers, deliver millions of pieces of PPE, and deploy hundreds of ventilators.

Without Surge & Flex, the impact of COVID on New York State would have been much worse. New York State has now institutionalized each of these four elements so Surge & Flex can be quickly operationalized should a new wave of COVID hit the state or we face another major health emergency.

NEW YORK STATE TESTING PROGRAM

New York State recognized early in the COVID-19 crisis that testing would be the single most important tool to combat and contain COVID-19. New York was the first state in the nation to develop its own diagnostic test and worked quickly to build a network of hundreds of local private labs to test, and set up access to more than 850 collection sites where New Yorkers can go get a test. As a result, as of this writing New York leads the United States and large nations in total tests performed per capita. New York's testing program is a national model that helped New York not only flatten the curve but actually reduce the infection rate since reopening the economy. The testing program established by New York State was instituted in part by executive order and Department of Health directives that are summarized below.

Creating New York State's Own Test

Early in the COVID crisis, America's testing capabilities were severely limited. Specimen samples had to be mailed from all fifty states to the CDC laboratory in Atlanta, where testing was conducted. By the end of January, New York had sent just eleven samples to the CDC. On February 4, the FDA issued an emergency use authorization that allowed a small number of CDC-designated clinical laboratories across the nation to test for coronavirus, using the same test that was being run in the CDC lab in Atlanta. That week, the CDC began to ship approximately two hundred CDC-developed coronavirus laboratory test kits to select U.S. labs, each kit capable of testing approximately seven hundred to eight hundred specimens.

New York's Wadsworth Center, the state's public health research lab, received the CDC test kits on Saturday, February 8. Upon examining the kits, the Wadsworth lab technicians realized they would not be able to rely on the CDC test kits. First, as the press later reported nationwide, the kits produced false positives—inaccurately reporting that someone was infected when in fact they were not. Second, the reagent chemicals needed to run the CDC test were in limited supply, available only from the CDC.

New York immediately mobilized to create our own COVID test, using different chemical reagents that were both more reliable to accurately find positive COVID cases and more commercially available than the reagents provided by the CDC—a potential "win-win-win" where New York State would have its own test with results reported within a day, a more reliable test than the CDC's, and the ability to scale up quickly by purchasing the chemical reagents from commercial suppliers. By the third week of February, Wadsworth had developed a test that passed the validation process—where known positive specimens are run and successfully detected on the new test. On February 29 the FDA sent over the official documents approving Wadsworth's test—the first non-CDC test to be approved by the FDA.

It is critical during a viral outbreak on the scale of COVID-19 that public health laboratories have the expertise, supplies, and equipment necessary to quickly develop in-state testing capabilities, helping ensure states are able to perform widespread testing in case the federal government fails to establish a national testing program.

Mobilizing a Network of Local Labs

The moment the FDA approved New York's test, the state mobilized to activate a network of hundreds of labs licensed by New York State to test. Within the first two weeks of March, New York State had helped eight top-quality labs in the state get the equipment, supplies, and necessary FDA approval to test for COVID. Finally, on March 13, the FDA gave New York's Department of Health the authority to approve all labs within New York State.

To mobilize the labs, the state issued an executive order directing all public and private labs in New York to coordinate with the Department of Health to prioritize coronavirus diagnostic testing. In addition, the state issued executive orders waiving regulatory burdens that constrained labs from reaching greater capacity. Together with a team of logistics and laboratory experts who coordinated with each lab in the state to help on issues including securing equipment, supplies, regulatory guidance, and staff, these measures helped activate more than 250 laboratories that now do COVID testing for New York State.

In addition, New York invested in manufacturers

to help develop lab equipment and supplies, including $750,000 for Rheonix, an Ithaca-based manufacturer of lab instruments and reagent kits, that have been deployed throughout New York State and now are relied upon for thousands of daily tests.

It is critical during a pandemic that states' public and private clinical laboratories are ready to direct their resources and priorities toward testing for whatever contagious disease is part of a global viral outbreak. Further, to avoid the problems with relying on national supply chains, U.S. manufacturers should be prepared, with assistance from the government, to retool operations to build lab equipment and supplies to help meet demand.

Building a Massive Sample Collection Network

As of this writing, the most popular way to test for COVID-19 is a nasal swab, where a health-care professional inserts a cotton swab into a patient's nose and then puts the swab in a glass vial that holds a liquid transport medium, similar to saline solution. This sample is then put on ice and transported to a laboratory to test.

New York State built a network of more than 850 collection sites located across the entire state and launched a website where New Yorkers could put in their address and find a site near them to get tested. This network of testing sites included walk-in locations in dense, urban communities and drive-through locations in rural and suburban communities. Further, New York State set up testing sites at dozens of churches in minority communities primarily in New York City. To support all these testing sites, the state provided PPE, test kits, and other resources to ensure all New Yorkers had access to testing.

In a public health crisis like COVID, states need the capacity to quickly mobilize hundreds of locations to give residents convenient locations to get tested, as well as be able to build and launch the IT systems needed for finding sites, scheduling appointments, and reporting results.

Setting Testing Criteria Based on Lab Capacity

As testing capacity expands or restricts, likewise the criteria of who is eligible for a test must be adjusted. On Friday, March 6, while New York still had very limited capacity, New York's eligibility included New Yorkers with symptoms who had traveled from hot-spot parts of the globe, contacts of known positives, individuals in quarantine, and individuals who had symptoms and tested negative for other influenzas. In June, when New York was doing more than sixty-five thousand tests a day, the state expanded testing criteria to all New Yorkers.

Since reopening on May 15, New York successfully capitalized on our expanded testing capacity to conduct widespread community surveillance testing—random testing of asymptomatic individuals without known exposure. Because 40 percent of infected people do not develop symptoms but may still be contagious, this approach helps identify where the virus may be spreading undetected. Community surveillance testing has been critical in identifying the virus early and controlling the spread through contact tracing before it reaches those who may become sick and require hospitalization—and is a testing approach that must be supported by the government in a widespread viral outbreak such as COVID.

Requiring Prompt Reporting of Results

New York State requires every laboratory in the nation that tests a New York resident for a communicable disease to report the results four times daily to the Department of Health. Known as the Electronic Clinical Laboratory Reporting System, this provides real-time insight into new cases throughout the entire pandemic. These reporting requirements will need to be activated immediately in future major outbreaks of communicable diseases. States should use their licensure authority to ensure accurate, timely reporting of testing data during a public health crisis.

10 WAYS TO AVOID COVID

People ask me all the time how they can keep themselves and their families safe from COVID. I am not a medical doctor, but here is what I do to stay safe—and what I ask my mother to do.

1. Stay indoors with a select group or go outside socially distanced. Do not have people coming to the home who have not been tested and have been circulating socially. Contact with health aides, a repairman, a deliveryman, a friend of a friend, all require caution. Contact with a young person also requires caution. No matter how many times I've said it, young people still put themselves in harm's way.

2. You do not have to have a fever to have COVID. If you feel any symptoms, especially respiratory, get tested. The older you are, the sooner you should be tested.

3. Before you go for a test, find out how long the testing site will take to turn

around the results. Three days is the ideal turnaround time. More and more testing sites use national laboratories to process the results. A nine-day turnaround to get results is problematic. In New York, in-state labs can turn around a test in three days.

4. Temperature checks are only somewhat helpful. People stress temperature checks because they're the only prophylactic we have right now, but asymptomatic spread is very real. And people who show no symptoms are very capable of spreading the virus. Don't take false comfort.

5. The experts first told us that the virus could remain viable on surfaces for up to forty-eight hours. This caused us to clean subways, buses, and my entire house. Experts now say that surface transmission is rare. I am still dubious. I have seen the so-called experts go back and forth on too many basic issues. Cleanliness is important, but not to the point of obsession. And cleaning surfaces is helpful during flu season regardless.

6. Hand sanitizer is important. As the state of New York is now a manufacturer of hand sanitizer, I feel that I have some level of expertise. While the marketing agencies have done a great job creating

the perception that hand sanitizer is a sophisticated product, it really isn't. Hand sanitizer is alcohol. The CDC says it must be at least 70 percent alcohol to be effective. Alcohol is available and much less expensive than hand sanitizer, although it does tend to dry out your skin. For people who are concerned about such things, that's why we have hand lotion.

7. Ventilation systems make a difference. While people don't normally pay much attention to air filters, they should now. HEPA filters are the best for equipment that can handle ventilation. After that, a MERV 15 filter is best and a MERV 13 filter is acceptable. Consider using them in your home and office.

8. Congregate settings are a real issue, especially for people who are in the vulnerable category. The "super-spreader" phenomenon has not gone away. One person in a public setting can infect dozens. Remember, an individual can be asymptomatic and not even know they have the virus. In a closed environment, such as a home or a car, opening windows and allowing circulation is helpful. Always exercise caution when inside with others.

9. If you feel symptomatic, isolate yourself and get a test. Testing doesn't hurt and it doesn't cost anything. Just make sure it's a site with a short turnaround. If you test positive, it is no fun calling all the people you have encountered over the past ten days and telling them they have to get a test because you may have infected them, but it is what must be done. Protect yourself and protect others.

10. Wearing a mask is common sense for everyone. Surgical masks are inexpensive and the burden is minimal. For people in the most vulnerable category, I have additional advice, and this is controversial, but it is my informed position. I advise my mother to wear an N95 mask when she leaves the house. I believe from all I have seen that a mask not only stops a person from spreading the virus but can be beneficial to prevent a person from inhaling the virus. It is true that a mask is most effective at stopping the spread from the person wearing the mask, but a mask can also protect a person from contracting the disease. Essential workers, including those in emergency rooms, have had a lower infection rate than the general population. That is a fact, and most experts will also agree that a

mask protects a person from inhaling the virus, to an extent. This is not to say it is foolproof, as the mask has to be worn correctly and fitted around the nose and cheeks. Health-care professionals do not recommend that the general public use N95 masks because they think it is over-kill and they think the N95 mask supply should be safeguarded for health-care professionals. I understand their point of view. However, we don't currently have a shortage of N95 masks, and I am sug-gesting that vulnerable people consider using them. I make sure my mother has them. Now, what she does with them is a different story. I am only her son, and in our house "mother knows best."

ACKNOWLEDGMENTS

———

I WOULD ESPECIALLY LIKE TO THANK THE incredibly talented team at Crown—Gina Centrello, David Drake, Gillian Blake, and Libby Burton—who worked closely with me to transform these reflections into print, as well as Bob Barnett for his wise counsel. **American Crisis** would not have been possible without their efforts.

ABOUT THE AUTHOR

ANDREW CUOMO is the fifty-sixth governor of New York, serving since 2011. He is the author of **All Things Possible: Setbacks and Success in Politics and Life** and the editor of **Crossroads: The Future of American Politics.**

Facebook.com/GovernorAndrewCuomo

Twitter: @NYGovCuomo

Instagram: @nygovcuomo